MY BODY, MY BUSINESS

MY BODY, my business

New Zealand sex workers in an era of change

CAREN WILTON

PHOTOGRAPHS BY
MADELEINE SLAVICK

OTAGO

*This book is dedicated to Dana de Milo,
trailblazer and wahine toa (1946–2018), and to the tireless workers
of the New Zealand Prostitutes' Collective*

Published by Otago University Press
Level 1, 398 Cumberland Street
Dunedin, New Zealand
university.press@otago.ac.nz
www.otago.ac.nz/press

First published 2018
Copyright © Caren Wilton
Photographs © Madeleine Slavick
The moral rights of the author have been asserted.

ISBN 978-1-98-853132-8
A catalogue record for this book is available from the National Library of New Zealand. This book is copyright. Except for the purpose of fair review, no part may be stored or transmitted in any form or by any means, electronic or mechanical, including recording or storage in any information retrieval system, without permission in writing from the publishers.

No reproduction may be made, whether by photocopying or by any other means, unless a licence has been obtained from the publisher.

Published with the assistance of Creative New Zealand.

Editor: Erika Büky
Design/layout: Fiona Moffat
Author photo: Colin Dowd

Printed in China through Asia Pacific Offset.

CONTENTS

PREFACE 7
INTRODUCTION: 19
A brief history of sex work in New Zealand

THE INTERVIEWS
Anna Reed 37
Shareda 61
Mistress Margaret 85
Kelly 107
Catherine Healy 127
Stevie 151
Dana de Milo 169
Allan 197
Jeanie 215
Misty 235
Poppy 253

EPILOGUE 273
GLOSSARY 277
THE PHOTOGRAPHS 279
FURTHER READING 282
ACKNOWLEDGEMENTS 286

PREFACE

One thing I'd like to see is the recognition of sex workers as ordinary, sometimes rather extraordinary, people.

– DAME CATHERINE HEALY, NATIONAL COORDINATOR,
NEW ZEALAND PROSTITUTES' COLLECTIVE

I HAVE OFTEN thought of the world of sex work as a world apart, a separate, secret world that can only be entered by those who – as in a fairytale – have been given the special key, or who know and utter a secret word. And then the walls dissolve, the curtains are pulled back, and the secret world is revealed as not so secret after all, as just another part of this world, just a breath or a step away. Just next door. Just ordinary, and yet not. A world that leaves its mark on those who have been there, so that they know each other, recognise each other as fellow travellers in a place that others don't always understand.

Over a period of almost eight years I interviewed people about New Zealand's sex industry, and about their lives in and out of the industry. I wanted to make visible the invisible, to bring the hidden into the light, at least a little bit, and to record a time and some places and ways of being that had existed but now were mostly gone. (And that, even when they were there, were often shadowy places, quiet places, places that only some people could recognise or gain access to.)

The decriminalisation of sex work in 2003 – 15 years later, New Zealand remains the only country to have done so – has meant considerable changes for the industry and for the climate in which sex work takes place.[1] I wanted to hear how this had affected people's lives; I wanted also to document the remarkable story of the New Zealand Prostitutes' Collective, and New Zealand's enlightened and world-leading law change.

In this book 11 sex workers and former workers tell their own stories in their own words. Too often other people have presumed to speak on behalf of sex workers, sometimes in inaccurate or slanted ways or with unhelpful agendas. In publishing these oral histories, I've been influenced by the work of other interviewers who have allowed interviewees to speak for themselves, including criminologist Jan Jordan (whose 1991 book of sex-worker interviews, *Working Girls*, stands as a precursor to this one), and – working with different subject matter – oral historians such as Alison Parr and Megan Hutching and authors such as Adrienne Jansen. I was also very much aware of the sex-worker advocates' catch-cry of 'Nothing about us without us'.

Having said that, I have edited the interviews considerably for publication – this book would be many, many times longer if I had not – sometimes reordering material from the original conversations in order to make the narratives more coherent, logical and chronological. The life stories that appear here have been shaped by my own sense of what was important and salient. As Megan Hutching notes of the 'act of translation' of editing oral history, 'We owe it to the narrator (and the reader) to present the story so that it is told in the way that the narrator and the oral historian feel remains faithful to the intent and tone of the interview.'[2] Each chapter has been approved by the interviewee it profiles, a sometimes complex and extended process – but a vital one, particularly when dealing with sensitive material.

In total I interviewed 19 people, whom I found through personal contacts, through the New Zealand Prostitutes' Collective (NZPC), and sometimes by one interviewee putting me in contact with another. I knew a couple of the interviewees already (and had known them for more than 20 years); the willingness of the others to trust me as an interviewer and then as an author is probably largely due to the fact that I came recommended, as it were, by people they already knew and trusted, and in some cases by people I had already interviewed. This was especially helpful with transgender interviewees – I had had little to do with the transgender community before beginning the project.

There was a range of topics I wanted to cover – people's early lives, how and why they began sex work, where and how they worked, their clients, health, interactions with police and the law, experiences of stigma and violence, any involvement with sex-worker advocacy, the impact of decriminalisation, when and why they stopped sex work (if they had done so), and what they were doing today. I typically finished interviews by asking about the positives and negatives of sex work, any regrets the interviewee had, and what they were most proud of in their lives. In reality, most interviews were far broader and more comprehensive than this list of topics suggests. Their shape and content were often determined by the story the interviewee wanted to tell and the meanings and interpretation they had ascribed to their experiences; as oral historian Anna Green has pointed out, 'We explain our lives as stories.'[3] Green also notes, 'Remembering is a complex process ... Memories are partial and fragmented, and in the process of reassembling them for others we decide what to include or exclude. We also seek to make meaningful connections between the present and the past.'[4]

Where interviews took place over more than one session (as happened in most cases), interviewees often came to later sessions finding that more memories had been prompted by the earlier interview. Some interviewees were clear about the subjects they were not prepared to discuss with me, or not prepared to have included in this book, and I welcomed this setting of boundaries – what oral historians elsewhere have described as 'the exercise of narrators' authority in the collaborative process of oral history making', or the 'assertion of a right to concealment'.[5]

Unsurprisingly, people varied greatly in their willingness to be 'out' about having done sex work; some of the full recorded interviews are freely available to researchers for listening and publication, while others require permission from the interviewee for either or both of these uses. Some are archived under the interviewee's real name, while others use a pseudonym or simply a first name. In this book, three interviewees – Anna Reed, Catherine Healy and Dana de Milo – appear under their full names, but the other eight included here chose to use just a first name, or a pseudonym – a clear illustration of the continuing stigmatisation of sex work and the potential negative effects of being found out, even many years later. The full interviews (comprising audio and detailed time-coded abstracts) have all been deposited in the Alexander Turnbull Library, and will be available to researchers, subject to any restrictions placed on the material by the interviewees.

Not all of the interviews appear in this book; some interviewees didn't want their stories published, while some had covered ground that was very similar to others. I opted for a smaller number of longer, more detailed stories that gave the full sense of a life, rather than a larger number of brief accounts. I wanted to include the stories of female, transgender and male sex workers, as well as people of different ethnicities, class backgrounds and sexual orientations, and a range of locations and eras. I wanted too to include people who had experienced different parts of the industry: massage parlours, brothels, street-based work, dominatrix work, escorting, private work, ship work. And some stories stood out as being particularly lively, vivid and well told; they were, essentially, great *stories*.

These stories are both extraordinary and ordinary, told by people who are themselves extraordinary and ordinary. They are in some ways stories of great bravery – of young transgender women choosing to live as their most authentic selves and build communities in an era when that meant being abused in the street and being unable to find employment. (For one interviewee, Poppy, who was barely in her teens at the time, it meant being subjected to horrific 'aversion therapy' in an attempt to change her gender identity.) They tell of the bravery of the small group of women from a Wellington massage parlour who decided that they deserved rights, as workers and as human beings, and who met to discuss setting up an organisation to advocate for those rights; and of the ground-breaking law change that was fought for and achieved by NZPC and its allies with the passing of the Prostitution Reform Act in 2003.

This book also tells of smaller, yet still powerful, acts of resistance and solidarity – the women in a Christchurch massage parlour doing a 'whip-around with the hat' to pay the fine of a colleague convicted of soliciting; the worker who refused to provide nude massages while receiving no pay for them (as was standard practice in 1980s massage parlours); the street-based worker resolutely turning down clients who wanted sex without a condom; the transgender woman explaining to a younger 'sister' where she could get hormone pills and how to find a place to live.

And these are stories of the things of ordinary life, too – of work, of parenting, of friendship, of money, of love. They tell of people who enjoyed the work, and people who found it boring or unpleasant. Some tended towards the 'job like any other' point of view: Catherine Healy noted, 'I was very conscious that sex work was work, and I felt very strong and empowered and happy and stimulated and all those things that you associate with a good job.' Others had a different take: 'You're not working in a fish-and-chip bar or selling Fisher and Paykel whiteware – you are selling your body,' said Kelly.

There were people who found camaraderie and community in the sex industry: 'What I remember is the women – there was a real sense of solidarity,' said Jeanie of her time in a Wellington massage parlour. Shareda, a transgender woman who worked on the street in Auckland and Wellington, thought of the street as 'where I met the people I came here to look for in the first place. And they ended up being lifetime friends.' These communities could serve as an alternative whānau, especially for people whose families didn't accept their gender or sexual identities. 'A lot of the girls were ostracised by their families, so we became family – we are family,' said Poppy. 'We're the transgender whānau.'

More than anything sex work is *work*, and work is, of course, always at least partly about money. For some people, sex work meant a way out of poverty. 'I'd had this thousand-dollar debt sitting there, and then I could pay that off. And I could have more food in the pantry than I would eat in a week,' said Stevie, who began sex work as a solo parent. 'It just made me feel like I had more say over my day-to-day life. I think it's real big stuff.' For transgender people in the later twentieth century, sex work was often the only way to survive. 'I lived as a woman all the time in Wellington,' remembered Dana de Milo, who came to the capital from Auckland in the early 1960s. 'That's why I had no work – no one would employ you. Most of us had to crack it [do sex work], or roll [steal], because we had to survive.' Margaret began operating as a dominatrix in Auckland at the age of 47 after her husband had a serious accident, leaving her with a child to support, while Kelly struggled to find a straight job after moving to Queensland with her young son in the 1970s. 'I flatly refused to be on the benefit, and my focus was to give my son and myself a better life. And we did, we had a wonderful life.' Yet before decriminalisation, the laws relating to sex work meant stress and subterfuge – or worse. The interviewees tell of entrapment by undercover police officers who came into massage parlours posing as clients, or who enticed street-based workers into their cars and then arrested them. As Anna Reed pointed out, under the Massage Parlours Act, women who were working in the comparative safety of a parlour could end up being forced onto the street if they were convicted of soliciting.

All but one of these interviewees worked in New Zealand before decriminalisation, and lived with the fear, if not the actuality, of arrest; several worked both before and after. 'As a worker you're so much more empowered,' mused Allan, who started sex work in his teens and returned to it in his forties, after the law changed. 'You can work, it is legal – that changes the energy that you're working with. You're not having to work under this shadow of darkness and seediness, actually it can be done in a place of light. It doesn't have to be all dodgy.' Kelly, who was working privately in Auckland when the law changed, said, 'That whole weight had been taken off your shoulders in many ways … you [had been] constantly living in that little arena of fear.'

However, there is still a high level of stigma attached to being – or having been – a sex worker. Misty was 'crucified' by her family when they found out about her job in a Christchurch massage parlour; Shareda remembered being pelted with bottles and rotten eggs by passersby on the street, while Kelly talked of workmates who were raped but never went to the police because they feared not being taken seriously. Anna Reed's daughters were bullied at school, and Catherine Healy points out that sex workers and former workers can still be excluded from some other occupations – highly ironic, given the insistence of the abolitionist lobby that sex workers should stop doing sex work. 'The industry is quite difficult to get out of, because what do you put on a CV? What do you say you've been doing for the last 10, 15, 20 years?' said Kelly.

The other side of the sex industry is the clients – another largely hidden group, and one also subject to a fair amount of stigma. (When did you last hear a man say he'd been to see a sex worker?) Several interviewees stressed that their clients were ordinary men, a cross-section of society. 'People think clients are dodgy, weird, or sad and lonely, or abusive, or can't have a girlfriend because they're horrible people who want to dominate women,' said Stevie. 'And it's totally not reality. Most of your clients are just very normal people.' The public health researcher Gillian Abel has noted that several pieces of New Zealand research found that clients were 'relatively benign', and that 'most [sex worker] participants … while able to cite at least some unpleasant experiences with clients, did on the whole say that they liked their clients and enjoyed contact with them'.[6]

Is it dangerous to be a sex worker? While several interviewees told me they felt they were 'protected', or that they could rely on their intuition to suss out bad clients, some (though by no means all) were threatened or assaulted while working. Misty, working on Auckland's streets, had 'a few incidents of ruffians and strangulations and stuff like that', largely from clients using methamphetamine, and Kelly was 'terrified' by a Vietnam-veteran client who freaked out during their session. Violence may also be perpetrated against sex workers by others as a hate crime, or with the assumption that the offender will get away with it because the victim is a sex worker. At least two interviewees in the project (neither of whom is included in this book, for various reasons) were raped in their off time because the rapists knew they were sex workers and that police were unlikely to take the assault seriously. One woman was sexually assaulted by a doctor during a consultation after she disclosed that she was a sex worker. (Decriminalisation of sex work, however, has meant that workers feel more able to turn to the police for protection and support.)[7]

But contrary to the opinions of some abolitionists, sex work as such is not necessarily abusive or harmful. The narrative suggesting that all sex work is violence, that all sex workers need rescuing, is a dangerous one; if all sex work is coerced, if consenting to sex work is not actually possible, then how can you identify incidents of actual abuse within the industry? This thinking is the flip side of the appalling old adage that a sex worker cannot be raped. And the insistence that all sex workers (or 'prostituted women', as the abolitionists typically have it) are victims and need to be rescued – even against their own will – denies workers autonomy and agency in their own lives.[8] 'Prostitution in itself is not synonymous with debasement,' notes the UK-based journalist Kate Belgrave, reflecting on her time working in a Wellington massage parlour. 'Stories of trafficked, bullied and beaten women are stories of abuse, not of prostitution per se.'[9]

The interviews strongly assert that sex work is indeed *work*, rather than a moral failure or an example of victimisation. It is true, however, that sex work is a particularly stigmatised and gendered kind of work – most workers are women, and almost all clients are men – and one that is intimately bound up with the sexual double standard. Psychology lecturer Panteá Farvid writes that men are seen as 'sex-needy and sex-driven, and women as passive and more interested in the relational, emotional or procreative outcomes of sex. The sex-needy model of male sexuality then positions men as legitimately requiring "uncomplicated" sexual release when and if needed … [C]ommercial sex is positioned as a viable option.' She also notes the parallels between sex work and traditional marriage, another arena in which women's sexual, emotional and domestic labour is exchanged for financial support from men.[10]

Several of the interviewees work or volunteer for the New Zealand Prostitutes' Collective; its long-time national coordinator, Dame Catherine Healy (whose damehood was announced as this book was about to go to print), tells of the collective's beginnings and the long campaign for law change. She suggested to me that this book could be titled 'From Police Cells to World Platforms', which exactly encapsulates the experience of some NZPC staff. There has been strong international interest in the New Zealand model of decriminalisation, and Catherine herself was invited to take part in (and won) an Oxford Union debate about decriminalisation of sex work – the first New Zealander to speak at the Oxford Union since David Lange debated the morality of nuclear weapons in 1985. Other interviewees talk of their pride in having been part of the campaign for decriminalisation.

The stories told here also illuminate other areas that have sometimes intersected with the world of sex work – the experience of newly urbanised Māori, the counter-cultural and protest movements of the 1970s and 1980s (including lesbian feminism), the difficulties faced by solo parents, the evolving culture of cities and their night life – and, in particular, the experience of being transgender in New Zealand.

While just four transgender people are included in this book – hardly a representative sample of the community – it's interesting to note the difference between the interviews with Dana (born in 1946) and Stevie (almost 40 years younger). Stevie, who uses the pronoun 'they', commented, 'I'm not a man or a woman … I'm a non-binary takatāpui transsexual,' employing terms (and probably concepts) that would have been completely unfamiliar to transgender people in the 1970s and 1980s. Dana's use of the terms 'queen' and 'real girl' for trans and cis women seems quite archaic now, but it's valuable to record them here – along with the 'back slang' used by ship girls and transgender women. Te reo Māori was also liberally mixed into their speech – even if, like Dana, they were Pākehā. (A glossary at the back of the book includes a number of terms particular to the sex-worker and transgender communities, along with some terms in te reo Māori used by the interviewees.) Stevie had been part of a politicised queer community before deciding to transition, whereas the older interviewees generally encountered other transgender people through street-based sex work or in clubs and bars. A full history of transgender life in New Zealand is yet to be written; it's an area ripe for exploration, and I hope someone from that community will do it.

As I worked on this project, people kept asking me what the interviewees had in common. I wondered too: was there any kind of generalisation I could make about the people I had interviewed? They were Pākehā, or Māori; they were 30, or 45, or 65, and had started sex work aged 20, or 14, or 34, or in one case 47. They came from working-class families, or middle-class ones; they had done poorly at school, or well. Some lacked qualifications, but others had a tertiary education. They were from the city, or from provincial towns, or from farms. They got on well with their families, or didn't. Some were single; some lived in long-term partnerships. Some were parents. A couple mentioned being sexually abused when young; others stressed that they had not been (countering the stereotype that sex work is a response to childhood abuse). Some had been sexually active early; some had had multiple partners before entering the industry; others had had remarkably little sexual experience before they started doing sex work. Some went into the industry because they had struggled to find other work and their choices were limited; some had had successful careers in other areas but wanted a change. A few loved sex work and saw it as a real vocation, while others had mixed feelings, or simply tolerated it because they needed the money.

Did they have anything in common? A lot of the interviewees found their way into the industry because they knew someone else who was working in it. They weren't groomed, they weren't forced, but they met someone who told them how this largely invisible, veiled world worked – who demystified it, perhaps took away some of the stigma and explained some of the benefits. A couple of the interviewees started out by working on reception at a massage parlour – jobs they found by answering newspaper ads – and then decided to 'jump the fence' for more money, once they knew more about what the work involved.

And of course money was usually a motivating factor. Sex workers made more money than women (cis or transgender) were typically otherwise able to. As Kate Belgrave has pointed out, sex work is 'enterprise in which many women have an unusual – for us – advantage. It's lucrative. It's one of the few occupations where women can expect a good fiscal return.'[11]

While I have included the stories of female, male and transgender workers, both Māori and Pākehā, heterosexual and LGBTI, from the 1940s to today, before and after decriminalisation, it is not possible for this book to represent the experience of every sex worker.

In particular, it does not represent people who have worked very briefly in the industry. It's not uncommon to do sex work for a short period and then move on, closing the door firmly behind oneself. Some former workers may not even tell their partners, friends, children and colleagues about a stint in the industry. This may be because they had difficult experiences that they want to forget, but more likely they simply want to avoid the misunderstandings and stigmatisation that could result from people knowing they were once sex workers, even if it was 20 or 30 years ago. They cut their ties with the industry completely. Migrant workers are another group who do not appear in this book – I have focused instead on those who have lived most or all of their lives in New Zealand, and I have given the book a predominantly New Zealand focus. It's also worth acknowledging that a majority of the interviewees here have had some involvement with NZPC.

Oral history allows an interviewer to take their time, to explore side alleys and interesting little winding paths, to ask an interviewee about what they wore and the colour of the wallpaper, to examine the domestic, the emotional and the private, as well as the so-called bigger issues.

Some of my interviews were very long – as much as 20 hours, recorded over many weeks – with talkative interviewees who had lived fascinating lives, full of irresistible and wonderful details. I hope that these edited versions of their interviews have preserved the integrity, vividness and individuality of their voices. They are people who entered sex work for many reasons – necessity, bravery, longing, rebelliousness, curiosity, sheer chance. I am deeply grateful to them for sharing their stories with me and allowing them to be published here. I hope that in some small way this book will help increase understanding of New Zealand sex workers, lessen the stigma still attached to the work, and demonstrate the impacts of decriminalisation on those in the sex industry.

NOTES

1. Decriminalisation of sex work is sometimes confused with legalisation (the approach taken in countries such as Germany and the Netherlands, and in some Australian states). Under legalised regimes, the sex industry is regulated by government, which may require measures such as mandatory sexual health testing or police registration of workers; in New Zealand, the sex industry is essentially treated like any other industry. For more on this see Gillian Abel and Lisa Fitzgerald, 'Introduction', in Gillian Abel, Lisa Fitzgerald and Catherine Healy with Aline Taylor, eds, *Taking the Crime out of Sex Work: New Zealand sex workers' fight for decriminalisation*. Bristol, UK: Policy Press, 2010, pp. 2–4; Bridie Sweetman, 'The judicial system and sex work in New Zealand', *Women's Studies Journal*, vol. 31, no. 2, December 2017, pp. 62–63.
2. Megan Hutching, 'The distance between voice and transcript', in Anna Green and Megan Hutching, eds, *Remembering: Writing oral history*. Auckland: Auckland University Press,

2004, p. 173. See also Linda Shopes, 'Editing oral history for publication', in Robert Perks and Alistair Thomson, eds, *The Oral History Reader*. 3rd edn. London; New York: Routledge/Taylor & Francis Group, 2016, pp. 470–89.

3 Anna Green, 'Oral history and history', in Green and Hutching, *Remembering*, p. 7. See also Melissa Matutina Williams, *Panguru and the City: Kāinga tahi, kāinga rua*. Wellington: Bridget Williams Books, 2015, p. 23.

4 Anna Green, '"Unpacking" the stories', in Green and Hutching, *Remembering*, p. 11.

5 Lenore Layman, 'Reticence in oral history interviews', in Perks and Thomson, *The Oral History Reader*, p. 248; Richard Cándida Smith, 'Publishing oral history: Oral exchange and print culture', in Thomas L. Charlton, Lois E. Myers and Rebecca Sharpless, eds, *Handbook of Oral History*. Lanham, MD: AltaMira Press, 2006, p. 423.

6 Gillian Abel, 'In search of a fair and free society: Sex work in New Zealand', in Eilís Ward and Gillian Wylie, eds, *Feminism, Prostitution and the State: The politics of neo-abolitionism*. Abingdon, Oxon; New York: Routledge, 2017, p. 143.

7 Catherine Healy, Ahi Wi-Hongi and Chanel Hati, 'It's work, it's working: The integration of sex workers and sex work in Aotearoa/New Zealand', *Women's Studies Journal*, vol. 31, no. 2, December 2017, p. 55.

8 See Juline A. Koken, 'The meaning of the "whore": How feminist theories on prostitution shape research on female sex workers', in Melissa Hope Ditmore, Antonia Levy and Alys Willman, eds, *Sex Work Matters: Exploring money, power, and intimacy in the sex industry*. London; New York: Zed Books, 2010, p. 34, for her suggestion that 'the small addition of the "d" following "prostitute" serves to imply coercion by a third party (or patriarchal system)'. Melissa Hope Ditmore notes of abolitionists, 'Prostitution as a condition is assumed to be so inherently intolerable that no rational person could freely choose it for themselves, therefore if anyone appears to have chosen it for themselves, it can only indicate that they are either not rational, or they are victims of coercion or deception … [This] opens the door to a paternalistic interpretation of "what is best for women"'. Quoted in Koken, 'The meaning of the "whore"', p. 38.

9 Kate Belgrave, 'My average life as an average whore', blog post, 7 October 2010, www.katebelgrave.com/2010/10/my-average-life-as-an-average-whore/

10 Panteá Farvid, 'The politics of sex work in Aotearoa/New Zealand and the Pacific: Tensions, debates and future directions', *Women's Studies Journal*, vol. 31, no. 2, December 2017, pp. 28–30.

11 Belgrave, 'My average life as an average whore'.

INTRODUCTION
A BRIEF HISTORY OF SEX WORK IN NEW ZEALAND

THERE IS NO EVIDENCE of prostitution among Māori before the arrival of Pākehā in New Zealand. However, once European explorers, whalers, sealers and traders began visiting the country, they were able to exchange muskets and other items for sexual services from Māori women (and sometimes men).

Over time these informal exchanges became increasingly systematic, with some chiefs organising prostitution to provide an income for their tribes. It became common for ports to offer sexual services to visiting Pākehā men, with young Māori women staying on board ships during their time in port. Kororāreka (later Russell) in the Bay of Islands – by the 1830s the largest whaling port in the Southern Hemisphere, with a reputation as the 'hell-hole of the Pacific' – was a particular hub for prostitution.[1]

As sailors and whalers were followed by more permanent settlers – at first, mostly male – prostitution flourished, by this time provided largely by European women. Bars and brothels sprang up in towns and cities, and were particularly numerous on the goldfields during the gold rush of the 1850s and 1860s.[2] Street sex work also emerged in the cities in the later nineteenth century.[3] An initial tolerance of the sex trade gave way to concern about its public visibility and about immigration by young Pākehā women who were thought to be entering into sex work rather than going into domestic service.[4]

With the signing of the Treaty of Waitangi in 1840, England's Vagrancy Act of 1824 – that country's main tool for controlling sex workers – came into force in New Zealand. In 1866 it was replaced by the Vagrant Act, under which a 'common prostitute' behaving in a 'riotous or indecent manner' in public could be deemed 'idle and disorderly' and imprisoned for up to three months.[5] This in turn was replaced in 1884 by the Police Offences Act, which made it an offence for 'common prostitutes' to publicly solicit for business.[6] Local authorities were responsible for control of brothels, with varying bylaws passed in different settlements.[7] However, the exchange of sex for money per se was not illegal, and sex workers were often tolerated, as long as they did not disturb the peace.[8]

Concern about prostitution as a 'social evil' drove the passage of the punitive Contagious Diseases Act 1869, echoing English legislation under which sex workers could be subjected to compulsory medical examination and then forcibly detained if they were found to be suffering from a venereal disease. Their male clients were not subject to this law.[9]

Social attitudes to sex work shifted in the late nineteenth century, with a growing number of people coming to see sex workers not as 'wicked harlots responsible for their own downfall, but as victims of injustice' in need of sympathy and support – and of rescue.[10] Church groups set up refuges and rescue missions, and sex workers were sent there to be reformed, though the harsh rules led many women to leave and return to sex work.[11] Feminist attitudes to sex work, then as now, were mixed – some feminist organisations identified sex workers and barmaids as posing a threat to the family and undertook a campaign to enhance the country's 'moral purity', while others were more sympathetic and lobbied for repeal of the Contagious Diseases Act.[12]

In the early twentieth century, notwithstanding concern over prostitution during World War I and the efforts of the health reformer Ettie Rout to prevent sexually transmitted infections among New Zealand troops overseas, the New Zealand sex industry seems to have dwindled.[13] American servicemen were stationed in New Zealand during World War II, and there was public concern about 'good time girls' and venereal diseases. There was also concern over the ship scene – in port cities, harking back to the earliest days of European ships in New Zealand, visiting seamen formed temporary (but sometimes recurring) relationships with 'ship girls', liaisons that might or might not involve the direct exchange of sex for money. In the 1950s and 1960s a number of young women who were part of this scene were sent to borstals in an attempt to reform them.[14] Around this time Flora MacKenzie, a dressmaker turned madam, ran a high-profile and flourishing brothel in Auckland's Ring Terrace. Between 1962 and 1976 MacKenzie faced six charges of brothel keeping and was imprisoned twice.[15]

In the 1960s and 1970s a commercial sex scene became more obvious and attracted media and public attention. In Auckland, Wellington and Christchurch, sex businesses defining themselves as 'massage parlours' proliferated. While they purported to provide just saunas and massage, it quickly became known that the women working in them also offered sexual services in the guise of 'extras'. Public concern flared over the parlours, and in 1978 the Massage Parlours Act was passed to regulate them. The act defined a massage parlour as a public place, making massage-parlour workers subject to existing laws against soliciting in public; it also placed limits on who could run a parlour, required workers to record their names and addresses for the police, and banned workers who had had prostitution- or drug-related convictions in the previous 10 years.

Transgender women – many of them Māori – formed communities in Wellington and Auckland, and some undertook street-based sex work, as it was almost impossible for them to find other employment.[16] They too were the subject of sometimes breathless media attention – 'Well developed breasts, make up and women's clothes make it difficult to tell the difference between the male prostitutes and real women. And Social Security is paying for the breast developer!' sputtered one Sunday newspaper in 1972.[17] The most visible face of the transgender community was the flamboyant and irrepressible Carmen Rupe, whose Wellington coffee lounge and nightclub – with sexual services offered on the side – were a magnet for straight punters as well as for young transgender people hoping to find others like themselves.[18] Interviewees for this book remembered Wellington as more transgender-friendly than Auckland, an attitude they ascribed to Carmen's high level of visibility.[19]

From the 1960s strip clubs also opened in the main centres, although at first performances were not allowed to include much movement, exposed nipples or complete nudity. While most strippers purported to be female, some were actually transgender.[20]

A few women worked on the street, while some worked for escort agencies, visiting clients in their homes, hotels and motels. These agencies weren't covered by the Massage Parlours Act; nor were private establishments such as the 'gentlemen's retreat' run by the former bandleader Bill Crowe in his faded-grandeur mansion overlooking Wellington's Oriental Bay (although in 1980 it was raided by police, and Crowe was prosecuted).[21] There was also a small number of male sex workers, who serviced male clients almost exclusively. They operated from 'beats' in public toilets or on the streets, on the waterfront, and, from the 1980s on, also through male escort agencies or privately.[22]

In the later twentieth century, while selling sex was not actually illegal, it was almost impossible to operate as a sex worker and not break the law. Under the Crimes Act 1961 it was an offence to keep a brothel, live off the earnings of prostitution or procure sexual services for another person. The Massage Parlours Act regulated massage parlours, and under the Summary Offences Act 1981 it was illegal to offer sex for money in a public place.[23] Clients of sex workers, however, were not subject to these laws. The criminologist Jan Jordan, writing in 1991, noted a 'double standard of morality – it is against the law for sex workers to solicit clients but not for clients to solicit sex workers. This reflects the bias of our early prostitution laws, which sought simultaneously to regulate women's lives while protecting men's interests.'[24]

From the 1970s to the 1990s the police operated 'vice squads', responsible for policing the sex industry, indecent publications and illegal gambling.[25] They targeted street-based sex workers, although only women were deemed capable of acts of prostitution: transgender (and male) workers were typically charged with offences such as frequenting with felonious intent, or being a rogue and a vagabond, until the Summary Offences Act 1981 altered the charge of soliciting to include men.[26] Undercover police also posed as clients in massage parlours in order to entrap workers. A Wellington journalist who accompanied two officers from the squad on a 'typical night patrol' in 1987 (in which both men had nude massages in city parlours and then entrapped two young transgender street workers, neither of whom had previous convictions) reported that the detectives 'joke and snigger at the prospect of a massage and proposition', and quoted one as saying, 'It's a good break to get out and have a night in the parlours or picking up "trannies" … It's a bit of a game. It revolts me.'[27]

In the same year, a group of Wellington massage-parlour workers began meeting in each other's homes and discussing the possibility of setting up an organisation for sex workers.[28] Since the 1970s, a number of organisations focusing on sex workers' rights had emerged internationally – these included COYOTE (an acronym for Call Off Your Old Tired Ethics) in California in 1973, the English Collective of Prostitutes in 1975, and EMPOWER in Thailand in 1985.[29] In 1975 sex workers occupied churches around France to protest repressive laws and police harassment; English sex workers took similar action in 1982.[30] In 1979 the American sex worker and activist Carol Leigh (also known as Scarlot Harlot) coined the term 'sex work'.[31]

The New Zealand Prostitutes' Collective (NZPC) emerged in a time of activism and social change in New Zealand. When sex workers began meeting in Wellington in 1987, it was six years since thousands of New Zealanders had swarmed onto the streets to protest against a tour by the South African Springboks rugby team. Sex between men, previously illegal, had been decriminalised in 1986, after a sometimes bitterly fought campaign; in 1987, again after considerable public protest, nuclear-powered vessels and those carrying nuclear weapons were banned from New Zealand waters. The women's liberation movement, active in New Zealand since the 1970s, was increasingly influential, and Māori activists were pushing for land, language and cultural rights.[32]

Another influence on the fledgling sex-worker activist movement was the arrival of HIV/Aids, with the first New Zealand case reported in 1984.[33] A moral panic over HIV/Aids scapegoated sex workers and gay men – but, as Jan Jordan points out, these public-health fears were to be usefully transformed into a campaign for sex workers' rights.[34]

'In terms of setting up the collective, the fact that sex work was a crime was a big motivating factor, and the idea that people didn't accept sex workers,' remembers Catherine Healy, a founding member of NZPC and national coordinator since the early days. 'We had HIV coming, and it was a scary, threatening thing for being a sex worker … Labour, management, stigma, recognising sex work as work, equal rights, equal protections, public health, HIV and Aids were the major themes – and of course the fact that sex workers were criminalised.'[35]

Transgender and male sex workers soon also became involved with the group, and in October 1988 NZPC received funding from the Department of Health to develop an HIV-prevention programme. The first NZPC drop-in centre opened in Cuba Street, Wellington, and the collective began producing a magazine, fostering peer-support networks and distributing condoms. In April 1988 Healy had been appointed to the National Council on AIDS, giving sex workers a voice and credibility at a national level.[36]

Work in the direction of law reform began in 1989, when NZPC made a submission on a bill that sought to criminalise escort agencies and outcall services.[37] Then in late 1991 a number of sex workers were arrested in a series of undercover police raids in massage parlours and on the street. This brought the conflict between the existing laws and the government's stated aim of HIV prevention into sharp relief: while the Health Department was funding the collective to promote safe sex and distribute condoms, police were seizing condoms and NZPC literature as evidence of illegal activity. After the 1991 raids NZPC wrote to the Department of Health, saying they would give back their funding and go underground unless a committee was set up to look at prostitution laws. As a result an interdepartmental committee was established, which included the Ministry of Women's Affairs, the police, the Department of Health and the Ministry of Justice; the Women's Affairs Ministry spoke out in support of sex workers, describing the law as 'discriminatory, because it criminalises prostitutes but not their clients'.[38]

The collective began networking with other organisations – inside and outside government – to push for decriminalisation of the sex industry, and a working group on law reform was set up in 1997 under the National government, whose MPs Maurice Williamson and Katherine O'Regan supported decriminalisation. The cause gained support from a number of organisations, among them the YWCA, the National Council of Women, the Council of Trade Unions and the Māori Women's Welfare League.[39] Catherine Healy, who spoke to many Rotary groups over this period, remembers the campaign for decriminalisation as 'a series of rolling events … It was just a constant chip, chip, chip, you know, almost obsessive. And using every situation that presented an opportunity to nudge it forward.'[40]

NZPC worked with lawyers to draft a bill, and in 1999 the Labour MP Tim Barnett introduced a private member's bill which would decriminalise sex work, promote public health and support the human rights of sex workers. After a sometimes fraught campaign, with increasingly fevered and vitriolic opposition, the Prostitution Reform Act eventually passed by one vote on 23 June 2003.[41] New Zealand became the first country to decriminalise sex work.

The Prostitution Reform Act repealed the laws that criminalised soliciting, brothel keeping and living off the earnings of prostitution. Its stated aims included safeguarding the human rights of sex workers and protecting them from exploitation, promoting their welfare and occupational health and safety, and supporting public health. The act made it an offence to pay for sex from someone aged under 18 or to force someone to provide sexual services. Sex workers and clients were required to practise safe sex, and business owners were to 'take all reasonable steps' to ensure safe sexual practices. Groups of up to four sex workers were able to work together as 'small owner-operated brothels', or SOOBs, without being registered. Non-residents of New Zealand were not permitted to work in the industry.[42]

The New Zealand sex industry operated under the same health and safety regulations as any other industry. Health and safety guidelines specific to the industry were developed in consultation with NZPC and with the Australian sex-worker organisation Scarlet Alliance.[43]

NZPC has commented that since the law was passed, it has been easier to discuss sexual-health issues and occupational safety and health with sex workers and brothel operators 'because conversations about sex work can be conducted more freely'. The once-fraught relationship between the sex industry and the police has improved hugely, and in Christchurch, where there has been violence against sex workers, including several murders, NZPC says the police have been 'outstanding'.[44]

The law change has also given workers a greater ability to stand up to unfair practices in brothels. In a ground-breaking case in 2014, the Human Rights Review Tribunal awarded damages of $25,000 to a sex worker who experienced ongoing verbal harassment from a brothel operator.[45]

Some local authorities have introduced bylaws regulating the location of sex-work businesses or street-based workers. In Christchurch, there has been ongoing conflict over sex workers in residential areas, after street-based sex workers were displaced from their central-city locations by the 2010 and 2011 earthquakes; in October 2017 the city council rejected a bylaw proposed by residents and opted instead for a community-based approach backed by NZPC and the police. However, at the time of writing, in early 2018, residents had appealed this decision, and the Ombudsman was investigating.[46]

A Christchurch School of Medicine study found that since decriminalisation, workers have felt more empowered in their negotiations with clients over matters such as condom use and sexual acts; these findings have been corroborated by later research.[47] While it is difficult to accurately assess numbers of sex workers, the Prostitution Law Review Committee, which reported on the impact of the act five years after it was passed, concluded that numbers of workers had not increased.[48] The committee reported 'increased confidence, well-being and a sense of validation amongst sex workers', a statement borne out by the comments of several interviewees who worked both before and after decriminalisation.[49] The committee also noted the 'absence of evidence of coercion' and concluded that there was no link between human trafficking and the sex industry in New Zealand (a conclusion endorsed by Catherine Healy, Ahi Wi-Hongi and Chanel Hati of NZPC, writing in 2017).[50] It also remarked on 'the stigma that still attaches to working in the sex industry, despite decriminalisation. This makes finding alternative employment and entering new social circles difficult for some.'[51] Violence remained a problem in some areas, particularly for street-based workers, and the prohibition on migrant sex workers meant that they had less access to the rights and protections provided under the Prostitution Reform Act.[52] Catherine Healy was made a dame in the Queen's Birthday honours of 2018 for services to the rights of sex workers. She commented that receiving the honour was 'like being brought in from the cold … I never, ever imagined this day would come.'[53]

Fifteen years after decriminalisation, there is a new generation of sex workers who have never known their work to be illegal and can hardly imagine that it once was.[54] Technology has also effected great change in the lives of sex workers, who are able to advertise on the internet (either on their own websites or via huge sites such as New Zealand Girls) and be contacted on mobile phones, giving them a once-unimaginable flexibility. Independent sex work – where people work for themselves, either alone or in a small group, from home or from a rented property – is increasingly common. Some workers travel to different towns, setting up shop temporarily in motels or hotels; there is also a growing number of 'boutique' brothels, where clients make an appointment rather than walking in off the street.[55] This shift towards independent contracting and flexible hours mirrors that of the wider labour market, and has meant an erosion of the support and camaraderie that previously existed among groups of workers in massage parlours or on the street (perhaps also mirroring the wider societal move away from unionisation and collective organising). There are fewer street-based workers;[56] the ship scene is also long gone, with increased mechanisation and the rise of container shipping since the 1970s meaning smaller crews and faster turnaround of cargo ships.[57]

While transgender people have more employment options than previously, and are less likely to see sex work as their only option, they still experience discrimination in employment.[58] The economic pressures that have sometimes made sex work the most attractive option for women remain, with women earning 12.5 per cent less than men per hour across the New Zealand labour market, while being three times as likely to be a sole parent and more likely to be unemployed or working in a low-paid industry.[59] In June 2018 it was reported that Immigration New Zealand had received a number of complaints about illegal migrant sex workers, and that 38 people had been served with deportation notices for doing sex work while on temporary visas; 27 had been deported, while as this book went to print the others were awaiting the outcomes of their cases.[60] Concerns were raised that the prohibition of migrant sex work placed these workers at increased risk of exploitation.[61]

In 2018 NZPC continues to have a contract with government to provide sex workers with sexual and reproductive health services and to advise government on policy.[62] Some other countries have expressed considerable interest in 'the New Zealand model' of decriminalisation.[63] Other approaches to regulating sex work internationally include criminalisation of the worker (as in New Zealand prior to 2003); legalisation, in which the government regulates the sex industry; and criminalisation of the client – the so-called Swedish or Nordic model – which draws on the radical-feminist belief that all sex work is violence against women and a human-rights violation, regardless of the actual claimed experience of sex workers.[64] This model, sometimes dubbed 'neo-abolitionism', has gained ground internationally, often through an 'unlikely collaboration of feminism and [Christian] fundamentalism'.[65] Sweden criminalised buyers of sex in 1999, and a similar approach has recently been adopted by other countries, including Norway (2009), Iceland (2009), Canada (2014), France (2016) and Ireland (2017).[66] However, many commentators and sex-worker organisations oppose criminalisation of clients on the basis that it forces the sex industry underground and makes sex workers vulnerable to more – not less – violence, discrimination and exploitation.[67]

Worldwide, organisations advocating for the rights of sex workers generally support decriminalising sex work, and in 2016 Amnesty International called for the decriminalisation of 'all aspects of adult consensual sex work', basing its policy on principles of 'harm reduction, gender equality, recognition of the personal agency of sex workers, and general international human rights principles'.[68] Agencies such as the United Nations Joint Programme on HIV/AIDS (UNAIDS) and the World Health Organisation also support decriminalisation.[69] However, in 2018 New Zealand remains the only country to have decriminalised sex work.

NOTES

1. See Jan Jordan, 'Of whalers, diggers and "soiled doves": A history of the sex industry in New Zealand', in Gillian Abel, Lisa Fitzgerald and Catherine Healy with Aline Taylor, eds, *Taking the Crime out of Sex Work: New Zealand sex workers' fight for decriminalisation*. Bristol, UK: Policy Press, 2010, pp. 26–28; Stevan Eldred-Grigg, *Pleasures of the Flesh: Sex & drugs in colonial New Zealand, 1840–1915*. Wellington: Reed, 1984, pp. 29–31; Jan Jordan, 'Sex work: 19th-century sex work', Te Ara – the Encyclopedia of New Zealand: www.TeAra.govt.nz/en/sex-work/page-1
2. See Jordan, 'Of whalers, diggers and "soiled doves"', pp. 28–30; Eldred-Grigg, *Pleasures of the Flesh*, p. 31.
3. Quoted in Ben Schrader, *The Big Smoke: New Zealand cities 1840–1920*. Wellington: Bridget Williams Books, 2016, p. 280.
4. Schrader, *The Big Smoke*, p. 282; Charlotte Macdonald, *A Woman of Good Character*. Wellington: Allen & Unwin; Historical Branch, Department of Internal Affairs, 1990, pp. 26–30; Charlotte Macdonald, 'The "social evil" : Prostitution and the passing of the Contagious Diseases Act (1869)', in Barbara Brookes, Charlotte Macdonald and Margaret Tennant, eds, *Women in History: Essays on European women in New Zealand*. Wellington: Allen & Unwin in association with Port Nicholson Press, 1986, pp. 17–18.
5. Eldred-Grigg, *Pleasures of the Flesh*, p. 31; Greg Newbold, *Crime, Law, and Justice in New Zealand*. New York: Routledge, 2016, p. 70; Vagrant Act 1866, New Zealand Legal Information Institute: www.nzlii.org/nz/legis/hist_bill/vb1866107.pdf
6. Jordan, 'Sex work: 19th-century sex work'.
7. Eldred-Grigg, *Pleasures of the Flesh*, p. 31.
8. Schrader, *The Big Smoke*, p. 283; Eldred-Grigg, *Pleasures of the Flesh*, pp. 35–36.
9. Macdonald, *A Woman of Good Character,* p. 17; Jordan, 'Of whalers, diggers and "soiled doves"', pp. 31–32.
10. Eldred-Grigg, *Pleasures of the Flesh*, p. 153.
11. Eldred-Grigg, *Pleasures of the Flesh*, pp. 153–55; Andrée Lévesque, 'Prescribers and rebels: Attitudes to European women's sexuality in New Zealand, 1860–1916', in Brookes, Macdonald and Tennant, *Women in History*, pp. 8–9.
12. Jordan, 'Of whalers, diggers and "soiled doves"', pp. 34–35; Eldred-Grigg, *Pleasures of the Flesh*, p. 154; Lévesque, 'Prescribers and rebels', pp. 9–10.
13. Eldred-Grigg, *Pleasures of the Flesh*, p. 164; Jordan, 'Of whalers, diggers and "soiled doves"', p. 36.
14. Jessica Weddell, 'Prostitutes are people too', *New Zealand Listener*, 4 December 1972, p. 13; Jan Jordan, *Working Girls: Women in the New Zealand sex industry talk to Jan Jordan*. Auckland: Penguin Books, 1991, p. 9; Jordan, 'Of whalers, diggers and "soiled doves"', p. 36; Jane Tolerton, *Ettie Rout: New Zealand's safer sex pioneer*. Rev. edn. Auckland: Penguin, 2015, pp. 92–173.
15. Jan Jordan, 'MacKenzie, Flora', first published in the Dictionary of New Zealand Biography, vol. 5, 2000, in Te Ara – the Encyclopedia of New Zealand: www.TeAra.govt.nz/en/biographies/5m19/mackenzie-flora; Jordan, 'Of whalers, diggers and "soiled doves"', p. 36.
16. See for instance Cathy Casey, *Change for the Better: The story of Georgina Beyer*. Auckland: Random House, 1999, p. 58; Johanna Schmidt, 'Gender diversity – Human rights and

discrimination', Te Ara – the Encyclopedia of New Zealand: www.TeAra.govt.nz/en/gender-diversity/page-6; Human Rights Commission, *To Be Who I Am: Report of the inquiry into discrimination experienced by transgender people*, 2008: www.hrc.co.nz/files/5714/2378/7661/15-Jan-2008_14-56-48_HRC_Transgender_FINAL.pdf, pp. 39–42.
17. 'Vice squad plans major crackdown', *Sunday Times*, 29 October 1972.
18. Paul Martin, *Carmen: My life*. Auckland: Benton Ross, 1988, pp. 119–44, 157–74.
19. Dana de Milo, interview by Caren Wilton for oral history project 'Selling Sex: The New Zealand sex industry', 2010, Alexander Turnbull Library, OHInt-0977-03; Poppy, interview by Caren Wilton for oral history project 'Selling Sex: The New Zealand sex industry', 2011, Alexander Turnbull Library, OHInt-0977-06.
20. Redmer Yska, 'Nightclubs: Strip clubs', Te Ara – the Encyclopedia of New Zealand: www.TeAra.govt.nz/en/nightclubs/page-5
21. Newbold, *Crime, Law, and Justice in New Zealand*, p. 71; Jan Jordan, 'Sex work: 20th-century sex work', Te Ara – the Encyclopedia of New Zealand: www.TeAra.govt.nz/en/sex-work/page-2; Leah Haines, 'A soul of discretion', *New Zealand Herald*, 10 September 2006: www.nzherald.co.nz/nz/news/article.cfm?c_id=1&objectid=10400637; Emily Watt, 'Mansion of secrets to close doors', *Dominion Post*, 2 September 2006: www.pressreader.com/new-zealand/the-dominion-post/20060902/281509336663880
22. Welby Ings, 'From the beat to the SOOB: The language of the male sex worker in New Zealand', *NZWords*, no. 12, May 2008, pp. 2–5.
23. Jan Jordan, 'Sex work: Legislation and decriminalisation', Te Ara – the Encyclopedia of New Zealand: www.TeAra.govt.nz/en/sex-work/page-4
24. Jordan, *Working Girls*, p. 10.
25. Jordan, 'Sex work: 20th-century sex work'.
26. 'Trevor Morley – Wellington vice squad', interview by Gareth Watkins, PrideNZ: www.pridenz.com/trevor_morley_wellington_vice_squad.html; Calum Bennachie, personal communication, 27 June 2017; Ings, 'From the beat to the SOOB', p. 2; Julie Hill, 'When the vice squad came calling', *The Spinoff*, 24 February 2017: https://thespinoff.co.nz/society/24-02-2017/when-the-vice-squad-came-calling
27. Ann Howarth, 'Keeping prostitution under control', *Dominion*, 22 July 1987, p. 13.
28. Catherine Healy, Calum Bennachie and Anna Reed, 'History of the New Zealand Prostitutes' Collective', in Abel et al., *Taking the Crime out of Sex Work*, p. 46.
29. Global Network of Sex Work Projects, 'History of the NSWP and the sex worker rights movement': www.nswp.org/timeline
30. Global Network of Sex Work Projects, 'Occupation of St Nizier church', www.nswp.org/timeline/event/occupation-st-nizier-church; Global Network of Sex Work Projects, 'The occupation of the Holy Church': www.nswp.org/timeline/event/the-occupation-the-holy-church
31. Carol Leigh, aka Scarlot Harlot, 'Inventing sex work', in Jill Nagle, ed., *Whores and Other Feminists*. New York: Routledge, 1997, pp. 229–30.
32. Ben Schrader, 'Public protest', Te Ara – the Encyclopedia of New Zealand: www.TeAra.govt.nz/en/public-protest
33. New Zealand AIDS Foundation, 'History of NZAF': www.nzaf.org.nz/about-us/history-of-nzaf/

34. Jordan, 'Of whalers, diggers and "soiled doves"', p. 37.
35. Catherine Healy, interview by Caren Wilton for oral history project 'Selling Sex: The New Zealand sex industry', 2011, Alexander Turnbull Library, OHInt-0977-13.
36. Healy, Bennachie and Reed, 'History of the New Zealand Prostitutes' Collective', pp. 47–52.
37. Healy, Bennachie and Reed, 'History of the New Zealand Prostitutes' Collective', pp. 51–52.
38. Healy, Bennachie and Reed, 'History of the New Zealand Prostitutes' Collective', pp. 52–53; Jordan, 'Sex work: Legislation and decriminalisation'.
39. Jordan, 'Sex work: Legislation and decriminalisation'; Tim Barnett, Catherine Healy, Anna Reed and Calum Bennachie, 'Lobbying for decriminalisation', in Abel et al., *Taking the Crime Out of Sex Work*, p. 61.
40. Catherine Healy, interview by Caren Wilton, 2011.
41. Jordan, 'Sex work: Legislation and decriminalisation'; Barnett et al., 'Lobbying for decriminalisation', pp. 63–64.
42. Gillian Abel, Catherine Healy, Calum Bennachie and Anna Reed, 'The Prostitution Reform Act', in Abel et al., *Taking the Crime out of Sex Work*, pp. 75–80; Jordan, 'Sex work: Legislation and decriminalisation'; Prostitution Reform Act 2003, New Zealand Legislation: www.legislation.govt.nz/act/public/2003/0028/latest/DLM197815.html
43. Abel et al., 'The Prostitution Reform Act', pp. 76–77.
44. Barnett et al., 'Lobbying for decriminalisation', pp. 69–70; Catherine Healy, Ahi Wi-Hongi and Chanel Hati, 'It's work, it's working: The integration of sex workers and sex work in Aotearoa/New Zealand', *Women's Studies Journal*, vol. 31, no. 2, December 2017, p. 55.
45. DML v. Montgomery (2014), New Zealand Human Rights Review Tribunal 6 (12 February 2014): www.nzlii.org/cgi-bin/download.cgi/cgi-bin/download.cgi/download/nz/cases/NZHRRT/2014/6.pdf
46. See Lynzi Armstrong, 'Hassling and shaming prostitutes no solutions to community's concerns', *Christchurch Press*, 24 May 2017; Tina Law, 'Pressure builds for Christchurch City Council to ban sex workers from residential areas', *Christchurch Press*, 12 April 2017; Logan Church, 'Ombudsman to investigate Chch sex worker decision', Radio New Zealand, 28 December 2017: www.radionz.co.nz/news/national/347130/ombudsman-to-investigate-chch-sex-worker-decision
47. Gillian Abel, Lisa Fitzgerald and Cheryl Brunton, *The Impact of the Prostitution Reform Act on the Health and Safety Practices of Sex Workers: Report to the Prostitution Law Review Committee*. Christchurch: Department of Public Health and General Practice, University of Otago, 2007, pp. 118–19; see also Johanna Schmidt, 'The regulation of sex work in Aotearoa/New Zealand: An overview', *Women's Studies Journal*, vol. 31, no. 2, December 2017, p. 46.
48. Prostitution Law Review Committee, *Report of the Prostitution Law Review Committee on the Operation of the Prostitution Reform Act 2003*. Wellington: Ministry of Justice, 2008, p. 41.
49. *Report of the Prostitution Law Review Committee*, p. 50; Allan, interview by Caren Wilton for oral history project 'Selling Sex: The New Zealand sex industry', 2016, Alexander Turnbull Library, OHInt-0977-19; Misty, interview by Caren Wilton for oral history project 'Selling Sex: The New Zealand sex industry', 2015, Alexander Turnbull Library, OHInt-0977-15.
50. *Report of the Prostitution Law Review Committee*, pp. 64, 167; Healy, Wi-Hongi and Hati, 'It's work, it's working', pp. 53–54.

51. *Report of the Prostitution Law Review Committee*, p. 77.
52. Lynzi Armstrong, 'Managing risks of violence in decriminalised street-based sex work: A feminist (sex worker rights) perspective.' PhD thesis, Victoria University of Wellington, 2011, pp. 75–81; Lynzi Armstrong, 'Decriminalisation and the rights of migrant sex workers in Aotearoa/New Zealand: Making a case for change', *Women's Studies Journal*, vol. 31, no. 2, December 2017, pp. 71–72.
53. Bess Manson, 'Dame Catherine Healy "brought in from the cold" after career advocating for sex workers', Stuff, 4 June 2018: www.stuff.co.nz/national/104330042/dame-catherine-healy-brought-in-from-the-cold-after-career-advocating-for-sex-workers
54. Catherine Healy, personal communication, May 2017.
55. Catherine Healy, interview by Caren Wilton; Healy, Wi-Hongi and Hati, 'It's work, it's working', p. 53.
56. Chanel Hati, interview by Caren Wilton for oral history project 'Selling Sex', 2012; Healy, Wi-Hongi and Hati, 'It's work, it's working', p. 54.
57. Gavin McLean, 'Shipping: The container revolution', Te Ara – the Encyclopedia of New Zealand: www.TeAra.govt.nz/en/shipping/page-9; Ings, 'From the beat to the SOOB', p. 4; 'Container shipping', NZHistory: https://nzhistory.govt.nz/culture/shipping-containers
58. Human Rights Commission, *To Be Who I Am*, pp. 39–42.
59. Ministry for Women, *Empirical evidence of the gender pay gap in New Zealand*, March 2017, pp. 7, 12: women.govt.nz/sites/public_files/Empirical%20evidence%20of%20GPG%20in%20NZ%20-%20Mar2017_0.pdf; Prue Hyman, *Hopes Dashed? The economics of gender equality*. Wellington: Bridget Williams Books, 2017, pp. 22–23, 49, 51.
60. Lincoln Tan, 'Illegal prostitution crackdown: 27 Asian sex workers deported', *New Zealand Herald*, 5 June 2018: www.nzherald.co.nz/nz/news/article.cfm?c_id=1&objectid=12064121; 'Illegal sex workers deported in visa crackdown', Newshub, 5 June 2018: www.newshub.co.nz/home/new-zealand/2018/06/illegal-sex-workers-deported-in-visa-crackdown.html
61. See Lynzi Armstrong, 'Almost legal: Migrant sex work in New Zealand', Open Democracy, 6 June 2018: www.opendemocracy.net/beyondslavery/lynzi-armstrong/almost-legal-migrant-sex-work-in-new-zealand; Armstrong, 'Decriminalisation and the rights of migrant sex workers in Aotearoa/New Zealand', pp. 71–75.
62. Hendrik Wagenaar, Sietske Altink and Helga Amesberger, *Designing Prostitution Policy: Intention and reality in regulating the sex trade*. Bristol, UK: Policy Press, 2017, pp. 251–53; Catherine Healy, interview by Caren Wilton, 2011.
63. Catherine Healy, interview by Caren Wilton, 2011.
64. Gillian Abel and Lisa Fitzgerald, 'Introduction', in Abel et al., *Taking the Crime out of Sex Work*, pp. 2–4; Bridie Sweetman, 'The judicial system and sex work in New Zealand', *Women's Studies Journal*, vol. 31, no. 2, December 2017, pp. 62–63.
65. Eilís Ward and Gillian Wylie, 'Introduction', in Eilís Ward and Gillian Wylie, eds, *Feminism, Prostitution and the State: The politics of neo-abolitionism*. Abingdon, Oxon; New York: Routledge, 2017, p. 3.
66. See Ward and Wylie, 'Introduction'; Josh Wingrove, 'Canada's new prostitution laws: everything you need to know', Toronto *Globe and Mail*, 15 July 2014: www.theglobeandmail.com/news/politics/canadas-new-prostitution-laws-everything-you-need-to-know/article19610318/; '"An historic day": It is now illegal to buy sex in Ireland', The Journal.ie, 27

March 2017: www.thejournal.ie/sex-laws-ireland-in-force-3309170-Mar2017/; Angelique Chrisafis, 'France passes law making it illegal to pay for sex', *Guardian*, 6 April 2016: www.theguardian.com/world/2016/apr/06/france-passes-law-illegal-to-pay-for-sex-criminalise-customers

67. See, for instance, 'The impact of "end demand" legislation on women sex workers', Global Network of Sex Work Projects, February 2018: www.nswp.org/sites/nswp.org/files/pb_impact_of_end_demand_on_women_sws_nswp_-_2018.pdf; 'Q & A: Policy to protect the human rights of sex workers', Amnesty International: www.amnesty.org/en/qa-policy-to-protect-the-human-rights-of-sex-workers; Schmidt, 'The regulation of sex work in Aotearoa/New Zealand', p. 43; Elizabeth Nolan Brown, 'What the Swedish model gets wrong about prostitution', *Time*, 19 July 2014: http://time.com/3005687/what-the-swedish-model-gets-wrong-about-prostitution/

68. Amnesty International Policy on State Obligations to Respect, Protect and Fulfil the Rights of Sex Workers, May 2016: www.amnesty.org/en/documents/pol30/4062/2016/en/

69. Ivana Radačić, 'New Zealand Prostitutes' Collective: An example of a successful policy actor', *Social Sciences*, vol. 6, no. 2 (2017), p. 3; Calum Bennachie, personal communication, 12 July 2017.

THE INTERVIEWS

ANNA REED

ANNA REED

I WAS BORN in Dunedin in 1943, and we moved to Wellington when I was five. My father's mother and stepfather were Polish Jews, and they came out to Dunedin as refugees in 1948. A lot of the European Jews had ended up in Wellington, and my grandparents went to Wellington to be around more of their own kind. We went too.

My father had come to New Zealand in 1938. He was very admiring of the Michael Joseph Savage government – equal opportunities and free education and health care. He was a communist and then a socialist, as many intellectuals were. He had gone to university in Zurich and studied architecture. He also went to university in Prague, and studied under Le Corbusier in Paris.

He came to Wellington and met my mother, and she got pregnant with my sister. I was born three years later, and my brother a year and a half after me. I think my parents got married on the understanding that if either of them wanted to have a relationship with anyone else, that was all right, as long as they were honest. We were aware that there were different people in their lives, and that was OK. They didn't seem to like each other that much, which had quite a strong effect on me. He was always putting my mother down. He was intelligent and witty and could be very cruel with his wit. She used to cry a lot, and I didn't like it at all.

In primary school I was the only child in my class that had a mother that went out to work. She could only do that because our grandparents lived with us. She worked in Wellington as a secretary for buyers for McKenzies, then secretary to biology professors at Victoria University. While she was there she did a degree in musical composition part-time. Then she went to library school. She ended up running the reference library at Victoria for many years. She was a composer, and she created a musical library database, and got a gong – a Queen's Service Medal – the year before she died.

My mother liked to sunbathe naked down the garden, and we often had holidays where we went to remote places and all ran around naked. I remember giving a morning talk at school and saying, 'The best thing about our holiday was we didn't have to wear any clothes!' Other people thought this was very strange. When I got older, my boyfriends could stay the night. I remember my father bringing us breakfast in bed on a tray, which wasn't commonplace in those days.

At school I was good at art, and at college I went into an arts-focused stream. But I came to grief a bit. My older sister had always been a good girl, so I rebelled. Also, I think in pictures – I'm a visual person. A lot of the learning we did was meaningless. Copying huge amounts of text and swotting it up – it was like a foreign language to me. I found secondary school very boring and meaningless, and I don't think it equipped me for what I needed in life. When I had children I vowed they would never go through a system like that.

I left school when I was just 16, at the end of the School Cert year. I didn't turn up for all the exams. The ones I knew I wasn't going to pass, I just didn't bother. I didn't do well at all – I passed English and I passed art. When I left school, my parents were horrified. Their children were all going to go to university – 'You can't leave school and get a job, Anna!'

I went to art school for a year. I didn't know what I wanted to do, but I liked art. I'd always been top of the class at school, then I got to art school and people were so good, I just gave up. I wasn't very focused. I used to sit around coffee bars – the Tete a Tete – with people like Bruno Lawrence and Mark Young. People who wrote poetry! I smoked my first dope. Had a lovely year doing nothing much, then my parents said they wouldn't support me any longer. So I got a job as a photographer's assistant for a studio in Wellington.

And I was planning to go to England with my friend and my mother. We booked, then I fell in love with somebody. So I decided not to go to England. My heart always won.

Then I got pregnant. And it was very tricky in those days – abortion was not legal at all. Finding a termination and somebody to do it was very difficult, and dangerous. It cost about 50 pounds, which was about three weeks' salary. A woman in Karori who we called Aunty Flo did it. She had been a nurse and had been shown how to do this procedure by a doctor. She was wonderful. I had to go home after she had inserted this flexible rubber tube into me, and ring her up when I started to feel some pains and let her know what was happening at each stage. It was good. The woman eventually got sent to jail, but I think she was as safe as you could get in those days.

After that, I didn't really feel connected to that man any more. So I decided to go to Europe. I got a ship to Italy, got off in Naples. I thought, 'Here I am! Here's the world!' I had 13, 15 pounds – not much, but I eked it out, hitched around. Sometimes teamed up with somebody, sometimes just stayed alone, slept in the fields and railway stations, didn't eat much. I didn't meet many young females on their own. My parents worried about me hitching round Europe, but I did it for years and I always felt very looked after. I looked a lot younger than I was – I wore my hair in two long plaits with flowers through them. I had a steel hair comb with a long thin handle as a weapon, but I never had to use it. I used to tell people I was 13.

In London I met my mother's cousin, Alison Grant Robertson, who was in her sixties, and was a huge influence on my life. She showed me that it didn't really matter what you did as long as you knew where you were going. You didn't have to fit inside the square. She certainly didn't.

Then I decided to have a baby. Some of my friends at primary school had had quite elderly parents, and I had a horror of being one of those grey-haired old mothers. I didn't really want a partner. I found it easy to love lots of people, and I always got sexually bored with one person. I liked the energy changes and having butterflies in my tummy, and that never seemed to last very long.

I went off to Wales and found a little cottage, moved everything down there and discovered I was pregnant. So that was absolutely perfect. I started meeting other hippies dotted around the hills, and I ended up in a commune in an old mansion, in the servants' quarters. The night Shanti was born I was sitting by the fire, as we all were, sitting and playing music and drumming. I stood up and my waters broke. Everyone else dropped another acid tab for the birth experience. I was lying naked by the fire and having contractions, and somebody went and phoned the midwife.

I came back to New Zealand when Shanti was about eight months old. Communities were taking off in New Zealand. Mum had heard of one in the Coromandel called Wilderland, so I went straight there, and stayed for maybe a year.

Later I moved up to Hokianga, and I had my second daughter, Ngahuia. Then we moved to a community near Nelson. When the Christchurch Rudolf Steiner school started up, I came and checked it out and moved down – though my children have never forgiven me for sending them to the Steiner school. They didn't have a good time at all, for different reasons.

I was always fascinated by the sex industry. I remember when I was about 14, 15, reading the court write-ups in the *Evening Post*. Women would be sentenced to imprisonment for something called procuring. I was fascinated by this whole concept – somebody was being sent to prison for having something to do with prostitution. I didn't really understand why that was wrong. I remember when the Profumo affair broke in England. This was a huge scandal, and there were these two prostitutes, Mandy Rice-Davies and Christine Keeler. I was absolutely fascinated by the whole thing.

The first time I went to Amsterdam, in the early 60s, I went one night and had a look at the window girls. I stood there, and I remember so clearly thinking, 'I would like to do what they're doing.' And that didn't mean sitting in the window. I knew that they were having sex. I liked having sex with different people, and you'd get paid for it. How wonderful. What a great way to make a living.

And that was really what sowed the seed. I did other things when I was living in the country, mulled over this and that. When I came to Christchurch, I used to make soybean coffee for health-food shops to pay the children's school fees. Then I ran into somebody who was working for an outcall massage service. And I said, 'You know, I'd love to do that. Could I work with you?' She said, 'Yeah, I'm sure you can.' So I borrowed all these clothes, because I didn't have anything that was right.

I remember the first client I had. He was a younger man. I was 34, and he was probably in his late twenties – he was a young rep staying in a motel. I remember him saying, 'How long have you been doing this?' I just said, 'A while.' A little while – that could be a few minutes, really. A few days, weeks, who knows.

And as soon as I had my first client, I thought, 'Ha! This is exactly what I should be doing.' I rang up my mother, the next morning. I said, 'Mum, I've got this wonderful job. I don't know what you'd call it, I just have hour-long love affairs with people and they give me all this money.' She said, 'Oh my god! Oh my god! I always have shocks from you, but now I know it can't get any worse.'

She was really upset. She'd come and stay with me sometimes – 'Don't tell me about your work, you know it shocks my Victorian soul to the nth degree. I don't want to know. I can't bear the thought of a daughter of mine sleeping with so many men.' I said, 'Mum, don't worry, I never sleep with them.' '*Oh!* That's worse!'

She said, 'Darling, you just don't seem to see that there's anything wrong with it.' I said, 'Well, I don't.' She couldn't quite get her head around that to begin with, but as years went by, she talked with a very few friends, and she said, 'They're quite envious actually of the way you've just gone ahead and done things when you wanted to do them. You wanted to have the baby without the partner – you've done what you wanted.'

Even though she did get used to it, she'd always say, 'Promise me I'll never see you on television.' I said, 'Why ever would I be on television?' It just seemed too remote a possibility. When I became involved with the New Zealand Prostitutes' Collective, I did it in a voluntary capacity for about three years. But as soon as I got a paid position, she accepted that television would be part of the job. In the end I think she was quite pleased with the way I turned out.

The first place I worked, in the summer of 1977, was called Pamper Visiting Massage Service. There were two outcall agencies in those days in Christchurch, and there were probably about four massage parlours and a handful of street workers. There was quite a lot of money around. It was before things happened that took a lot of money out of the economy – before we had a big drought, which affected a lot of farming money. When I was first working we saw a lot of farmers. Then we had the share-market crash, so that took away a lot of income that might have gone to the sex industry. Then the casino opened. People coming to town might have once upon a time got an escort or gone to a massage parlour, but now might take that money to the casino.

A call would come in to the base, and we would go out to wherever that person was, in their hotel, motel or home. So we would turn up with a towel and talcum powder or oil, you gave the client the choice. You laid him down and gave him his massage, and generally that would extend to something we called extras. You had to be very careful about how you worded anything, because you could be arrested for soliciting. So you played this silly little verbal ping-pong game. He'd say, 'What extras do you offer?' and you'd say, 'Well, what do you have in mind?' Always trying to get him to say it. It was silly. And you couldn't say anything on the telephone at all.

Usually they wanted sex, or sometimes oral. Men often think that because they're not having a full sexual service they're not being unfaithful to their partner or wife. Or, especially with older men, they haven't had oral sex with their wives ever, so that's a whole new thing for them.

We used to stay an hour. We had a driver, and you'd be picked up and taken to another job. We'd go from job to job to job. The driver would come in and take the money for the agency, $30 or $40. You would ring in to say that you were OK, using the client's phone – this was the days before cellphones. When you were ready to be picked up, if it was before an hour, you'd ring the agency and say 'I'm ready now,' and wait for the driver to pick you up.

The first person I worked for was the best person. He was an ex-policeman. He had a very strong sense of service in what we were doing, and I did too. Clients loved him. They would ring up and tell him all their problems – he'd spend ages on the phone. After that, I went to work for a woman, actually a transsexual. That's when I first met trans people. She had worked in a little rap parlour. Rap parlours were places that hadn't managed to get a massage parlour licence for whatever reason. You had to have a licence under the Massage Parlours Act 1978. She worked for this rap parlour, and she decided, no no no, she'd just set up a little house and have a couple of people working there and do jobs herself, and keep all the money rather than have to give some to the agency.

I worked for her for two or three years – I didn't want to work in a parlour. Then she and I fell out, and that was that.

When I was first working, I would always say, 'I'm a whore. I think this is great.' 'Oh, don't say that! That's terrible!' I'd say, 'I think it's a great word. That's how I feel.' Then I decided I was a paid lover.

I've always been addicted to love in whatever form it takes. It was just very natural and easy for me to go off on that little tangent, the dance you do with somebody. But really it's because when I was 27, when Shanti was a baby, a beautiful, beautiful being came into my life and showed me who I was. His name is Maharaji.[1] He was only 13. I went to London and somebody I knew said, 'Anna, you've got to see him.' I went into this room and he came in and sat down, and I was just totally bowled over by him. He was kind of golden. I'd never seen a golden person before. He was just emanating something. He started talking, speaking in parables, all relating to your inner person. I thought, he knows more about me than I do myself.

He showed me how to look inside myself, and it was a total revelation. I didn't understand it at the time. But after a while I noticed that I was relating to people in a different way. I knew who I was, and I could see who they were. Not all this stuff that you think you are and you think you might be, but just going into a deeper place with them. So that was great for working, because there would be somebody who would come into my domain who I might not be physically attracted to at all. And every single time I'd just look into those eyes and see what I wanted to see, and it turns into a beautiful thing. It's always, always been like that. If it stopped, I would have stopped working.

I believe some sex workers have a colder approach. But I don't know how you could do something that's really intimate without being intimate yourself. I'd come out of a room looking like I'd been in bed with somebody for a weekend. And I'd sing. I'm also a very noisy lover, and every parlour I worked at, people would say, 'I could hear you down the corridor.' I'm just very noisy, always have been. Some men really like that, and some people didn't like it.

People think I must know all this stuff and have all these secrets. But I wouldn't ever do anything to anyone that I wouldn't like done to myself. That was really my bottom line. Some people would want me to stick my fingers up their bums, and I don't like that myself, so, 'I'd rather not do that.' I was into major kissing for a long time. I always thought, how can you make love

---

1   The spiritual teacher Prem Rawat, then known as Maharaji.

with somebody without kissing them? When I had to become more health-conscious, I had to revise that, learn to kiss in different ways.

Sexually I've always been very multi-orgasmic. With clients it was often better than with lovers, because it was all new and exciting. I always got bored with one person – I don't like predictability. Sex work just was made for me, I tell you. And I believe that in other civilisations, other times, that we were highly revered, we were the wise women. We were often nurtured into this role. And I really understood that.

Years later I went to a workshop with Annie Sprinkle at an international sex workers' symposium in LA. There were various streams of things you could do, and one was Annie Sprinkle, who's a porn star. She did this workshop on sacred sex, and it was a very profound experience for me. It was the first time I had been in a room with other sex workers who were going along a similar path – they had an understanding of sex work that was deep inside. It was great. I didn't feel alone any more.

I hadn't realised that I felt alone until I went to that workshop. It's just doing sex work from a place of love inside yourself. A lot of people that I worked with had a totally different experience. The word 'love' would never have entered the equation in their understanding of what they were doing. But the workshop was very enlightening – it was like, yay! There are lots of us out there!

When I worked from the trans woman's house we also did outcalls, and I did my own driving. I had a funky old two-tone purple bus, which was very noticeable. I used to park it down the street from where I was going, so the neighbours wouldn't say, 'What was that bus doing outside your house?' I drove myself to deserted old factories and all sorts of things. Looking back now, I did go to some pretty strange situations, and there were a couple of times that could have been challenging. But I always felt looked after. I think that if something is happening and you react with fear or anger, it's likely to manifest and grow into something else.

I remember being at a motel. I was in the shower, and the man took my money out of my bag. I knew he had, and he totally denied it. It was money he had given me, and then it wasn't there. I was so hurt that I had given him my love and he had done that to me. That was probably the most overwhelming feeling that I had. How could you do this to me, when I've given you my love? Because that's how I always was with my clients.

I wanted him to pay for it in some way. Part of me was really angry. I remember coming down the steps – it was about two o'clock in the morning – and I screamed out, 'You're a liar! You're a thief! And what's more' – I was trying to think, what's the worst thing I could say to him – 'and what's more, you've got no love in you whatsoever, no love in you!'

Another time I went to a motel. I'd seen the man before, and there was something a wee bit odd about him, but at the same time I didn't feel scared or that I didn't trust him. He said, 'I thought we'd try something a little different tonight, Anna.' He said, 'I'm going to tie you up.' I said, 'Oh, are you?' He pulled out these stockings, and he tied my legs and arms spread-eagled onto the bed. I thought, this is a bit odd. He said, 'How are you feeling, Anna?' It was just this very quiet way he said it. He said, 'Are you scared?' I said, 'No.' Then he suddenly turned off the light, and it was pitch black. He said, 'Are you scared now?' I said, 'Well, I just need to tell you that my driver will be coming to the door in about five minutes.' 'Oh my goodness, oh my goodness!' He started untying me, snapped into another kind of mode. I actually had to wait for the driver for a while, but I'd thought, you've got to change this situation. But if I'd reacted really differently, it could have been worse.

When I worked in parlours, occasionally people would have bad experiences with somebody that I'd been with, who had been OK with me. It's an awful thing to say, but I think some people do attract certain things.

I had moved into a house with another woman from the Steiner school and her two children. It was pretty chaotic, with four children and two mothers. Then the house next door became available – they both were old villas, large properties. So I moved next door and we took a section of the fence down and had this big communal garden. We would eat an evening meal together, and when I was working my girls would stay over there. I'd come home and make their lunches and she'd see them off to school. I gave her 10 per cent of my earnings.

I wasn't very good at charging, I must say. I was quite overwhelmed by all this money. It was more than I needed, and I did tend to give quite a lot of it away. It just went wherever it was needed. My mother used to say, 'Why don't you keep your money? You might need to buy a house!' I'd say, 'Property! I'll never own property!' I was a hippie – you didn't do things like that. But a lot of money went on going to festivals, mostly in America, to be with my spiritual teacher.

In the beginning I used to just say, 'Here's my bag. Feel free to put whatever you want into it.' That was how I liked to operate best of all. Most people would put in what they would normally pay, and occasionally they put in more, and occasionally they put in much less. I remember a man putting in a dollar. I did think that was a bit stingy. Then when I started working with other people in a parlour, I had to learn to charge what they were charging, because they would get really pissed off. I was always very popular. It was because I enjoyed sex – they were my lovers for that time. But the others were convinced I was undercharging, because why else would I be popular?

Clothes were a problem. I'm an op shopper from way back, so I'd get various outfits together. I didn't wear makeup for a year or two, because I just didn't wear makeup. I didn't wear a bra – I had quite good breasts, they were quite high. I didn't normally wear underwear at all actually, so I had to buy some. I remember going into a dress shop and buying a dress. I'd never done anything like that before as an adult, just bought a new dress. And I wore that pretty solidly for a long time. When I went to parlours, we used to wear robes. I had a selection of really nice robes. I bought a lovely Christian Dior one in America, I made one. Just something that was easy and fast to put on, you tied it up round your waist, and could be naked underneath. Long, with high heels – got to wear your high heels.

I used to sit and dream about how if I was running a place I'd like a piano in the corner. I liked the saloon-girl kind of image. I wore clothes like that a lot too – coloured petticoats, flouncy silk things. A flower in my hair and corsety things, I liked that idea.

I do remember with the clothes thing, especially in the last 10 years or so, when I was in my fifties, I'd score some outfit from an op shop and think, this'd be OK for work. Then I'd get terribly anxious that I looked like the mother of the bride. That was the worst look I could possibly have.

In terms of safe sex, I was a hippie, and condoms were so unnatural. I thought they were revolting. I always had them with me, but I didn't instigate their use much. In my first year of working, I had gonorrhoea seven times. I used to go down to the sexual health clinic every second Friday for a check-up. They were really good to me – they knew what I was doing and they never preached at me. They would just give me my shot of antibiotics. Then I'd think, I should use condoms, but sometimes I would and sometimes I wouldn't. I had gonorrhoea in my throat twice. It wasn't until I was sitting there waiting for my appointment one day, and I saw the nurse leading out this woman who was in tears. I went in and said, 'That poor woman.' She said, 'Oh, her husband went astray, went to a massage parlour and gave her something.' Suddenly the penny dropped and I understood my responsibility in society.

After a few years working as an escort and privately, I was with a friend in the States, in Kansas City, and I was mugged and beaten by a man in the street. When I came back, I became aware of my personal safety for the first time. We didn't even have a lock on our back door. I was probably a bit naive, but that experience took away a lot of my innocence and trust. I thought, 'There are some awful people out there. I didn't know they existed before. I think I'll work in a parlour with other people around.'

The one I really wanted to go to was called the Boutique. It was a small place, but reportedly very busy. In order to go there I had to start at a bigger place that had the same owner. He said, 'We want you at the Man Tuam.' So I was at the Man Tuam. One night I was the only person there and I did 17 massages, one after the other after the other. I could hardly walk. I came home and couldn't believe it.

I eventually went to the Boutique. There had been two people working there for years and years, and unbeknownst to anybody they were creating a parlour right next door, so they took all their clientele with them. But the Boutique was busy. We saw a lot of farmers in those early days. Mondays and Tuesdays they came to town. So from then on I worked the same shifts for years and years, no matter where I was. I worked Tuesdays and Thursdays, double shifts. I would go in at 10 or 11am when they opened and work right through till 3, 4, 5am. I found it easier to do that than work a night then get up in the morning. All my regular clients knew I worked Tuesdays and Thursdays, didn't matter whether it was day or night. And I worked right through, with two weeks off every summer for a family holiday.

Two of the parlours I worked in had open fires. They were upstairs and you had to carry the bags of coal up the stairs. They gave a lovely feeling in the lounge areas. The massage tables – these were the days before decriminalisation, so you were supposedly only performing massages – were always quite high and narrow. So to do the sex bit we had sheepskin rugs on the floor. Looking back, those rugs would never be washed. You'd put a towel on top. But it was not so easy having sex on those tiny narrow beds. Then I went to a parlour called the Sunrise, and their beds were wider. They were still high, but they were big enough for you to fit side by side.

Then I worked at the Lily of the Valley, which became Club Lily, then Gavincy's, but that's closed now too. They were the first place in Christchurch to have double beds. When I saw them, I was like, what would you want a bed for if you weren't doing sex? Hope we don't get busted! Just this idea of having a bed rather than a massage table, where you could euphemistically assume that you were just doing massage.

The client would have a half-hour or three-quarter-hour or hour massage. In those days we got wages – $4 for a half-hour massage, $8 for an hour. Because they were quite busy times, my pay packet would be about $60 a week. That was good declarable income, especially if you were on a benefit, as I was in the early days. Anything else – if he wanted a hand relief it was generally $30 – this is around 1980. I think sex was $60, and sex with oral was $80. I always did oral – I put the condom on with my mouth anyway.

Occasionally you'd get what we called straight massages. We hated them. They were people that just had the massage money – they didn't want to or couldn't afford to pay for anything more. You had to spend that time with them, give them a massage. You'd be nude, they'd be nude. At the same time you were always aware of the fact that they could be a cop, because that's what the cops did. We always thought we knew by the look of their shoes whether they were police or not.

I never got busted, but I knew people that did. The cop would come in for a massage, and lie there, and if she offered anything else, they'd come back at the same time the following week with a search warrant, and arrest her. She'd go to court, her name would be in the paper. Two hundred dollar fine, and we'd always do a whip-around with the hat, because we knew she wouldn't be able to work in a massage parlour for 10 years. It was terrible. Terrible. If you had a drug- or prostitution-related offence you couldn't work in a parlour. So that put people onto the street. It was very, very unfair.

The police loved visiting the parlours and taking down everybody's names, and making out in their jokey kind of way that they were your mates, and then they'd turn around and bust you. We just hated that. You had to put your true name and date of birth in the police book. In those early days they would come and regularly uplift pages of those books. Then computers came in and they would just enter the details on their computers.

People started leaving massage parlours because they felt they weren't being treated well, or that they had to pay too much of the money they should have had themselves. So they started working privately, and there were no laws around that, except the soliciting law. If you went outside the Massage Parlours Act you weren't controlled by the police.

The head of the vice squad decided that, gosh, there's people starting to advertise and I don't know who they are. So he reached a deal with the *Press*, that they would only accept your advertisement if you had registered with the police. And he would take a Polaroid photograph of you. We were outraged. I rang everyone that was advertising in the *Press* to see how they felt about having their photographs taken. Some people were like, 'It's for our own safety, it's all right,' while others thought it was a breach of their human rights.

We got the police commissioner to look into the fact that he was taking photographs, insisting on them. The commissioner wrote back to say, 'If the police in a particular region develop a new initiative that they believe is in the interests and safety of the people, fine.' And after that, registration crept through New Zealand.

We were always concerned about who had access to that information. You'd go to put your advertisement in the *Press* and they'd take this folder off the shelf and open it up. There were people's personal details there – who has access to them? It took a lot of work to get them to at least put it under lock and key.

When the Prostitution Reform Act was passed, it was recommended that those old lists get destroyed. Well, in Wellington they mixed them into the general police database. Nobody knows how they might come up. Christchurch assures us they've been destroyed, but I don't believe the police will ever destroy intelligence. People have told us over the years that when they've applied for jobs that require stringent security checks, they haven't got them. Everyone that applied for a job at the casino got turned down – and then someone we knew who had worked but hadn't been on any register, went for a job there and got it.

One woman, a professional cleaner, applied for work cleaning at the police station. She's been in no trouble, nothing on her record, except that she'd been on the escort list. And she got turned down. She rang up – she wanted to know why. They said, 'You're not a suitable person.' She's convinced that it's the only thing that could have got in the way. So, who knows.

The police started taking down details and photographs of street-based workers at the same time. We'd go up and down the streets saying, 'If the police want to take your photograph you don't have to. You don't have to tell them anything.' People get scared of the police and they feel as if they have to comply. And the police can make it quite tricky.

Generally, relationships in the parlours were good. There was always the odd one or two that were having permanent crises or were troublemakers. But mostly the camaraderie was really good. I didn't form strong relationships with people that I worked with. I was probably seen as a wee bit aloof. I love reading, and I used to read between clients, whereas a lot of other people would just be playing pool, if there was a pool table, or sitting round talking, at the most reading women's magazines. I'd buy the *Listener* on Tuesday and I'd read all the reviews, get my book from the library. And they were all younger – I was always older than anyone.

At first, we got paid for massaging. And then there was quite a long period where we didn't. Then the parlour owner came down from Auckland and said that we were going to have to pay shift fees. It was going to be $10 per shift – you paid to go to work. We were outraged. We had a meeting at somebody's house, and we decided unanimously that we would not be paying shift fees. I rang Catherine Healy[2] – this is probably about 92. I said, 'You won't believe this. The owner of our parlour is trying to charge us money to be there.' She said, 'We've been paying them in Wellington for ages.' I said, 'What?! Well,

---

2   National coordinator of the New Zealand Prostitutes' Collective.

we're not paying them.' We put our foot down. Turned out Auckland and Wellington had had shift fees for a long time. So we held out for a year – we all threatened to leave if it was installed. Then, it's happening whether we like it or not, so we had to bite the bullet and do it. Slowly other places in Christchurch started charging shift fees too.

Then there were fines. You're 10 minutes late, $100 fine. Anything to get any money out of people. The woman that managed the place where they introduced shift fees used to hire and fire and fine arbitrarily. Every day people would turn up for work – got a taxi, had to pay child care – to be told they were no longer on the roster. They wouldn't even get a phone call. No reason – her little whim. I was always good, I was always on time and did lots of the cleaning and laundry. And I was popular in those days. But the first thing I did as soon as I got there was look to see if I was still on the roster. And that's a horrible way to work, in fear.

In 2009, most places charge about $15 for a shift in Christchurch. The odd one, if you don't get a job you don't have to pay a shift fee. Others, you pay a shift fee whether you get a job or not. Then there's the whole bond thing. A bond is where you've got to pay say $200 to start work at a place. They say, 'That's so if you don't turn up we've got you covered. If you leave and give us two weeks' notice, we give it back.' Some people never got their bond back, although they hadn't done anything. Some of those owner-operators had terrible practices.

I always had more money than I needed. My mother kept saying, 'You should buy a house, darling!' 'No, I don't want to buy a house.' I rented a house for six years – I always thought I owned that house. I knocked out walls, put in mezzanine floors, a potbelly stove. It and the house next door got sold to the Housing Corporation, who bowled them. I was mortified – that was my home! It was fabulous. It always had lovely people staying – so many memories. I couldn't believe it. That was when I thought, 'I've got to buy a house. I don't want this to happen again.' So I started saving money. I saved and saved, and looked at about 150 houses. Eventually I found this house – and I've just pretty much paid it all off. It's a lovely house.

When I first started work I was on a benefit. I began paying tax after about five or six years. In those days you could go down to Inland Revenue, go into a little cubicle. I'd just have a little book made up of what I'd earned and what I'd spent for advertising. I put my own ad in the paper. I always had 'Tuesdays and Thursdays, Anna, for a loving massage today.' And they'd do my tax for me. I remember when I first wanted to go off the benefit, and I told this caseworker, 'I'm going to do escorting.' I said, 'I'll probably go out for dinner and meet people, it'll be quite good.' She said, 'Are you going to make enough? We're only thinking of the children here. I don't think you should go off the benefit.' I thought, dammit, I'm trying. She said, 'Just give it a couple of weeks.' I rang her and said, 'It's going really well, I'm making lots of money.' She said, 'I don't think you should go off the benefit. You tell me how much you've earned and I'll deduct it.'

First of all I told Inland Revenue I was a masseuse. Then I put 'sex worker/educator' because I felt that was what I was doing. When I came on board here with the collective I became an educator. Whenever I re-entered New Zealand from anywhere and you had to fill in your entry form, that's what I would put. Sex worker/educator. And I would always be searched. Sometimes the only one on a plane searched. I'd be so pissed off. They'd be peering down my toothpaste tubes. I'd say, 'Just look at me. I'm this middle-aged woman. Do you really think if I was bringing drugs in I'd be drawing attention to myself?' I said, 'It's just because of what I've put on the form.' And they'd usually admit it. I'd say, 'Get over yourself. I'm trying to just be honest here.' It really used to make me angry. Mum would say, 'What do you expect, dear?' and I'd say, 'I expect people to accept me the way I am.'

When I didn't need a babysitter every time I walked out the door, I thought, it's time to do some voluntary work. The AIDS Foundation was advertising for volunteers. It was about 1989, and in those days there were a lot of sick people, people were dying. I thought, well, there but for the grace of God go I, looking back and seeing how loose I'd been in terms of not using condoms.

Rodger Wright – who our needle exchange is named after – was appointed as a representative, a person living with Aids, onto a committee that met in Wellington every couple of months. Catherine Healy, our national coordinator, was appointed as a representative of the sex industry. Rodger said to her, 'There's a volunteer in Christchurch who's had Aids training, and she's a sex worker.' This was of great interest to Catherine, so she made contact with me. I went to Wellington. I remember walking into that first office they had in Cuba Street. I saw a filing cabinet and I thought, 'Oh! Information on the sex industry!' I was so impressed by that filing cabinet – that's what sold the collective to me.

The first issue of the magazine had come out and it had been called *Fallen Angel*. And I was appalled. I said, 'I do not consider myself fallen. I have risen! And I will not contribute to this magazine while it has this title.'

Anyway they paid for a separate telephone line, a fax and an answer machine for me. That gave the media a point of contact, if they wanted to know anything – and the media is always fascinated by the sex industry. Then other people started ringing, saying they wanted to be involved. So we started meeting at the AIDS Foundation every week, then at the needle exchange.

Rodger came to live at our house because he couldn't live on his own any longer, he was too unwell. So my daughter Ngahuia and I spent a lot of time looking after Rodger. He and I had a few battles in the beginning, but we grew to love each other. My other daughter, Shanti, had been working in Japan and made a lot of money, and she wanted to pay for me to go to Europe. There was a big HIV/Aids conference in Berlin, and Catherine Healy said, 'If you get there, we'll fund you to attend it.' It was a huge conference – there was something like 17,000 delegates. I said, 'I can't go because I can't leave Rodger.' In the end, a house for terminally ill people had been set up, and Rodger agreed to stay there.

I went to the conference, and there were a lot of international sex workers there. We had major meetings and it was really good. That's what conferences are all about – it's the networking. Anyway I came back and Rodger had decided to stay in the house. I was with him when he died – that was very special.

After he died, we looked for premises, and set up our drop-in centre in early 1994. We were trying to build up our networks, make contacts. We would visit parlours and ring round the escorts, and do street visits. I've done street outreach weekly for all those years, still do, one night a week. We have packs we give out with condoms and sachets of lubricant. We used to give out printed stuff about ugly mugs; now we have a text alert system in Christchurch, so if people tell us about anything we can bulk text.

In the old days, people would give us any information about any bad clients they'd had. They mostly came from the street sector – occasionally private workers, but not much happens in parlours. Although sometimes somebody'll try and rip the condom off – definitely an act of violence. A client has been charged in Christchurch for that. But it's mostly in the street sector where people are more vulnerable. We would get as much information out as was safe for us to publish. We would make a little booklet and photocopy it. Another region put too much information about somebody and he recognised himself and decided to sue us. Catherine got very anxious about this and said all the ugly mugs had to be withdrawn.

In Christchurch, for some reason, we have more violence reported than any other region. So we had a worker who worked alongside Telecom to develop this system. It's wonderful. Somebody can say, 'This green van pulled up and the guy had a knife and wanted me to get in,' and we can text that information, and everybody that's subscribed – we've got 270 people – gets that text. The police think it's wonderful. We have a very good relationship with the police in Christchurch, and we like to work with key police personnel.

I had a lot of regular clients. I had some for about 15 years. Although, interestingly, when I started doing public stuff and my face went out there, some of those regulars stopped coming. At first I thought, it's because I'm getting old. I was probably in my early fifties. You'd see someone come in and think, that's funny, I used to go through with him a lot, I haven't been with him for ages. I think they just felt it was getting a bit confrontational for them.

I fell in love with my favourite client. He was absolutely gorgeous. He was about 15 years older than me, and he had grown up and married the girl next door in a fairly remote farming area. It was the first time he'd ever been in love, and it was so beautiful to be on the receiving end of his love. He had a fabulous heart, a beautiful heart. He left his wife and came and lived with me. My children liked him. He was the first person that they didn't see as a threat. I didn't stop working – he wouldn't have expected me to. He used to get out of bed and come and pick me up, 3 or 4 in the morning, from wherever I was working. There were difficulties, but I just loved that man. Then the difficulties started to get more dominant, and I thought, I think I need time on my own again. He went back to live with his wife, and he'd come and see me about once a year, say, 'That was the best year of my life.' I'd say, 'I know.' He was the last person I lived with.

I thought sex work was a great thing to do. I was open with everybody. And I think my friends probably just thought, strange thing to do, but she doesn't seem to be damaged by it. They got used to it. Women are often very interested and ask all sorts of questions, think you know all these secrets that you don't.

I used to tell my daughters that I went to massage people. I used to massage friends too, so that wasn't any revelation. Shanti found out when she was nine. Children can be very cruel. There was a girl that was older than her, and Shanti came home crying, saying, 'She says you're a prostitute, you're dirty and you do dirty things with men with no clothes on.' I thought, well, it's time for the big talk. We sat down, and it was quite easy to talk to her. I said, 'Look, there are some people out there that have got nobody to love. And you know me' – there had been people in and out of my bed in my private life for years – 'I like loving people and having sex with them.' She said, 'Yeah, you do.' I said, 'A lot of people have problems about people having sex with different people. I don't. And a lot of people have problems about money. Sex and money are the biggest things for a lot of people, and when you're paid to have sex, that's when you're called a prostitute or a sex worker. A lot of people think that's a bit much, they can't cope with it or they don't understand it.' She thought about it and she said, 'You're probably quite good at it.' I said, 'I think I am too.' She said, 'The only thing is that I might not be invited to people's places because they might not like it.' I said, 'Well, it hasn't happened yet.' She coped with it and on she went.

It was very different with Ngahuia. She had no idea what they were talking about. She found out when she was nine, same kind of thing, other kids. Boys, I think, who bullied her and made her life hell. There was a television ad at the time – 'My mum's a Maggi mum and Maggi mums have much more fun.' They sang, 'Your mum's a prosti mum.' Poor wee thing. She would always bottle things up – she would never ever tell me what she was thinking. So she would lash out at people physically, and would sulk and not speak for days.

But they both grew up, and they both have a totally different understanding of it now. They think it's shit hot. Well, they think the work I do, especially with the Prostitutes' Collective, is wonderful. They both got me to speak to their women's studies classes at Hagley High. It was the first school in New Zealand to do women's studies. Shanti asked me to talk to the group, and it was good. People asked questions and I was as candid as I could be. Then Ngahuia did women's studies three years later – same thing. Now my girls tell everyone what I do, because they think it's fabulous.

I've been the collective's regional coordinator for Christchurch since 1988 – 21 years. Sometimes I think, maybe I'm getting a bit old, my wrinkly old face in the media. I get embarrassed when I see my face – the face of the sex industry. Not exactly a Barbie doll lookalike. The cameras are never kind. I make demands now – I tell them to bring their soft focus camera.

I retired from sex work when I was 58. It happened very suddenly. I wasn't planning on it – I thought I'd probably work till 60 or 65. I used to joke, 'I'll work till I'm 65, get the pension.' I only worked for places that didn't allow shoppers – people that sell stolen goods. When I first worked at the Boutique somebody came in with all these diamond rings he'd obviously got from a burglary. People swooped on them. I was appalled – I could not believe it. If I went to work for a place I would ask them about that, and make sure they were strict about not letting those people in.

I was at the parlour next door for eight years. They had this policy of not letting shoppers in. Then management changed – this guy took it over and his mates started coming in with stolen property. I stood up and said, 'I can't believe this. I've spent the last 10 years trying to get the general public to believe that we're not part of some criminal fraternity.' I walked out. I went next door to NZPC and said, 'I've left! I've left! That's it!' I thought, I'd rather leave on a principle than because nobody wanted me any more. I've retired! Instant retirement! I've done it!

After a couple of weeks the management changed back, and they said, 'Come back.' I said, 'No, too late. I've done it now.' I saw a few clients – they said I could take any clients I arranged to see. So I did that for a little while.

Some clients clearly didn't want somebody older, and some did. I had some regulars that were much younger than me, who liked older women. There's somebody out there for everyone. Some people who come into our drop-in to get their condoms and lube, I look at them and think, goodness me, she's getting clients and she's morbidly obese, or not attractive at all. There's somebody out there for everybody, I know that.

I missed working at first. Now my body's changed – I've put on weight around my stomach and hips, and I don't know if I could cope with anyone seeing me naked. I always had a really good body.

The biggest positive was really that it just gave me so much. It gave me so much inside. It was all a joy, really. I know that my story isn't common. I do know that. I love great sex, no commitment. Brilliant. Great combination. And getting paid really well for it.

The biggest negative would be what happened with my children. And I still feel really sad that people have to tell so many lies, pretending that they're not working, or not wanting to tell people because they fear they're going to be judged or treated differently. That's the reality for a lot of people and it makes me sad, because I know it doesn't have to be like that. With partners, when somebody works and they hide it and the partner finds out, it's always the lie that is the biggest part of it. If you're open about it when you first meet somebody, if that person wants to be with you they'll be with you. What really gets my goat is clients that have relationships with working girls, 'Oh no, it's all fine,' then they live with them and want them to stop working. That pisses me off. If she wants to work she should be able to.

I look forward to the day when you can apply for a job and you can say to your prospective employer, 'I worked at such-and-such a parlour, brothel, for five years.' And that person can see – 'Ha! This person's going to be a good communicator. This person's going to be a very good reader of body language. This person's going to have a sympathetic disposition.' All those little things that you actually learn from doing that kind of work. The assets, rather than 'Oh my god, we're not going to have anyone like her here.' I want people to be able to be open about who they are and what they do, and it makes me sad when they can't be.

Anna was interviewed in Christchurch in June 2009.

SHAREDA

SHAREDA

AS A CHILD I thought about myself as just being one of the girls. You don't wake up one day and go, 'Oh, I think I'm transgender.' It doesn't work like that. For me, it's always been there. It's part of who you are as a person. It's where you're comfortable in yourself. Even as a young person – boys know where they should be, over there with the boys. Girls know they should be with the girls. When you're transgender, you know exactly where you want to be. You don't want to be over there where it's rough and tumble – you want to be over *there*, where it's soft and feminine and more fun.

I always stayed with the girls, because I like girls' company. It's more therapeutic, more relaxing – not stressful, like kicking a ball, playing rough, tag, tumble. I'd go and play elastic and hopscotch. I loved girls, and they were just my friends. They came to me – I was just friendly. If I saw a girl in the playground I'd just go, 'Hi!'

I loved school – I like drawing. Music and art, that was me. Mind you, it was most Māori kids – they all sang, all played the guitar, they all drew. Maths was the one we hated.

My teacher was really good – but that's not to say I didn't get teased. It's only natural for kids to be nasty to one another. I got teased a lot, but I never struck out at anybody. My brothers used to say, 'If they say anything to you ...' and I'd be like, 'No, no, don't do that. I don't need your help.' Brothers are very protective.

I was born in Auckland in 1962. I lived there till I was about five, then I moved to Whāngārei, and that's where I spent most of my growing-up years. I'm from Ngāti Hine, a little subtribe of the northern region, and Ngāti Tūwharetoa. I feel I belong to two marae – one on my mum's side and one on my father's side. One is called Rangimārie, it's up in Moerewa, and the other is Maniaiti, it's a quaint little marae in Taumarunui. They called it the Wallace Pā, after my grandmother and grandfather, who used to run it.

My dad died when he was 33, when I was about seven. So I never had that father figure, but I had an uncle – he was sort of like my father. My mum married three times, and altogether there were 16 of us kids. When you've got a big family like mine, from the north, you all get on. If you go to school and get bullied, you just look to the next one up. Māori families are very close, especially up north.

Carmen came up on the black-and-white TV one day, back in the 1970s. My mum goes, 'See? See who that is? That's Carmen,' because my mum went to school with Carmen and her sister, Tess. My mum said, 'See that person there?' I go, 'Do you know her?' She goes, 'That's Carmen – that's my friend from school.' She goes, 'That's who you want to be like.'

That was my first glimpse of Carmen. And I thought to myself, 'She's like me, but she's really brave, dressing up like that. And if she can be brave, and dress up and be a woman ...' I didn't actually realise that the 70s was pretty scary even for transgender like Carmen, because New Zealand was very heterosexual. It wasn't until Carmen came out, that all these middle-class New Zealanders were like, 'Oh, who's that brave person?' She's got these big huge knockers, and yet she was born a man. She stands on the steps of parliament with her big hooters hanging out, and she's running for mayor, with her candidacy sticker saying 'Get in behind' on the back of the car. Carmen broke down those barriers.

Living with my stepfather, there was a lot of drinking and physical abuse of my mum and of us. I went to stay with my uncle in Auckland when I was 13. I'd never in my life seen so many Pākehā neighbours, and at school there were heaps of Pākehās, but they were nice. There were 10 kids in my uncle's family, including myself. We had a whole crocodile of us walking down to the dairy, and we'd be walking back all carrying a loaf of bread each.

My uncle beat me as well – but I still loved him. I think he was trying to bash the tranny out of me – 'You're a man, you always will be.' He died a few years ago. I miss my uncle. I lived with him and his family till I was about 17. My cousins and I were the same age, and we went to school together. My uncle had his good points. He just had a really quick temper. He used to say things like, 'We're going to change you whether you like it or not.' Never worked. When people try and force things on you it only makes you more rebellious.

It's always the mother who's supportive. The father's the hardest. For European transgender, the father is just like, '*No*.' My Pākehā friend said, 'You Māori queens and Pacific Island queens are lucky – your families say, go and do what you want as long as you're happy.' When you're European, your dad wants you to be something. He wants some grandchildren. If you're the only boy, it's not a good thing to be transgendered – you're meant to be carrying on the line. Māori families are more accepting. If you've got a little boy running round being girly, you just get used to the fact, that's how he is, leave him alone. Some people think, maybe they'll grow out of it – and some do.

At high school I had to wear the boys' uniform, but I still had plucked eyebrows, I wore earrings and eyeliner. My uncle didn't like it – but the older I got, the more he backed off. He could see it in my face. I'd put eyeliner on when I went to school, but I'd take it off when I went home.

My uncle even let me go over to the city to the disco with the other kids, but he didn't know I had a dress in the bush. I had a dress ready to put on to hop on the bus. I'd see all my friends, and they'd go, 'Oh, you look really cool!' 'Thank you.' They'd go, 'We're going to this disco.' 'Oh, I've got to meet a friend.' And do you know where I went? To Myers Park, at the top of Queen Street.

I'd been for a walk up there one night, and I saw these tranny girls in these really stunning outfits, and their big titties, and I was curious. I didn't really know about prostitution. They took me into a coffee bar and bought me a coffee, sat down. When you're young, everything is beautiful – people are just so beautiful. And they *were* beautiful. They were in their twenties, thirties, so they looked pretty good. Stunning wigs, eyelashes – I was like, 'Oh, so pretty, I want to be like this.'

In the 1970s there was a club called Mojo's on the corner of Queen Street, and it was a drag show. I walked past, and I didn't need to know they were transgender – you can tell. It's that instinct. And they look at you. You just know instinctively that they're like you are. So I made my way up to Myers Park, wandering around, and found them all doing that work. I thought, 'Oh, look at those pretty girls! Men give them money to look pretty! Wow! I could do that.'

I didn't know anything about how horrible people could be to you as transgender. I didn't know the difficulties of finding a job, or anything like that. The world was just starting to open up to me, and it was all exciting, as it is when you're that age. I didn't know about hormones – but I remember asking them about their titties. 'How do you get those?' 'These? Oh, you take a few pills.' Some of them had very nice breasts. Some of them I didn't even know were transgender because they looked so pretty. It was all a big eye-opener.

I got started doing sex work from going over to the city and walking and looking around, exploring. That's how I met the girls, wandering around – the bright lights, and seeing these men wanting these pretty girls that were like me. I was like, 'Oh my gosh, I can do that too.'

So I tried it and it worked. I took a sexy dress with me – put it in my bag – and changed in the toilet. When I'd met the girls, I didn't know what they were doing, and they took me for a coffee and explained. I thought, that could be something I'd like to try. I was about 14 – think I was still in the third form. Once I did it, I was like, 'Wow, that man just gave me more money than I've ever had before, and it was only for a few minutes, and he told me that I looked pretty, I looked nice.'

So when I got a chance to go into town, that's where I used to go, up to Myers Park, and make me some money. I wasn't nervous – I was excited. It was like a whole new world – I've got a nice outfit on, everything's moving so fast. I can remember girls' faces. They're probably all gone by now.

There were heaps of girls working in Myers Park – Queen Street is a long street. Customs Street down the bottom, that was a beat as well. There would be about 20, and then down at Customs Street, Fort Street, you've got another set of workers working the bottom, outside the Great Northern Tavern. That was a hangout for transgender. Altogether there were probably about 40 girls working, maybe more.

The only thing that scared me was the stories the girls told me about the police. They were horrible, horrible. You had to run from the police in those days. The older girls would tell me, 'If you see a big brown Kingswood, run.' I said, 'Where?' They said, 'Anywhere. Just get off the street. Go down Myers Park to the toilets.'

And as soon as the police car came, the pig wagon behind it, everybody would just disappear. Those who didn't run fast enough got arrested. Those police, they didn't stand for any crap from anybody, not even a bad word. You just shut up, did what you were told, because if you didn't, you'd get it. Transgender girls were always getting beaten up in the police station. They said to me, 'If you get caught by the police, get a hiding from the Auckland police, don't get a hiding from the wharf police.' The wharf police were well known for throwing tranny girls into the water, off the wharf. Wake them up.

I did get caught one time. I was about 14. They said, 'Move,' and I didn't move fast enough. Next thing this Kingswood pulled up alongside me, and these big huge detectives hopped out, with big scary moustaches. They didn't talk nicely to you – they'd go, 'Who the F are you? Got any ID? What's your name? You look a bit young to be hanging round here. You know what the charge is for somebody your age? If you don't have $2 on you, that tells us that you have no means of support, and we're going to charge you with frequenting with felonious intent.'

They took me back to the police station. I'm like, 'Oh my god, all those horrible stories are going to come true.' But luckily, my age probably saved me. They threatened me, but they didn't beat me up. They took me into a room with a spotlight. It was dark and I had to stand on a platform, and they asked me all these stupid questions. It was like a game. I had a big Samoan police officer standing next to me in the dark, saying things like, 'Don't grin, or I'll wipe that smile off your face.' They'd go, 'Are you a boy or a girl? How long have you been queer?' Stupid things like that.

Then they put me in a cell, and the next morning I was taken to court in a police wagon with gang members from Mt Eden prison. They were really nice. I was sitting next to a really big one, and he said, 'Are you all right?' I went, 'I'm all right.' They took us and put us in the holding cells at the bottom, me and these gang members.

I stood up in court, and they said, '*He's* charged with frequenting with felonious intent. He's under-age, so we recommend that we put this person into care.' So they put me into Ōwairaka Boys' Home for two weeks. They had no cells – just beds where you slept, with curtains. The guys would get you up, you'd line up, shower, do some exercises. After two weeks my uncle came to get me. I tell you, I've never been so glad to see his face. There was another trans girl that was in there, caught for the same thing – frequenting with felonious intent, being a rogue and a vagabond. Those charges were mainly used against street workers.

Time went quite fast in the home. It was a bit like a prison, but not a prison. They were fine – I just didn't have access to makeup. But I found a way – I'd learnt it from an old queen who had been in Mt Eden Prison. She goes, 'If you ever need eyeliner, just turn a glass or a piece of metal over, light a match underneath – that charcoal will do you.' So I used that. A little jail trick, she called it.

When I was back at my uncle's, I went to a vocational guidance course. You learnt what it was to be in work, and if work came up and they needed young people with no training, they'd take them in. I met five beautiful girls and we made friends really quickly. Then one day they came up to me and they go, 'We're leaving. There's a job at the Collins Brothers printing factory.' They got jobs as collators – the women do the collating. Then those girls called me and said, 'There's one more vacancy, would you like to come in?' I said, 'Have you told them what I am? That I'm a queen?' And they said, 'Yeah, we did. He wants you to come in.'

The man was very nice – he said, 'The girls told me about you.' I said, 'Really? You don't mind, do you?' He goes, 'No. Are you here to work, or what?' I said, 'I want to work.' He called in this big lady with glasses. 'Give her a smock.' All the girls had them on. It wasn't just the job – somebody was accepting me for who I was. He was a gorgeous man – he had no qualms about me. To him it was about the work.

So I saw the girls from the course – 'Hi!' Hug, hug, hug, all in the tearoom. I felt really, really complete – like, this is where I want to be, and this is who I want to be with. I stayed there for a year, but unfortunately those girls didn't last very long. They dropped off one by one and I was still there.

Then I thought to myself, you're getting older. It's time to go somewhere else. So I went to Queen Street, and caught up at a coffee bar with one of the older girls. She said, 'Go to Wellington, Shareda. Don't stay here. Look at me, I'm still here. I've been beaten up so many times. You're still young, go to Wellington.' She goes, 'The police are nicer down there. You'll see Carmen.' She goes, 'Don't live here, it's horrible.'

So I did. I left my job and caught a bus to Wellington.

When you're transgender, back in those days, you don't have community support. You don't have groups like Genderbridge, Rainbow Youth, Agender. Those things weren't possible back then. The only place you could find transgender were down on the street, and that's where I found them.

That was the first thing I asked people around Wellington. I asked anybody, 'Excuse me, do you know where the queens hang out?' They'd go, 'There's a tavern down there, it's called the Royal Oak.' It was the most notorious pub, especially for the tranny girls. I talked to the barman outside because I wasn't allowed in – I was under age. He goes, 'They come in here at night.' So, I'm hanging around. Next thing a taxi opens up and out they get – all I can see is these big huge wigs. Bernie, the man that owned the pub, goes, 'There they are. That's one household.' I go, 'Are they in households?' He goes, 'Yeah. That's 80 Pirie Street. See the big one hopping out? Don't go near her. That's the boss. She's rough.'

As the years went on I had my own household, me and the other girls. We were 40 Colombo Street, everybody knew us.

I went up to Pirie Street the next day. I'd met one of the other queens, but she wasn't from any of the households, she was an independent girl. She goes, 'I know that lot, I'll take you up tomorrow.' She goes, 'By the way, don't be intimidated by the big boss. She's a pussycat.'

So we went up there. One of the girls answered the door, curlers in her hair. My friend went, 'Is the boss home? I've got a girl here wants to meet her.' So she took me upstairs to meet the boss – sitting there with these big size-44 knockers under her nightie. She looked really scary because she had no makeup on. She goes, 'Go and meet the boys downstairs.' That's the way she was with her household.

One was in charge of the washing, one was in charge of the cooking, getting everything ready. Everybody had a job to do – that's how the house ran. They didn't serve her, but they did everything. That was how they paid their rent. And the house was immaculate. It was just spotless. Because the one who ruled the house was a hairdresser, nobody could get their hair done professionally, except by her. And they looked stunning when I saw them getting out of the taxi.

So that's how I came to know some girls down here. They didn't have paid work. Some did the ships – the boats that came into port, like the Japanese. Others worked on the street. Some were on benefits. If you live in a bigger group, it makes living easier, so that household never really did the streets. It was more those who worked independently.

When I first arrived, I made friends with two young queens, the same age as me. I met them out on the street, and we hit it off. Julie had this fox stole on, and she had this petite little figure, and this gorgeous Chinese dress and beautiful thick hair with goldy-brown highlights. She walked up to me and said, 'Hi,' and I was like, 'Hi.' She goes, 'Oh, you're new! I was just going for a walk, I've just made some money.' I said, 'I'm new to this.' She goes, 'Come on, we'll go somewhere for a coffee. I'll shout you, don't worry about it.'

That's how we became friends, then flatmates. She asked me to live with her, then another one came along, then another, and then my poor friend goes, 'Girl, it's getting a bit heavy. It was all right with me and you, but now everyone is trying to jump on.' She said, 'I think we need to go somewhere else, just me and you, because we're losing our privacy.'

We moved to Colombo Street in Newtown, which was a bigger space. Other girls were coming into town, doing exactly what I was doing – looking for sisters, looking for a new life. Next thing there was a household of seven or eight of us in a two-bedroomed flat. We all made money – sometimes we had so much money we had too much food. Sometimes I'd give their rent back. We had a good household.

Everybody was doing sex work – birds of a feather flock together, as they say. Everybody was happy. All you had to do was be nice, get on with everybody. If you didn't – get out. And I never had to say get out. There were seven of us in two bedrooms – that was why we were all in the sitting room. But one more? No. No, you tell her to find somewhere else.

Our street's always been Marion. Always. In the 80s the women moved up to Abel Smith Street, and that became their bit. The trans girls mixed more with the ship girls than with the street girls. The Sunset nightclub on Cuba Street was where all the Jap seamen went, and it was just flooded with ship molls. Them and the tranny girls got on so well – all intermingled in the same thing. And sometimes the seamen would want a trans girl, so the girls would hook up a trans girl.

The street for the trans girls, nightclub for the girls. Very few women worked on the street. It meant the girls were safer, even though the gangs used to go round and stand over them and their Japanese seamen, and rob them outside the club. It was the Nomads – they were bad, bad news. They started off as rejects from the Black Power, because the Black Power have always been good. They have rules, and if you didn't abide by them, well, get out. So they just wandered – hence the name. And they caused havoc on that street for a long time, even with us. But they couldn't rob us, because we were harder to get it off than the ship girls. They basically left us alone. But at the same time, you didn't cross paths with them.

The first time I went up to the Sunset, there were these great big trannies, wider than anything I'd ever seen, huge. One on the door, she had this scary baritone voice. I went, 'Hi!' She went, 'Hullo girl. Haven't seen your face.' I go, 'I'm new.' She goes, 'Where have you just come from?' 'I've come from Auckland.' 'You're not a roller, are you?' I go, 'What's that?' Dumb me. She goes, 'You'll find out.'

I paid my money, went upstairs. There's another huge one cleaning the tables, looked like a wrestler. Same thing – 'New face on the block, what's your name? Where you from?' I said, 'Auckland.' 'You'd better not be rolling.' I said, 'What's that?' 'You don't know? That's stealing. Taking money.' I go, 'I don't do that.' I found out that Auckland transgender had a reputation for coming down, rolling the clients on the street, then the Wellington ones would get the blame and the cops would come down on them. They'd go up to the Sunset, roll a drunk Japanese sailor who belonged to somebody else, then take off back up to Auckland.

Everybody who went to the Royal Oak went to the Sunset. The Royal Oak was the daylight to the evening, and the Sunset was from the evening till the morning. The same people went. There were ship girls, trannies, seamen, gay men, gang members, lesbians. I knew a few butch girls whose partners were with the Jap sailors. The butch girls just sat around, made sure nothing happened, but their girlfriends were ship girls.

All sorts of people. There was an ugly phrase – 'a can of worms'. It's not a very nice thing to say, a can of worms. They should have just said, a fruit bowl. A fruity fruit bowl of people, all different colours, shapes and sizes. Māori, Pākehā ... the Japanese seamen were quite fond of European women. The Māori girls they liked, yeah, but Asian men are quite prone to European girls. There were a lot of Pākehā girls – and if you were blonde, well, that was even better. You'd have no problem with Japanese seamen. There were Māori, two Samoan girls, couple of Indian girls, but no Asian girls that I can remember.

So that was the Jap seamen's hangout, the Sunset. For the ship girls, it was work. It was a mixture of work and good times. For us, it was a good time. We made our money on the street – up at the Sunset, have a good time. That's what we were there for, nothing else. I wasn't out to pick up any seamen. Bad enough I couldn't speak the language. Mind you, neither could the ship girls.

I've been on ships. I was always scared – I heard that people who steal get thrown overboard. I'd seen a tranny girl thrown overboard from a fishing trawler because she stole some money.

When you go on a ship, and you're with somebody, they had a term – 'boxed off' with someone. The best one to be boxed off with was the cook. And if you were friends with the captain, you could sail with them. It was called ringbolting. I've done it.

I just went on the ship, sat in a bar, all the girls sitting around. It was so beautiful – it was the old-style 70s, early 80s, and all you saw were those fluorescent fantasy pictures that felt like velvet. They glowed in the dark, and they were shocking pink and green. I remember going on and hearing Pink Floyd. I didn't go on to make money – just when I was invited on. I only drank Coke, because I didn't drink. We just sat around, smoked a bit of pot.

A lot of the ship girls actually fell in love with the guys. Some of them got married. A lot of the girls are still in Wellington, and their half-Japanese children are all grown up. The Japanese were the most popular – they had the money, and they were generous if you were good to them. Very clean people.

Boats came from everywhere, but the ones with the money were the Japanese. When the laws changed, that was the end of the Jap days.

Girls would stay on the boat while it was in port. The guys would give them money, buy them something nice. I'd go over to some girls' places and there'd be about five Japanese seamen in the living room. Always lots of money, and quite happy to spend it on these girls. The girls would go, 'I'm going shopping, me and my Jap man. He's leaving tomorrow, so he's getting rid of his New Zealand money.'

But it wasn't a trans girl thing, the boats. It was the street the trans girls liked – especially me. It was where I belonged – it was where everybody else was.

I didn't really enjoy selling myself. It's business, really, but there are some guys that are nice. You make friendships as well – some guys are just so sweet. Sometimes over the years it's not just about money any more. You don't have sex, it's become a friendship. You forget about the money. No sex, though.

I never ever heard of a girl that married her client. Fancy having a relationship based on the fact that he picked you up on the street. That's not a relationship, that's a client, and he always will be. You didn't fall in love, you got paid. Imagine if he threw that back in your face when you had an argument. Wouldn't that be horrible?

I didn't have attachments to guys – they were just clients. They were just here, and then, 'See you later.' It's hard. You say to yourself, 'Oh, it's just business,' but then somebody comes along that's so sweet and nice, and you can't help yourself. There's always one. And I've met one or two. Just sweethearts. Never fell in love, though. No. You can't fall in love with someone that belongs to somebody else. Whether the relationship is working or not – they still don't belong to you. And if they have children, they definitely will never belong to you, because their commitment will always be to their kids. So I just go, 'Oh no, I'll just do my business. See you later, catch you around next time.' But sometimes it can be hard, when those golden men come along.

Some clients are really terrible. We used to laugh – we called them secret squirrel. They'd look over at you, and when you looked back at them, they'd be looking in a shop window. There were tortuous ones in cars – they'd go around and around in circles all night, the windows down.

The ones looking in the window were just being discreet, but they were clients. As they got closer, you'd walk across and go, 'Hi.' They'd look back at the window. You'd go, 'Are you looking for something?' They'd go, 'Oh, I was just wondering how much.' So you'd tell them. I'd say, 'If you pay for a taxi, I'll go and get one and come round.' It always worked. I never asked them to walk with me – they're paranoid enough just standing there.

I'd take them home to my flat with six flatmates, all tranny girls. If you got sick of the client and he had more money, you'd just give him to the next girl. I've been woken up a few times – 'He's got another $60!' 'Oh, OK. Throw him in here.' The clients have got money, they want some more – well, got a whole smorgasbord there.

I didn't always take them home. Not everybody wanted an hour – some wanted five minutes. But then you had the quick ones, behind a building, which was quite good. If you wanted to go home and take your clothes off it was to stay there – not go out and do it all again. I'd rather come home with one, go to sleep. Quickies were less time, less trouble.

I didn't like going in cars. They were tricky and uncomfortable. I got sprung twice by the police – they pulled up behind. You hear the door, the torch goes on, tap tap tap on the window. They were quite blunt – they'd go, 'You know that's not a woman?' They'd go, 'Did you solicit him for money?' I'd be like, 'No, we just came for a ride.'

I think it's cheap in a car, cheap behind a building. To do oral sex behind a building is fine, but when it comes to having to take your clothes down and all of that – no, no. I couldn't. There's only one place to have sex, and that's in a bed. Don't just bend you over some dirty yukky drum – yuk! No, no, no. You need to be comfortable. The person needs to be nice too.

I could handle probably three clients in one night – no more than that. And they're not all young, handsome and good looking, some of them are fat and yukky, but I just treated them all the same.

Sixty for a blow job or a hand job, 120 for sex. But I didn't like to give sex – I preferred blow jobs, that's what I was good at. Once I was dressed, I didn't want to take my clothes off, because I spent about an hour getting them on, doing my hair. I'd be like, 'Don't touch my hair,' because you've set it and put hairspray in it. You touch it, it's going to look like the cat jumped on it. That's why I didn't like going to bed with guys. Some guys are like they're in their fantasy dream – 'You're so sexy, you're so beautiful,' and I'd be like, 'Time.'

To me it was a business. If the guy was nice I always saved him for last, so if I went home it didn't matter – I wasn't going back out anyway. I never took home drunk guys. I had bad experiences with drunk guys. You've got to keep them active, because if they hit that back position on the pillow, they're out. One spewed in my bed. I was like, 'Get out.' It was my fault, I was desperate for money. 'Out!' I got him a taxi, the driver wouldn't take him. He fell asleep on our stairs.

They were mostly middle-aged married men with families. Heterosexual, not gay men. They probably didn't have a very exciting sexual life, or they were closely bisexual, not attracted to guys, but attracted to trans girls. I think just coming out to fulfil a fantasy, for some. Some, because sex in the marriage isn't working, which is why a lot of clients come, whether you're a girl or a tranny. They're all going there for a reason – usually because they're not getting what they require at home, or because of their desires – their wife is not going to do it. So you go somewhere where somebody can.

I always found the older they were, the easier to do. Less trouble. Young men are tortuous. They wanted the whole world, they wanted the works for 40 bucks, whereas a mature man was quite happy, if he didn't want sex, to have a cuddle and a cup of tea. That's not much to ask. They were much more pleasant. They had more time – young guys were just bam, bam, then gone. Take what they can get and run.

The men I avoided most were men from my race and Samoan men. I've got nothing against them, but when you're Māori, the last thing you want to think about is sleeping with a client, then you go on a marae and find out that's your uncle. New Zealand's a small place, and a lot of Māori transgender girls avoided Māori guys for that very reason – it's a small country, we're all interrelated somehow. We avoided our own people like the plague. And I was accosted by a lot of Māori guys. But I found that a lot of Māori and Samoan guys were quite arrogant compared to European guys. They don't like that word 'No'. I'd rather not say no, I'd rather avoid having to say it. You'd make up excuses, but they're quite pushy, especially Māori guys. European men were much easier, much nicer to work with.

Clients tried to get out of paying all the time. But that's the girl's fault. When you go with a client, you always ask for the money first, who cares if you've been with him 10 times. There's been cases – 'Oh, left my wallet in the car.' But that's not his fault, that's hers. I've done that once. Just tired, couldn't be bothered, just wanted to go to sleep. Took him home. 'Can I pay you later?' 'OK.' So, do the deed. He goes, 'I'll just go and get my wallet.' I was thinking, you're quite a nice guy, I'll see how genuine you really are. We'd had a cup of tea. He goes, 'I'll go and get the money.' I said, 'Thanks for being really really nice,' thinking, 'We'll see.' Next thing, vvvvrrrrooom – gone. Thanks very much, that's what I needed to know, now I'll go to sleep.

So I had a rule – always ask for the money first. Don't trust somebody you've just met. That's the way business is – when you do a job, you get paid for it. The clients I went with didn't bargain. I've heard the worst are Indians, Mediterranean men – bargain you down to two cents. Indians – terrible. I said, 'You're not in a market in India bargaining.' They go, 'Twenty, twenty.' 'No. I told you what it is.' 'Twenty, twenty.'

I must say, I have done it, behind a building, really quick. I'm like, 'You've only got 20 bucks? OK, five minutes. Let's go.' Five minutes, bang, back out. And every girl has. They can't tell me they haven't, that they weren't hungry for a burger or a packet of cigarettes. I did feel like a bit of a cheapskate actually – but back in those days 20 dollars was 20 dollars. You really couldn't argue with that.

Sometimes I'd approach clients, if I knew them. But some guys, you didn't know they were undercover police officers … I got caught about eight times. There are times I'd go out and I'm a bit overexcited because I'm out for a good night and I feel confident, I've got a nice dress on, looking forward to making a bit of money and going out to a nightclub and having fun – but then hop in a car, don't really care who it is, just being greedy really. You hop in a car, ask for business, and out comes this card – 'Undercover police officer, you're under arrest for soliciting,' which is really, really tortuous. You know you can't get out of it, you can't deny it, because the other policeman on the other end of the radio is listening. You get driven to the back of a building, to a waiting police wagon, and you know you're going to be in that police cell till about eight o'clock in the morning. So you can kiss your good night goodbye.

All that frustration of all dressed up, and all you're doing is sitting in a stinky cell with 13 other girls, all waiting to be processed. It's cold and all you can hear is clanking of keys and policemen calling the next person who's going to be processed. By the time you get let go in the morning, you're like, I hope I never get caught again. But I did.

The maximum was $200, the normal was $100 plus $10 court costs. I don't know why they couldn't have picked on somebody else, a murderer. They harassed working girls that did nobody any harm. The massage parlours got busted as well.

I got picked up about eight times. Just my stupidity – getting out of it and not using my good sense of judgment that I have when I'm straight. I didn't drink, so I got stoned instead, or took some pills. That's what got me caught, my carelessness. We all knew it was risky, we all knew it was illegal, we knew we could get caught – but that made it exciting. That made us want to go out there even more. Decriminalisation is the best thing that ever happened – but at the same time, there was all that excitement you had when you went out, the excitement of getting away with it.

Some of the nicest people I've met were on the streets. Some really nice men hung around. They weren't clients per se – they were just guys who enjoyed a tranny girl's company and would drive them around like a taxi. When you didn't have a ride home, somebody would say, 'There's one of our chariots.' 'Could you take me home?' And you'd give him a cup of tea. They weren't clients, they were just lonely, nice, lovely men that had nothing to do with their time, so they'd be a chauffeur for us. They came in very handy when it was freezing cold and all you wanted to do was go home.

There were dramas, as there always are. I remember seeing older queens fighting. Paddings would go flying, wigs would come off. Us younger ones didn't wear wigs, but the older ones did, it came out of the 70s fashion. I saw a few brawls. Not a nice thing to see, but that's what the older girls used to do, they always had conflicts, and the only way they could settle them was to fight each other. I stayed away from that.

My favourite outfit was black – black, frilly, short skirt. Black stockings and black, sexy, shiny patent-leather stilettos. A tight-fitting dress was always sexy. And it had to be black. I think every tranny girl I know had what we in our circles called a money-making dress. We all had one outfit that worked. That's what we'd say to each other – 'You've got your money-making dress on!' She'd be like, 'Yeah. Where's *your* money-making dress?' 'Oh, I decided to change, I'm just wearing something different tonight.' 'Oh, you going to wear it tomorrow?' 'Yeah, probably.' So we all had a money-making dress. And it *was* a money-making dress, because every time you wore it – boom. Everybody wanted you.

There were nights like that – some nights I had so many clients I couldn't deal with them all. As soon as you came back from one, another one wanted you. It was like heaven, for the money. But then there were nights when it was somebody else's night. Things go in runs, and while your run is good – milk it. I did. Then sometimes it was another girl's night. She'd come and go, 'Oh girl, I just did four!' and I'd go, 'Good on you. Your night.' She'd go, 'Do you want to go out later?' and I'd go, 'No. You keep going while your run is good.'

The Evergreen coffee bar that used to be on Vivian Street – that used to be Carmen's Coffee Lounge. Unfortunately when I got here Carmen was gone, and her niece had it. I just got the last taste of what it was like. It became the Owl's Retreat, then it became the Evergreen, which it stayed all those years when Chris Witoko had it. Quite a history, that little place. Chris lived upstairs – she took it and called it the Evergreen.

The Evergreen was a wonderful place. It was a drop-in centre, and there was always a place to sit. It was the girls that kept that coffee bar going, so it was good on both sides, for Chris and us. We spent our money in there – we could go in and keep warm. When there were tortuous people outside we could go there, just chill out for a little while. Just somewhere to go, company. It was the only transgender gathering place that transgender people liked to go to. The Evergreen was theirs.

It was always a business – Chrissy was money-minded. The older girls would talk to her and remind her that these girls on the street are the ones that keep your business going, so don't be nasty and go throwing them out the door. Mind you, some of them needed to be thrown out, just drunk and being loud, one or two attacking a customer, another two rolling somebody's wallet out the back. She'd say to me, 'Why can't they be like you?'

The decor was Jurassic – that's a queens' saying, it means very old. She had a retro cage with a parrot in it. It was plastic – we used to laugh at it, go and flick it. She was such a character, she had these plastic vines hanging everywhere. And the whole wall was photos – all the way from the back to the front. She even had photos of me. The photos down the front were all black and white, they were from the 60s. All the ones at the back were from the Sunset nightclub days. To stop people stealing them she had it all laminated.[1]

She sold whisky – she'd put it in the steel milk jug and teapot. She was real tight, she'd have this Lemon and Paeroa bottle filled with whisky, with lines on it, so whoever's on that counter, she'd know how many shots there should be by reading the bottle.

The sandwiches were the best in the whole world. That's all she sold as food, because that's all everybody wanted – Chrissy's famous toasted sandwiches. And believe me, they were so yummy after a night out. I'd go in there – 'Hi Chris!' She goes, 'Toasted sandwich?' I went, 'Yeah.' She goes, 'Your favourite?' And I went, 'Ham, cheese and sweet corn.' I said, 'Can you flip it on both sides?' She goes, 'Yes, dear.' I go, 'Flip it on both sides and butter it vigorously with lots of butter.' That's it, she knew me. She goes, 'And that's with one coffee with two sugars?' 'Yes please.'

There were fishermen, businessmen, general public. Guys came in that played drunk: 'I've had a hard night, I don't know where I am.' That number. They were the funniest – I'd just play along too. 'Oh my gosh – are you sure you're all right?' 'Yeah … what's this place called?' I said, 'It's the same place you were last week, my dear.'

It was probably about 84, 85 that Chrissy took it over. Then she started getting sick – well, she was diabetic anyway, had been for years. Then she had to go on dialysis. After she died it lasted maybe a year, not even that. Then it was closed. All of a sudden, there was a whole change on the street. Brian Le Gros, who owned Tiffany's and Liks strip clubs, left and opened the White House in Auckland. Emmanuel Papadopoulos, who owned the Club Exotique in Vivian Street, passed away. There was a massage parlour next to Chrissy's called Angelique's. It was empty, Chris's was empty, and then all the squatters

---

1   Chrissy Witoko's laminated panels from the Evergreen were acquired by the Museum of New Zealand Te Papa Tongarewa in 2012, and can be viewed online (along with a biography of Chrissy) at 'Queen of the Evergreen': collections.tepapa.govt.nz/topic/3751. For more about Chrissy's life, see Tapatoru, 'Witoko – Chrissy': www.tapatoru.org.nz/witoko---chrissy

got in through the back and were living upstairs, and they set it on fire. I don't know if it was purposely. I don't think so. I sat there watching it burn, watching the firemen, thinking, all those memories gone up in smoke. But no lives were taken – just the end of an era. Old places like that, one spark and it goes up like paper.

The only thing on Vivian and Cuba Street that's still there is that expresso bar. Midnight Expresso. A lot of memories on Vivian Street.

I encountered the Prostitutes' Collective when it first started, 1988, at the top of Cuba Street. At first they didn't have an outreach. Everybody knew they had free condoms. We were using safe sex anyway – we used to go to the chemist and buy ours, but when we found out about the drop-in centre, it was good. Go in there, pick up some free condoms. Saved us a lot of money, and we could sit down and chat, talk about who got plucked the other night, who went to court, how much they got fined.

'Plucked' is a street word for undercover operations – 'What happened to you the other night?' 'Oh, I got plucked.' It's funny how words get invented. Like 'crack it'. 'Where are you going?' 'Oh, I'm going to crack it.' 'Where's she gone?' 'She's gone to crack it.' Crack it – make some money.

'Don't be tortuous.' A hamoxial is somebody who's annoying, obnoxious and horrible – all those things. I don't know how you spell it. 'Oh my gosh, he's a hamoxial, don't go with him.' 'How bad is he?' 'He's tortuous!' Some queens would speak gibberish, which was so annoying.

Some transgender girls, it's hard to tell. But for me, I'm not going to play hide and seek. I'd rather you can tell I'm transgender than a transgender who's totally flawless. Because that's dangerous – I've met a lot of transgender who we'd call 'unspring'. I knew two girls who got put in hospital because they looked too good but they got sprung. We were out there, and the guys were like, 'We know what you are, no problem.' But when you have somebody who's really stunning, and an ultra-straight man, he's trying to feel her up and she's telling him she's got her period, and he puts his hand down there – at least if he knows what you are, that's not a problem. But if he doesn't know, and he's a super-straight man – two girls got put in hospital. When you're that good, you have to be honest.

In the gay world they have a saying that when somebody's not out, they're in the closet. In our world, we say somebody like that is living in stealth. And it can be quite dangerous.

There was verbal harassment – sometimes physical. I had to defend myself a few times. People say, if someone gives you a hard time, just walk away. But some people just won't go away – walk down the end of the street, they follow you. I felt terrible about defending myself, because I'm not that kind of person. You're just ready for any kind of situation. Even from cars, you've got to be careful – there's bottles, there's rotten eggs. I've been hit by eggs, hit in the head by a Steinie bottle. It was my fault because I wasn't paying attention. It's not clients – it's just normal public. If you want to know what some of the public really think about prostitutes, well, go out there.

At least inside, you're safe. Outside is a whole different story – you're exposed to the elements, to everybody. But I couldn't have worked in a parlour. Transgender girls have minds of their own, they're not going to work for anybody. They like the freedom, the independence. Anyway, the clientele for transgender aren't going to be seen walking into a building. It's sort of an in-the-closet thing with transgender girls, so the best way to do it is to cruise around, pull up in a dark spot.

I was always Shareda – the tranny girls never changed their names to work. Girls in brothels do. I don't know why – it's all an act, I suppose. On the street they don't have those insecurities about their names – you're who you are. Can you imagine a client – 'Oh, Sandy!' 'Oh no, it's Mary.' 'You told me it was Sandy a minute ago!'

I used drugs to work, because of the pressure. You don't know what's coming. When you go to work, you know what you're doing, you know what's expected. It's not the same on the street. Every night is different, and you've got to learn to deal with it. You can have a wonderful night, you can have a real shitty night, you can have an extra horrible night with people throwing eggs and bottles at you. So it blocks it off. It blocks everything out when you're going out to work. You're out of it, you can laugh it off. It takes all those nerves away. Walking up to cars isn't easy either, unless you know the client. Walking up to somebody new is really scary, because you know what he might be – a police officer. You've got to have a lot of guts, and if you don't try, someone else will.

It's not a job you go into easily. You know the risks, and you know the kind of people that will be out there later in the evening. Drunk people, gangs, tortuous people. So, get a bit of armour, drop a few pills – makes the night go a little bit better. A bit of a booster. Valium and all those downers were the best ones to go out on, because you don't even hear anything else. All you know is just work, work, work, business, business, business. The only thing you never did was work lying down – you got him to lie down and you sat up and did the work, because as soon as you lie down, boom. Many a girl's been robbed that way – even myself. I woke up, my purse was gone. A few rules you learn from experience.

Everybody did drugs. They were doing uppers and downers – people would go to the doctor and score them. There was speed, there was Valium, Pipanol. Marijuana wasn't really a big thing. No heroin – that's Sydney. We never had drugs that bad. We didn't even have needle users – pill poppers and dope smokers, that's all.

I stopped doing sex work about 10 years ago. It was only a means to an end for me after the 90s. The 80s were fine, they were good years, then you got into the 90s and things were changing. The environment around the street was changing. In 1987 they banned American war boats – they were another source of income when they came in, the American sailors. Then they stopped the Japanese trawlers from coming, which meant there was no work for ship girls. So that was the end of that. The whole environment was changing. The club where the seamen went, the Sunset, closed about 92.

As much as we wish things could stay the same, they don't. Things change, people change, environments change, and that's what happened. Decriminalisation came along in 2003. That was a good thing for all sex workers – it was safer, you didn't have to register with the police any more.

But the street scene changed, it lost its excitement. It got boring, like everything gets boring after a while. You don't get gold medals. And you can't stay out there forever – there's no retirement thing for you. You need to get your mind sorted and get out of there, because it doesn't last forever, and we all get older. The good thing for older sex workers now is that they can work privately, they don't have to stand out there and freeze to death.

The weather was horrible. It was colder in Wellington than it is now. God, those southerlies – and you're standing out there in a swimsuit! Swimsuits were a craze for a little while. And then there were leg warmers, and matching jumpers – those were pretty cool. My friend had the meanest legs, nice figure – she'd have this baby blue jersey on, and matching leg warmers, and black stilettos, she looked stunning. That was the craze. The less you had on, probably the more money you made. It was cold – but having some pills and some smoke, that kept you warm. You didn't feel it if you took a few pills, you didn't feel any of the cold.

I had a job in a factory for a year, but the owner died, so back to the streets for a long time. During that time I went into Social Welfare, and they had a job for a cleaner. So I did that for two years, for $80 on top of my benefit, because I really didn't want to be out there. Then they sold the building and the contract ran out. Back to the streets.

Then this lovely lady called Catherine Healy called me. I knew what NZPC was about, I knew about Catherine through the news, but I'd never met her. She said, 'I've heard some good things about you. Did you use to take a lot of stray transgender queens in, give them a home?' I went, 'I've been doing that for years.' She goes, 'You know, we need someone like you.' I was like, 'You mean a job? That sounds so cool!' She's like, 'But you'd have to learn to use a computer. That's the catch.' So I went, 'OK, I'll learn.'

I've been here for eight years, and I'm so happy. I'm in a place with good people, and I help people out who are where I used to be. It's a lot easier for transgender girls now – they can go to university. They can go to courses. People are a lot more tolerant about transgender.

I've done a lot since I've been here – been to meetings, spoken at the Out Games. I make up condom and lube packs in plastic bags, do outreach on the street. But our numbers on the street have just gone right down. I'm lucky if I see one person on Sunday. The law might have changed, but the abuse hasn't – it's still the same. There's still bottle throwers, things like that. At least the girls can call the police, and the police are really good. They're always there. They come up here, say if you need extra patrols out there, just let us know. Our connection with the police is much better, even with street girls.

I liked it when it was good, the sex industry – the good times. As I got older, I didn't regret it, but it's a bit like a drug, it didn't have the oomph of when you first did it. You have that first boom, and it's like, Wow! Then later, well, it's sort of wow, but it's sort of not as wow as it used to be. But it shaped my growing-up years as far as learning about life, the sex industry. And the people that I met.

The best thing I got from the industry was friends. Life experience – because you have to grow up really fast when you're on the street, when you're in the sex industry. I had my run-ins with guys – but it comes with the territory. Even before we go on the street, we know what kind of people are out there. We know what to expect. Sometimes it used to get too much for me, so I'd go home and cry and then go back out there again. Sometimes you can't believe what horrible things people say to you or to other people.

The downsides were the people. The weather. Horrible people. Bottle throwers, cake throwers, egg throwers. Drunk people. They came with the territory. Gangs, people fighting, walking around with bloody noses, just been beaten up. That's what I mean about it being a life experience and having to grow up fast, because it's happening in front of your eyes and you're like, 'Oh my gosh, that guy's got a big gash in his face and nobody's helping him.' Or one of the older queens that was walking across Cuba Street and this sports car just came through the lights – boom, she just went up in the air and dropped like a bag of potatoes. Luckily a police car was coming round the corner. They caught the guy – he handed himself in. She wasn't really the same after that accident. Those are the kind of things I saw. People getting hit by cars. People cut up and bruised, people getting mugged – Japanese sailors getting mugged in alleyways, that kind of thing. But I just put it down to life. I'm lucky I wasn't in there, I was outside looking in, which is a lot easier.

But life experience, mainly, and friends. That's where I met the people I came here to look for in the first place. And they ended up being lifetime friends. Other trans girls. When you're in your twenties every day is a moment. You remember bits and pieces of things, different faces. And some of them are really special, and that's what you remember. Especially friends, the ones that have come and gone. That's what I got out of it. The money – nah, that just went with the territory. The money just made it sweeter.

Shareda was interviewed at the Wellington office of the New Zealand Prostitutes' Collective between March and May 2012.

MISTRESS MARGARET

MISTRESS MARGARET

I WAS BORN in 1946 in England, in Hemel Hempstead. Hemel Hempstead was a new town built after the war as a satellite town of London, around an old village that went back to Roman times.

My father was Welsh and my mother was English. He was a bus driver and she was a school cleaner. She had three children, and my grandfather was senile so she looked after him as well. I was the eldest. My father had been away at the war for years and years, then he came back and was living in my grandparents' house with a screaming child. I don't think happiness was an enormous goal – survival was, really. People who have been through a hard time, all they really want to do is keep the house clean, keep everyone fed and watered. Fun was not really high on the agenda.

I never really liked my dad, but I look back and see the war things and now I understand why he was probably like he was. I just kept out of his way. If you were reading a book – he didn't like you doing anything which wasn't productive. I think he wanted sons but he ended up with three daughters. He was not a happy man.

My mum was much more reasonable. I think she was a lot brighter than my father. She spent a lot of her time keeping between us and him, which is an awful position to be in. She was quite a private person as well.

School was really good – because of the new town, they built these fantastic modern schools. It was really nice and the teachers were good. I enjoyed creative things, writing poetry and art, but I really just liked the environment. I probably struggled with some things but I did enjoy it.

When I was 16 I got a lot of O levels, and I transferred to the grammar school, which was probably quite a radical move in those days. It was quite scary because grammar schools did Latin, French, German. It was a much freer type of environment, we had a sixth-form common room and the Beatles were all the rage. There were very witty boys there instead of the rather coarse boys at the secondary modern. They'd make witty, intellectual jokes. The teachers were fantastic, and they were quite eccentric, which was wonderful.

My mother believed in education for women, because she could see it was better than what she got landed with. So myself and my two sisters all got a tertiary education. I was probably the first after my mother's generation to go on to college – for women it was even more unusual. I went to St Loyes School of Occupational Therapy in Exeter.

Living in my home town, I was not very aware of what was going on in London, which was only 24 miles away. We were really restricted – we listened to a bit of radio, a bit of TV, and visited my aunties, who weren't political. They were lovely and friendly and baked cakes. It wasn't a very stimulating environment.

When I got my period I could hardly bring myself to tell my mother. I had no words really, so we dithered around each other for hours. I finally told her, and she said, 'You'll be all right as long as you keep away from boys.' Well, our market was very busy on a Saturday and I didn't know how far I had to keep away from them. You'd see someone coming up the aisle and you'd think, oh god, and you'd go a different way. It was ridiculous.

I'm not quite sure when the penny really dropped, but the most helpful person was my art teacher. He was a man of 27 when I was 16. He was this wonderful outspoken Derbyshire man, extremely handsome. Anyway he would call a breast a breast. We had never heard anatomical words in our life. I used to pose for him, and he used to pose for me nude. It was a marvellous education. Also to be with someone who was creative, the first person who questioned what went on in life, as opposed to everyone around me who just seemed to follow like a herd of sheep.

I first had sex when I was about 19. I met someone at a bus stop, we went out a few times and went back to some grotty flat. It was all a bit gruesome really – the thought of sheets which aren't pristine and clean. So then I launched into a whole series of affairs – I think it's the thing about women searching for affection and men searching for sex and the two collide.

I was bamboozled by the world, really. It was a very limited world. I can't remember having huge expectations – it was very day-to-day, without a long-term plan. I think this is partly a lack of role models. I didn't know any successful women apart from the teachers at the college, who seemed to be all spinsters.

I came to New Zealand in 1969. I had been living with a Biafran chap, which was never going to work. It would have broken my mother's heart that I was living with a Biafran, if she ever found out. The Biafran war was on, and he was totally unreliable, so I decided I'd be safer at the ends of the earth. I had a friend who was working for the hospital board here, so I got the free passage and came for a two-year contract.

I landed in Auckland on the 1st of January in 69. I walked out of the door and there was no one anywhere. I couldn't understand it. I'd been in London and there were always people about. I walked to Symonds Street and I don't think I saw anyone the whole way. Everyone had gone away. It was weird.

I went to a party, and the women were at one end and the men were around the keg, and at 11 o'clock they all chose their piece of meat to take home. In London men and women did speak to each other a lot. You were treated like a human being. I was indignant – I just didn't know what to make of it. It was like being on another planet. I didn't know the language, I didn't know what people talked about. It certainly wasn't the things we talked about in London.

I met my future husband very soon after that, so a lot of the mysteries of life got solved. He was quite a worldly New Zealander. He certainly thought outside the box. He was a patient of mine at the Ōtara rehab centre – it was the classic thing you're not meant to do. I had to wait for him to get divorced, which took four years. He had been unhappy for years and leading a separate life. So about 1974 I got married. By then I was working in a geriatric hospital in Cornwall Park, then my team got moved to Auckland Hospital. I worked there for a while. Then we went to England for a year.

My son was born in 1982. I had six weeks off to have him, and went back to work, and carried on for about six years, by which time I really was worn out. I resigned and did odd jobs for a bit, and then helped to set up a clinic for people with low vision.

Then my husband had a very big accident, and he was in hospital and was unlikely to come out. That was when I realised that I've got to take charge of providing an income that would look after my son and myself long term. And I realised I needed to be around the house because my son was only about 13. For years I'd been looking to get out of the working environment I'd been in. I'd thought of all different things, but really couldn't think how to get into them or get the experience.

Then I met a man who said on our first meeting – we had a sedate cup of coffee – that he liked to be caned. And that was probably the best thing anybody has ever said to me. I was a bit surprised. I did it a couple of times and I couldn't really get into it, but then I was quite angry about something. I would never now see a client if I was angry, it's not the right space to be in, but at that time it caused me to give him a very good caning, which he was very pleased about. So after that, I said to myself, I can do it, he wants it, what's my problem?

The man that I caned introduced me to a man that became my mentor. He was a lot more serious about what domination does for men, why they want it and the type of woman they would like to do the domination part, and he was prepared to give me practical help. He was a very refined, honourable man, which made it a lot easier to take what he said seriously.

I knew nothing about domination. I'd had one relationship that had elements of bondage, where I was tied up, but with someone who I would now not let come anywhere near me. He had very little empathy, which is the last thing you want really with someone tying you up. So that wasn't a good introduction, it didn't have the basic elements of safety and sensuality.

When I met the man who became my mentor I was 47. I felt worn out and unattractive, as though I was just a machine providing domestic services, childcare and all the rest of it, running up and down to the hospital. But my mentor said, you will be very good at this. He said men don't want to go to someone very young, inexperienced, frivolous. He probably liked what we call mummy figures – fuller-figured women. I fit into that category, and so he could see me being quite popular in that sort of role. I was desperate to find a way of earning a living that didn't take all day, that I could be creative in. I just had to believe him until I got the hang of it.

He was a person who helped women set themselves up, gave them the confidence, experience. He said you earn reasonable money, you have a lot of freedom, it fits in with your childcare and you meet lovely men. I think he felt that a lot of men need these services, and he had empathy with them because it was so hard to find someone to fill the role of a good dominatrix. He was incredibly generous with his time, facilities, experience, everything. He wasn't a pimp in any way at all.

So I placed an ad in *Truth* asking men to meet me to tell me their domination fantasies. This was the only way I could think of to actually meet men who would be interested. What are they like? Have they got two heads? Are they wearing dirty raincoats? I had no idea. So I drank lots of cups of coffee in public places with them and we'd have a general talk and at the end I'd say, 'Would I be acceptable to dominate you in the fantasy you've described?' And all of them, I must have met 20, said yes. They were virtually on their knees in the coffee bar begging me to take them home.

I had no idea what a dominatrix was. Now you'd look on the internet and within three minutes you'd have some idea, but then you had no idea. There were a few books, but books are either sensational or they don't give you an idea of the practical steps. I was terrified, but I thought, OK, I've got some good backing.

My mentor had a very good rapport with men who he'd met previously in his attempts to help other women. He had a little black book and he would contact these people saying, 'I have a new woman in training, and she will be available on a certain date, in a certain location.' And then he would set things up for me. My technique of course was terrible – I was very stiff, because I had this image that you had to be stiff and powerful. But I had to start somewhere, and I think the lovely thing about men is that you may not be particularly skilled, but if you have good intention and they don't feel as if they're being ripped off and used, they're very accommodating, very understanding.

I was extremely nervous. Everyone thinks a dominatrix is full of self-confidence, but I think to doubt and to have human feelings is very good, because you can put yourself in someone else's shoes, and most of the guys who have come to a dominatrix are shaking in their shoes. But you have to be able to act confident, so on top you're very much in control. Just like in a lot of hospital situations, you're covering it up until you relax together, and then hopefully your creative side takes over.

If they walk in here and they're blasé, there's nothing in it for them really. They're coming to someone for the first time, they don't know them. They don't know who may be lurking about. Have you got hidden cameras? Are they going to bump into their friend coming out? They've got all these things on their mind. Will the dominatrix get them in a vulnerable situation and take advantage of them? The other thing is if a person's held a fantasy for a very long time and they have got the courage up to come to someone, the fear of that fantasy being ruined is very strong.

I think now with the internet, they find a lot of people have got a similar thing to them, and it's calmed people down a little bit. But some have things that they can't explain to themselves, like this desire to wear nappies or something. They think, I'm a grown man, why have I got this thing that I can't control and that gives me so much pleasure? They can read about other people, but it doesn't affect how they feel about themselves. Before the internet it was much worse. I was often the first person that they'd spoken to about their fantasy.

I finally got courage up to put my ad in *Truth*, and started using my house. It had spacious rooms, high ceilings, two huge rooms, bathroom facilities for my work, easy access from the motorway, it was perfect.

It was 1994 when I started work. And the first three months it was a massive learning curve and I was so busy I couldn't believe it. Some days I'd be exhausted mentally, because I wasn't switched on enough to just use the imagination as we go along. You're writing the play as you're going along, you're moving the scenery, you're moving the characters and trying to work it all out and make it end within an hour. Exhausting.

It got better, but every night I'd go to bed and think, I'm sure I'll wake up in the morning and I won't want to do this anymore. But 18 years later it might have calmed down a bit, but the excitement is still there. No day is ever the same, no person is ever the same, no client is ever the same on a different day.

My ad said something along the lines of 'refined English mistress'. The English is very important in some people's mind in terms of finding the perfect dominatrix. I'd put CP, for corporal punishment. Cross dressing. I probably said 'bondage'. *Truth* wouldn't allow me to write the words 'adult baby', they said we might get paedophiles. So I'd put 'mothering', they didn't seem to mind mothering. Clean drug-free premises, something like that. It was concise.

I'd always say, 'Good morning, Margaret speaking.' If someone said, 'Hullo, what do you charge?', I'd say, 'Are you looking for a sex worker?' And they'd say, 'Yeah.' I'd say, 'Sorry, I'm a dominatrix, you need someone else.' So that's one conversation which doesn't go very far.

Then you get others who are much more gracious. You say good morning, they say good morning back, and they might say, 'I've never done this before.' And I say, 'Have you got something on your mind?' If they hesitate I might say, 'Is it easier if I run through the sort of things we can do?' Because nice men on the whole don't want to offend you, so they won't say 'I want anal' in case it horrifies you. It's better to offer and lay out your limits.

Within about 20 seconds I can tell if that person may ever come to me. Some are dismissed, they're not suitable, got a bad attitude, whatever. And then there are shy people who need a little longer, and sometimes people who know exactly what they want. If they tell me then I'll say, 'Yes, we can do that', or I might put them onto someone else who is a different age or shape or demeanour.

I never push people into making appointments. It doesn't work, basically. If you push people they'll make an appointment, not turn up, waste your time. And the fact that you're relaxed, the genuine people will appreciate that and they'll come to you whenever they're ready. Some people say, 'Are you free this afternoon?' They've enjoyed talking, they feel safer and ready to go.

Possibly 40 per cent have got a fantasy in their mind – for example an aunty catching them in her lingerie drawer, dressing them up or giving them sex education or a spank or whatever. It's quite hard to know what is exactly in someone's mind. What does she look like? How does she act? So I have to elicit that.

Other people want activities, so it's the bondage, the tying, the blindfold, it's more events. I'm surprised even at my age that having a woman of a certain shape or size is secondary to having someone they have empathy with and feel safe with. If they're too apprehensive they're not going to relax into it. I think having worked in health, feeling safe is something I am able to engender fairly quickly.

I had a bed with legs, so I got some chain and looped it round the legs, then got some cuffs for ankles and wrists. I got a blindfold. And then I went to a funny shop in Herne Bay that had all these leather genital-tying-up devices. I bought a handful of these at vast expense only to find that one size does not fit all, so they've languished in the drawer in pristine condition. Things like shoelaces are much more flexible. Again because of lack of experience I bought stuff that people say you need, but it was not really very useful.

As I went along I began to make things. Adapt clothes for cross-dressers, make the bras broader across the back, or adapt the slips so the shoulder straps don't keep falling off wide shoulders. And you visit op shops and find shoes and high heels.

I started looking at clothing in a completely different way. I'm a plain dresser. But I began to find shapes which enhance my figure. White skin against black lingerie. High heels do wonderful things for women. I started buying leather jackets and leather skirts, which normally I wouldn't be seen dead in, and enjoying them.

I always ask a person how they want me to be dressed. It shows you're willing to listen to what they're saying. And you learn a bit about what their mind is saying to them. If they say, 'I want a leather-clad bitch', and I'm thinking high heels, black stockings, black leather skirt, black jacket, it puts me in a different theatrical frame of mind from if they want their aunty in a pink slip and a pair of beige stockings.

For adult babies, it depends who is looking after the baby. Are you a classic nanny? You might have a white blouse and dark skirt and be quite distant or frosty, or you might be quite motherly, an aunty who's rushing around looking after the baby wearing their slip or whatever. Most men do love the feel of something silky, so at some stage they're going to want to touch the slip or slinky garment over your thigh, or be lying across it. The texture of things as well as the look is important.

A tarty aunty is someone who'd taunt and be very provocative to a 14, 15-year-old boy. A tarty aunty might be all sort of tits and bum and short skirts and her knickers showing. I'm often more of a motherly aunty, an aunty who finds the boys masturbating in a magazine or in her lingerie drawer, but is quite understanding that at their age it's bound to be a bit like this, and that may lead on to 'This is what women like in the way of stroking,' or 'I bet those magazines don't tell you what it feels like,' and you run their hands over lingerie and breasts. Everything is so different with each person.

Or I might be a prison guard who's got a prisoner and is taking advantage of the situation. If it's a fetish I could be wearing a great big old mohair cardigan. I've got quite a bit of rubber, some PVC, a black bodice and skirt. I've got a white PVC nurse's uniform and a cloth nurse's uniform. I could be a tarty schoolmistress.

There is a fantastic range of scenes that people want. One is where they want to replay something that happened in their past, usually something that had an impact on them at the time. They may have been quite young, say eight or nine, and over the years they have developed it into an erotic fantasy. An older man came to me and said, 'When I was about 10 my aunty used to take me away on a holiday every year and we'd go to a caravan.' It was in England, so I could just picture this, and he said, 'One day we turned up at the caravan that she'd pre-booked, and it was absolutely tiny.' And she said, 'We can't stay here, we'll have to go home.' And being young, and it was his holidays, he said, 'No, please let's stay?'

So they had these two single beds very close together and a tiny little wash handbasin at the head of his bed. So in the morning he wakes up, and there is Aunty, bent over washing her face, under her arms and between her legs in this tiny little bowl with her bottom over his face because it was so cramped. So he said, 'I saw this looming moon above me, but pretended to be asleep.' And he said the same thing happened the following morning, but the morning after that, 'I couldn't control myself, and I stuck my head up between her legs.'

The poor woman must have gone through the caravan roof – children are impulsive. So he wanted to replay this wonderful scene in the caravan, which was quite fun.

I often say to people, 'That's what actually happened, but you've been thinking about this for a while, haven't you?' And they'll say, 'Fifty years.' So we'll talk about what sort of ending it might be. I'd ask people how they want it to develop.

A lot of women have abused boys, young men, by using their superior power. I've had men who've been seduced by their stepmothers or who've slept in the same bed as their mother until they're 22 or whatever. And unless there is any heavy, cruel abuse, men tend to not think of these things as abuse, but convert it to some erotic way of dealing with it. I've played out being seductive stepmother.

Then there are schoolmistress fantasies. That's more being stripped naked in front of a fully dressed woman in a role they remember from their past, where someone has the power over them and they might want to feel smaller and insignificant and controlled and punished, berated. And sometimes there are reasons they'll identify, that you've had these things happen to you and you didn't have any control over it, but now you pay someone to do this to you and you've got the control. When we're humiliated, we think, god wouldn't it be awful if that happened and my knickers fell down in the supermarket? But here when I make the worst possible thing that they can think of happen, they survive it and they're empowered in a way.

Ordinary sex is fine for the men who come here. They say, 'I love my wife, we have a great sex life, but she can't do this for me.' And they're not being critical. It's just a fact of life, and you can understand why women can't do it. They cook, clean, are taxi drivers, they go to work and then you expect them to be an experienced dominatrix as well. The men will often say, 'The orgasms I get in this situation are far more intense than in ordinary sex.' Ordinary domestic sex might take 15 minutes if you're lucky. But here you've had someone in various stages of excitement for an hour or so and you've built them up and let them down a little bit and built them up – and they've been away from reality. No domestic thing has got in the way, they haven't had an argument with me two days ago, we're not worried about the finances. It's a capsule of sheer delight, or should be.

I think you've got to treat it like any business, especially if you're self-employed. You need to be well organised, on time, probably work pretty regular hours. You need private, quiet premises where people can come and go very discreetly. From a personal point of view you need to be fairly sane. You've got to have a good sense of theatre, but it can't be theatre which is detached from the actual client. It's got to be invoking the feeling of the fantasy in someone, but still having your own personality and humanity available to them as well. When I started I was very stiff. I was acting a part and the relating was probably very hit-and-miss, whereas now I think the relating is really important and being able to set the scene and the theatre is a close second.

You have to make the best of whatever shape you are. When men come in the room they're not looking at you as though you are a catwalk model; they really focus on something which attracts them. It can be a smile, or a very nice cleavage set off by the right clothing, or high heels, and they sort of fill in the bits in between in their own mind.

I think my favourite part is when someone stands up at the end of a session, they're looking a little shell-shocked often, and in a rather disconnected way they say that was great and they mean it. If they haven't enjoyed themselves they'll just pay you and say goodbye, but when they've had a marvellous time they look absolutely stunned, and often they tell you over and over. People ring up the next day and say, 'I couldn't think of anything to say, but I had a marvellous time and I'll be back.'

The youngest man who ever came to me was 19. I turned him down on the phone. Then a few days later I'd forgotten his voice, and he phoned up and said he was 22 and I thought, he sounds very sensible, I will take him. Later on when he visited me he said, 'I'm the 19-year-old.' But he was a fantastic player. And the oldest was something like 84 when he started coming to me and about 87 when he stopped.

The only common denominator is that they have a slightly evident softer side, and a confidence that allows them to put themselves in the hands of a woman and get sensation and feeling. Professionally they're everything from doctors, plumbers, professors of sociology, beneficiaries to multi-millionaires. People who come with an envelope full of five-dollar notes that they've been saving up for three months, just a whole range.

Money is obviously a motivation to me, but I don't look at people thinking, they're rich, I'll get extra money out of them. I look at them as, 'What's your imagination like?' I have had some people who are very high-profile. They've come for years, and they've obviously found that someone would have to torture me to tell anyone else who they were.

Most of my clients are married, and they would describe themselves as happily married. I had a very intelligent man who said, 'I've had this thing about wearing nappies and being dressed up as a baby.' He was a lovely, honourable married man, and finally he got to bursting point. He visited me and I gave him a little talk afterwards. I said, 'When you let this out of the bag and you find someone like me, you'll want to be here every hour of every day. But after a month or six weeks it will start wearing off. When you've been to someone like me and experienced it a few times you'll start calming down, because you know you can come, have your private time and then go home.'

After a few weeks he said, 'I am so much nicer to my wife because I'm not so strung out.' So I think I'm an escape valve to the men who have got things they find hard to raise with their wife. Or they've raised it and she's not interested, and they say, 'I don't want to force her into anything she doesn't want to do.' I'm discreet. I never phone them afterwards. They have to phone me. I'm not going to interfere in their life. I'm a total safety valve.

I always say, 'I'm a dominatrix, I do not have intercourse with my clients,' because it saves the clients asking. Some people who do so-called domination are also having fairly ordinary sex as well, which confuses the type of men who come to me. I try to present myself as offering domination only. But for 95 per cent of the men who come to me eroticism and sex of some sort is the driver. So if you're taking sex as touching, stroking, masturbation, I suppose there is a lot of sex, but it's sex where I am in control of what they get. It's the parcelling out – you get a little bit of this and then you long for more. You might be caning someone, but they are interpreting it as sexual. For 95 per cent of people it ends in masturbation and orgasm.

In terms of safety, the first thing is interviewing people properly on the phone. If a person shows respect, they're prepared to listen to you. If they say, 'I want to lick you,' and I say, 'I don't do that, if I catch herpes I can give it to hundreds of men,' and they say, 'Oh all right then,' they have listened and taken your limit on board. Although I'm still cautious to a degree, in 17 years I've probably only had two people I really wanted to get out of the place. That was when I was new, and I was trying to be open-minded, thinking not everyone can phrase everything perfectly on the phone.

The other really good thing about domination is that a man who wants to come to a dominatrix wants to surrender control, he doesn't want to control you. You hope you're more safe than someone in the ordinary sex industry taking a random client.

Once someone's here I talk to them about the safety issues which are relevant to their session. If I'm going to be doing anal on them I always use a surgical glove on my hand, lots of lube, two condoms on all equipment. If I'm going to put someone in bondage – I could drop dead, I could have a heart attack, trip over on equipment, bang my head, whatever – I text my friend who works locally and knows how to get into the house. That's my safety set-up. I always say, I will be texting you back before 12.30, whatever the time is.

With caning, it's a case of using the muscular part of the buttock, not letting the cane or the strap wrap around the sides because men haven't got very much fat there. I used to practise with my cane on a hard pillow and aim for a certain part of the pillow over and over again. Once there's any danger of drawing blood I stop. Some people go into blood sports and they don't appeal to me at all, that's things like needles, nipple piercing, scrotal piercings in the session. I'm not keen on getting a needle stick injury, so I just avoid those.

I do water sports, which could transmit hepatitis, but I haven't got hepatitis and I haven't got practices that would lead me to get hepatitis. I talk to people about the possible implications, but you're normally doing it on the skin so you're not around mucous membranes, and so far, so good.

When I started I had no idea. I used to think I'm around all these men, surely I'll catch something, and every six months I'd trot off and get myself tested. But I'm not doing things that transmit disease, so after a while I just realised that this was my paranoia rather than reality.

Before the law change[1] I asked a barrister friend about what I was doing. He said if it came to it, he thought the way the law was worded that I would be guilty of soliciting for sex. He said a judge would find it very hard to say you are not contravening the law, but everyone I spoke to in practice at that time said unless you're really rifling through men's pockets, stealing from them, doing something stupid, you're most unlikely to be visited by the police. They could find me in *Truth* and do swoops I suppose, but it never happened. If they did come and visit an elderly lady operating as a dominatrix, I think they really ought to have better things to do.

I did worry, because I'd come from a different world, and I didn't really have anyone to talk to about it. When I started work I didn't know a single person who had also done this. Probably the first person I ever met was a woman who worked from a brothel in Hamilton. Quite a mature woman, incredibly popular, both for her sexual services and as a dominatrix. By then I'd built my own persona and skills and I thought she was very ordinary, but having met

---

1. The Prostitution Reform Act 2003, which decriminalised sex work in New Zealand.

other dominatrices now, when you're in your tracksuit or whatever and you're just sitting being ordinary, of course you're ordinary. Somehow you expect a dominatrix to have a certain fire or something that comes through, but everyone needs a day off.

Then through a woman I was training I met other women who were working in Auckland as dominatrices. We'd get together and have dinner occasionally. But we are all so different as people – just because we have the same occupation doesn't mean we're going to necessarily get on or want to meet every week.

I think there are probably about six people who take it seriously in New Zealand. Then on websites such as New Zealand Girls you'll get people who are doing a bit of crossover between sex work and domination. I'm not sure that they really understand it. They tend to be very young and they might put B&D in their advert. It may be that they've got a paddle or something and they'll give someone a couple of whacks across the bottom. If you're a good dominatrix you earn a lot more than the average sex worker in a shorter time, so why would you want to be having a bonk for 60 bucks when you can be earning a lot more an hour?

I thought at one stage about renting an apartment and doing sex work, because there are a lot of nice men, perhaps a bit older, 45 to 75, 80, and they're not looking for a young person for a quick energetic bonk. They would like someone to talk with, laugh, have some physical contact, not necessarily intercourse but they may want masturbating or closeness. There are a lot of people who are divorced or bereaved, or like some of my clients say, 'I've been married three times, I'm not very good at it, I'm not going there again.' I think that's a sensible man. People say, 'I'd rather go and pay someone, it's cheaper.'

So I did think about it. But however carefully you word an advert, there will always be a lot of calls from people who have totally misunderstood, and those calls wear me down. Things like, 'Hullo, what do you charge?' This is after you've said good morning, so I immediately get cross. It's frustration at the lack of manners, being a bit British. So I knew I might not be able to keep up the enthusiasm. And I met my partner and it went off my agenda for a while. I felt I can't have three lives. Partner, dominatrix and sex worker, that's all a bit too much for me.

I have tried to be helpful to women who are interested in becoming a dominatrix. But out of 10 I've tried to help I'd say there was only one who made a real go of it, and took it seriously and took learning seriously, and then started using her own imagination.

She and I started by having clients who were willing to have two of us there. I would brief her on what we were going to do, and I would use hand signals slightly out of sight. Or the client may be blindfolded or she could be standing behind them. She was very perceptive. When there are two mistresses in a room one of them has got to be in charge – she was really good at stepping back a little, and then joining in when it was appropriate. Then we did the physical things like learning how to spank, strap, cane, tie up genitals, all the practical things you've got to do. We had a few lessons on our own doing that, and we used the book *The Mistress Manual,* which was a very simple book written with some enthusiasm by I think a happy amateur, but one who'd really thought about what she did. And after a while she went and set up on her own.

She was intelligent and had been around men, felt totally comfortable with naked bodies and men in various states, so I didn't have to get her past that stage or anything. You could say she was a bit of a natural.

I tried to help women, but they either haven't got the demeanour or they don't understand. If they've come from the sex industry they tend to have a different demeanour, very hard to change. Or they didn't turn up, or they haven't got the right gear, even though on the phone they've said, 'Yes I'm wearing this, yes I'll wear red lipstick', all the things that are important to the session. You've made it as simple as possible, and they can't comply with the simplest thing, so they're not going to make it on their own.

About half of them had worked in the sex industry. And then at the other end are women who are quite bright, and they've got their own career and they're wondering whether to change from something which has got a good income, independence, social acceptability, to doing this. That's quite a hard step to take.

I had a brief foray into running the Domina Reform School for Good Girls Who Wish They Were Bad, with a friend. She was very good at seeking publicity. She got a radio spot and we offered one woman a free session. Eight to 10 was an ideal group size, and we would talk to them about very simple things designed to enhance the ordinary suburban bedroom experience. That was very good, getting that publicity and offering a prize. Obviously a lot of women were listening, and they managed to get our phone number and booked.

So it was very handy to have three compliant slaves who were blindfolded and tied to the bed lightly, and we would instruct groups of women on how to do genital tying, how to stroke, how to do body slide type things, how to tease. Then we would have a little light time where we showed how to put a condom on a carrot with your mouth. It was great, female bonding is wonderful.

The sessions would last about three hours. We'd finish with a glass of wine, at which stage we'd say to the women, how would you feel about having the slaves that you've been tormenting all afternoon join in? And usually they said, oh yes let's see them, because they hadn't seen their faces. And the men would get dressed and come and join in and it was remarkably relaxed by that stage. They'd be talking about all sorts of things they like to try. It was great fun.

We did one in Australia and three or four here, but it was the expense of advertising, and getting women to commit. Women don't earn as much as men – for them to pay $100 for three hours was a lot of money. It took us a whole day to organise it, organise the men, pay for the wine, get set up, miss out on a whole lot of work ourselves. So in the end it faded out. It was great, and if I had a suitable person who wanted to do it I'd love to do it again, because it's so rewarding giving women confidence.

I've had a website for about 11 years, which I haven't changed very much because it works really well. A lot of websites for mistresses are very dark, they make them black, dungeony, hard to read. A lot of my best clients are fairly timid and safety-conscious. It may be very exciting to be dark and dungeony, but I have always promoted a sense of safety. It's a quiet, clean, safe, smoke- and drug-free premises.

To people who ask what my current premises are like, I say it's a spacious room, five by seven. It has two areas. One is for domestic fantasies, that's the area we're sitting in, a couple of chairs, desk, chest of drawers for cross-dressers' clothes, a bed, lamp. It's quite cosy when the blinds are down. And the other end has got the bondage equipment in, a bench, two overhead winches, a horse and lots of things I can pull out of cupboards. The mistress needs to be able to see what she's doing. If you're tying up genitals and you're getting hairs caught, or you've got to undo everything you've tied, you do need to be able to see. I can make things dark by putting a blindfold on someone, but I really do need to see. I have dimmers on all the lights so I adjust the lighting up and down as the session goes on.

There are people who like to be impressed by equipment. I don't display equipment because not everyone wants to walk into a room of huge dildos or vicious-looking equipment. I like to pull it out of hidden places. It suits my way of working, and you never know what will offend or frighten someone.

I have a very compliant saddler in Hamilton, and good equipment lasts for years so I have been building it up. I hardly buy anything now. I've got some stuff made by metal workers, I've got steel bars and things, but the equipment used most frequently comes from ordinary hardware shops. Lengths of chain, double-ended dog clips, rope.

I make some things that I particularly like, like silky hoods out of double-thickness silky material, much more pleasant than a blindfold for novices. Men love to have their head stroked, and if it's silky it feels nice, as opposed to a blindfold which often just gets caught behind the ears. I adapt a lot of stuff for cross dressers, which comes from op shops and discards from girlfriends. Obviously men are quite a different shape to us. Silicone breasts off the internet, shoes from op shops for clients. Expensive shoes for Mistress, of course.

I don't think the neighbours know. I don't want to be upset by neighbours doing things and I wouldn't do that to anyone else, so my clients come and go very quietly. People think there's a lot of noise in dungeons, deathly screams and the like. When I'm working it's extremely quiet, the odd groan. Ordinary conversation is about the level we're at. I don't play loud music. I don't do anything to annoy neighbours. Keep the place free of rubbish, sweep up the leaves.

A man who owned a brothel told me if your neighbours talk to you they have no idea what you do. He said, 'My neighbours will not talk to me. They all turn away.' He was a brothel owner in town and he lived in the suburbs quite discreetly, but they took offence at him.

My son was about 13 when I started. He knew that before, I used to work all the hours God sent. Kids are great in that they are self-centred. They want you there to cook the meals, and so when I told him very simply what I was planning to do, he said, 'Good, you won't have to work on Christmas Day.'

That as far as he was concerned was the end of it, as long as I didn't do anything that would enable his schoolmates to know. My mentor took my son aside and very simply told him what this was about. He said, 'What your mother is doing is a very honourable thing, it's not a dirty thing at all.'

My son has always been able to keep a secret, even when he was little. We used to have a saying, this is for inside the house, this is something we don't talk about outside, and he really got this concept. He would come in the back, clients would come in the front, they'd never meet. If a certain door was shut he'd know I was busy, he'd never come that way. As long as he had access to food and the computer what other cares did he have?

My sisters and their respective families are all abroad. The sister I'm very fond of and her husband were very open-minded and very funny about it. In one of Tom Scott's books a minister is tied up as an adult baby or whatever and the mistress goes out and leaves him. My brother-in-law loved Tom Scott's books and so if he met me at a station he would be carrying this huge sign, 'Nanny Whip'. My other sister, who is much more strait-laced, has never asked me a single question about the mechanics of what happens, even how much I earn.

In terms of friends, I've weeded out people who can't accept me for what I do and who I am a long time ago. I have a wonderful girlfriend who said, 'I can't understand why any man would come and pay you money, but I'm glad you're happy.' She has no comprehension of this sort of fantasy or what's in it for men. She's very easy going, she's met some of my cross dressers. People dress up in all sorts of funny things and it doesn't faze her at all because she loves fancy dress.

When I started doing this I was having a bit of an identity crisis. I'd been a responsible health worker for 25 years and then I started doing this. I was also fairly newly widowed, and after a few years I did start meeting men. Most of them thought it was a bit of a laugh to begin with and that you had all these exotic clothes, they thought that was fun. But once that stage passed, they really failed to see who you were as a person.

I'd think, really does it matter, I'm very happy. I've got my son to look after, he's getting older but I need to be around quite a bit. I was quite established, I was busy, nice girlfriends, I could do pretty much what I wanted. Then I met someone who was a client and I just rather liked him as a person, he obviously liked me as a person. That set us off on a different basis and it cleared the air; he knew what I did, I knew what he liked and we could either talk about it or just put it to one side.

That developed into an ordinary later-life relationship. I don't think he gets jealous. I can quite understand why a lot of men would not want you round men all day long. If he said, 'I want to be a male escort,' I guess I would have my thoughts on it, but he seems to be quite happy. It's worked for 10 or 11 years, so I guess he'd have spat the dummy if it was not working for him.

When I first started this I was about 47, and the mentor said to me, 'If you're good at this you can be doing it when you're 70, if you're fit and well.' I thought, I'll never be doing this when I'm 70, this is a short-term solution to my present difficulties. But I can see if I want to I could be doing it at 70.

I'm not going to be every client's delight, but there are people who have been coming to me for years and we've all been getting older at the same rate. There are some people who like older women, and you can dress to grab the eye of the man to direct it where your best features are, and you're clean fresh, your makeup's on, your high heels are on.

They're not very good at age, a lot of men, and so if I want to be doing it I will. I'd like to work until I'm 70 because I have no idea what I'd be doing every day without it. I've got interests, but I can't walk all day and I can't read all day.

I have all the way along thought, well, perhaps I'll do this for five years. Then I got to about 53 and there was no sign that clients were dropping off, so perhaps another couple of years. It went on like this and now I'm 65 and I've really given up worrying. There may come a time when I break a hip or get backache or something but until that time I'm quite happy.

About six months ago I had a man come to me. He was about 38, and on the phone I'd been a bit naughty and said I was 58 or something. He said afterwards, 'I hope you don't mind me saying, you don't look at all 58.' So I thought, gosh. I said, 'How old do you think I am?' He said, 'Mid-forties.'

And I thought, the darlings. It's not that a woman would think I look mid-forties, but the fact that there are some men who think you look mid-forties and they've had such a wonderful time, they've got the rosy glow and the pink glasses on. Isn't it wonderful, and he's a young chap. It was a mystery. But I think what men like, it's part of my persona when I'm doing this and I do blossom. It's like women get a glow after sex, I get a glow with power, the gentle power that I can exert. Often clients will say, 'You're lovely, aren't you.' I think that's quite nice, they've perceived me as quite human despite what we've done. They don't see me as a leather-clad bitch, even though I might have been acting the part.

Margaret was interviewed at her Auckland home in August 2011.

KELLY

KELLY

I WAS BORN in Huntly in 1952. I am Scottish, Portuguese and Māori – the Māori side of my family are from Whanganui. I have two older sisters and a brother, and we grew up farming in the country.

I had a very good, safe upbringing. We didn't have a lot, but we had everything we needed. Very loving parents. It was a good upbringing. We saw lots of things that kids today don't even know happen, like the birth of different animals. You had to travel a distance to get to a town, so we used to only shop once a month. Women in that era who were farmers worked hard. We'd have the shearers in, so Mum would be cooking and would be in the shearing sheds helping with the fleecing and stuff like that. There was no such thing as washing machines, you had the old coppers, so the women worked very hard. Mum knitted all our jerseys – she was always cooking, always preserving. My father was a very strong man who would be out on the farm at night pulling sheep from the peat, but you'd see him at home helping Mum knit the bands on the jumpers. There was no TV, so you'd listen to the radio. We used to play board games, we all sat at the table as a family.

They were Labour people. My father was not dark, but my mum had the darker-looking blood in her, so she couldn't even get into a hotel. Women, especially Māori women, did have boundaries put on them a bit back then. They were brought up to respect European and Māori cultures, so that's why I'm very happy in my skin. People say to me, 'Are you Māori?' and I say to them, 'I have a Māori heritage, yes.' I'm very happy with both of my cultures

– I don't acknowledge myself purely as one or the other. I would like to have been able to speak Māori. I did try about five years ago but I'm too old to learn those things now. When I grew up, you didn't speak Māori unless you were in the real back bushes. The whole thing was, to be educated, you've got to speak English.

When I was about 10 we moved to the city, to Auckland, and Dad went to work for the abattoirs. I thought, 'Yoo hoo, bright lights, this is me.' We were in Papakura to start with, then Ōtāhuhu, I went to Ōtāhuhu College. School was OK. In hindsight I wish I'd done things a little bit differently, but it was OK. I didn't go through to School C [Certificate]. It was like, 'I'm out of here,' and you could get jobs then, so it didn't matter. When I look back now, I would have liked to have entered the medical arena, maybe as a nurse. I have no regrets, but that's the only thing I would change. You don't see those things until you get older.

We didn't really get sex education, very little was ever spoken about sex. You learnt by what you heard at school more than anything, whether that was the right information or the wrong information. You couldn't get condoms – you had to go into a chemist, and they would be hidden underneath the counter. When I met the father of my son we did try and get condoms, and the chemist just laughed at us and said, 'You're too young, go away.'

When I was 17 I got pregnant. You were expected to get married, so we did, we got married and we had a wonderful son. Our marriage lasted about six years and then I left, and of course that was something you didn't do. I was a bit of a black sheep from the beginning – I always did things that were not socially acceptable. I knew I was going to leave him a couple of years before I did, but I had to wait until my son started school. When he started school I was able to return to work full-time. You couldn't get bank loans for houses – there was nothing really available for you, so I was very grateful Mum and Dad always gave me good support. This was the mid-70s.

Then we moved to Australia. It was really just for a change – I went first because I knew nobody there. I flew to Brisbane and didn't really like Brisbane, so I hired a car and drove down to the Gold Coast and thought, wow, this is me, this is lovely, the beach, the sunshine. I fell in love with the Gold Coast, and the caravan parks were just beautiful. So I bought a caravan and hitched it up there and my son came over. We had a 26-foot caravan in the park. You've got your power, it's got TV, it's got everything there. It was just a great place for a young boy to meet other kids.

I looked for work for about five months, applied for everything you could possibly apply for, office work, reception at hotels, whatever. Five months had gone past, and I was running out of income and thinking, my gosh, I've got to do something. Then I saw this ad in a local rag for a receptionist for a massage parlour, and I said to one of the ladies I was friendly with, 'I think I'll go and have a look at that.' There was a chuckle, a laugh, oh why not, so I went and had an interview. I said to the owner, 'I hope you're not expecting me to do this.' And he said, 'No, no, I want my receptionist to not be doing it.' So I took the job. I'd had nothing at all to do with the sex industry. I came back to the park and I said to the ladies, 'Well, that's me, I'm in the massage parlour,' and there was a chuckle.

I was there a few months, and I thought, I can do this. And some of the ladies that I befriended while I was running the massage parlour were absolutely wonderful women. One lady, her father was an inspector in the police force in Victoria. Another woman's husband had gone bankrupt so she'd left, she had kids to raise. They were very well educated, amazing women. I had a wonderful rapport with them. I thought, I can do this, and I decided to jump the fence and earn far more money than I was as a receptionist.

I was in my late twenties and I was very focused on why I was doing it. I had a child to raise, I had to feed my son and myself. I flatly refused to be on the benefit, and my focus was to give my son and myself a better life. And we did, we had a wonderful life.

I told him only what I thought his brain at that time could handle – that I used to go out and have lunch with gentlemen, I was hired to be escorted to lunch. We used to have barbecues, so my son got to meet other children of women that were working in the industry and realised that they were just like anyone else. As he got older I told him a little bit more, then a little bit more. He was absolutely fine because I was still his mother, I was his caregiver, I was still everything that I was before. Right up until I retired out of the industry I used to say to him, 'Are you still OK with where I'm at?' 'Oh Mum, god yes, doesn't bother me in the slightest.' So he was never, ever tainted by it as people think.

That's probably the part that upsets me the most, when I read that sex workers are not good parents. Back in that day you could have lost your child. I don't believe that children get tainted from the sex industry. It's a job. I've not associated myself with the drug scene, and not everybody is a drug addict in the sex industry.

I was very able to do my job, go home and leave it there and just get on with another day. Wake up in the morning and be like everyone else that thinks they're normal, read the paper, have breakfast, get ready for work. Send your kids to school, whatever. I was no different to anyone else. My choice of work may have been a bit different. And it was my choice of work; it was not something that somebody talked me into doing. It was a choice I made for a better financial life.

With my first client I was shaking at the knees. It was hard. I guess as I was receptioning there, it wasn't like going in cold. I had listened to the girls, we used to sit round in the lounge when it was quiet, have a coffee and a laugh and talk about different things, so it was an open book, what was happening inside those doors. But as they always said, your first client is your hardest – after that it's a breeze. And it was. After that it was not a problem at all.

We used to be checked once a week, the doctors would come into the parlour and you'd have a check-up. There were no condoms being used in the early 80s, only if a client requested it. The girls would check the clients in the best way they could. The slightest suspicion, if a doctor could see that there was something maybe wrong while giving you an internal physical he would suggest you didn't work until your results came back. They also taught us how to look for things, how to feel for warts, how to look for herpes. You couldn't always get it right, of course, but it was the best we had at the time. When HIV hit, that was mid-80s, very strongly the sex industry turned the corner and said let's utilise condoms. From there on I never ever did unsafe sex. Sex workers educated people – they were the strong advocates of education around safe sex.

I worked mostly days; I didn't really do nights because I preferred to be home for my son. I pretty much worked when he was at school. If we needed to work at night for whatever reason, one of us would have the kids at our place for the night. We had our own little babysitting community. That was a priority of the women there, making sure their kids were safe. The majority of them were mothers. It was about money, they'd been left in situations that were very hard for them with a family. A lioness will do anything to feed its cubs, that's what we used to say. We were very protective of our kids.

I'd probably been working about two years when I told my family. I was always coming back to New Zealand for holidays, and I just sat them down one day and said, 'I need to tell you that this is what I'm doing. I'm OK, I'm keeping myself as safe as I can. My son is safe, he's not put into any unsafe situations.' So it was not an issue. Actually my mother said, 'If I was 40 years younger I'd probably do it myself.'

They were just concerned that I stayed safe and looked after myself, and made sure that my son was safe. My parents always knew I was never a follower. I was more of a leader than a follower, and nobody could really make me do anything that I didn't want to do. I was just a daredevil – the others were the goody two shoes. I was the one doing all sorts of things that was out of the norm.

I always paid tax – it was just part and parcel of me working. But during the Fitzgerald Inquiry in Queensland I lost my assets.[1] It was classed as illegal gain, it was illegal money – it was considered no different to a drug dealer. It didn't matter that you'd paid tax, it didn't mean a damn thing, it was criminal. During that time lots of women got hit. It was very tough – it was a time that I don't really like to go back and look at. I lost my home, I lost my assets, so when I came back to this country I decided I was going to fight for sex workers' rights.

I came back to New Zealand about 1990; my parents were getting older and my father was a bit unwell. I went to NZPC in Auckland to see what was happening in the industry. I knew a couple of ladies that owned a place in Rotorua, so I ended up going there to work. I stayed up in Auckland with Mum and Dad, and then I'd go down to Rotorua for two weeks and work in a brothel there and then come back for a couple of weeks.

Then I worked in Auckland. And you get the brothel owner that wants to take you to bed and see if you know what you're doing and how you can please

---

1. The Fitzgerald Inquiry was a judicial inquiry held in the late 1980s, which looked into allegations of police corruption, gambling and prostitution in Queensland and led to the conviction and imprisonment of several high-profile politicians.

a man, all this sort of carry-on. I was in my thirties, and I said to him, 'I've worked now for a very long time, I am very aware of what I'm doing. I don't need to take you to the room to show you anything. This won't be happening.'

I found out the truth of how New Zealand massage parlours were working in those days. The client would be paying so much at the door and then you'd have to negotiate your money in the room, and sometimes you didn't get paid at all. I couldn't believe how crazy it was. They were introducing fines if people were late, and shift fees and all sorts of ridiculous things. Sometimes the girls wouldn't earn any money, and they still had to pay that fee. I'm thinking to myself, I don't believe this.

All the girls were giving nude massages. The client would pay a fee at the door, $40, and he got a nude massage, and then it was up to him to negotiate any extras with the girl. So of course a lot of them didn't have the money. They've already seen you in the nude, they've had you massaging them and quite often they've already ejaculated on the towel, then all of a sudden there's no money, they've got what they've needed, and you don't get paid. I couldn't believe it.

I had my first one of those, a straight. You've gone through that nude massage and he's got no money, so I said 'Right, in the shower.' I wrapped a towel around myself and came out. The owner was sitting in the office and I was absolutely furious. I said to him, 'How dare you?' I said, 'I did not get into this industry for you to get paid and me get nothing. If you think I'm going to go through this again you are wrong and if any girl I work with goes through this you're wrong.'

I said, 'I'm going to tell the staff right now that they don't get their clothes off until they're getting money. If he wants a massage, do it in your knickers, your bra and a cami, do not get fully nude until you're getting some money.' I never ever worked again nude, unless I'd got money up front.

I used to sit the young women down and say to them, 'You're in the sex industry now. You don't have to do anything you're morally uncomfortable with. The main things in the industry are hand relief, oral or sex. Anything over and above that, if you're not comfortable with it, don't do it. But if you can't do those then you shouldn't be in the sex industry.' I used to make that very clear. A lot of the ladies over the years have thanked me for that.

I did a few outcalls in Australia, but in New Zealand, I flatly refused to after an experience I had in Australia, at a hotel in Surfers Paradise. He was an ex-Vietnam vet and a helicopter flew over. We were up on the 15th floor, 20th floor, and that helicopter was to do with Sea World, where they have chopper flights. To him he was back in Vietnam, he did a complete spin-out and was picking up the body bags and bodies and shit like that. I was the enemy. I was very close to being thrown off the balcony, to be honest.

I think if it had been somebody young – don't get me wrong, I was terrified – but if it was somebody that was young and didn't handle it in the right manner it could have been detrimental to them. I was only in my late twenties, but I still was able to talk him down. Thankfully that ended up in a better space after about three hours, and I managed to get out of there. He was very apologetic the next day. He sent a huge bouquet of flowers.

There were a lot of those risks when people went to private houses or whatever on their own. I chose after that not to do any. I thought, you're too vulnerable. You'd turn up at these places and you never really knew that you were on your own. There could have been somebody else in another room; other people could have turned up later. A lot of brothels in Auckland used to make girls do outcalls. I would have walked out. I had a son to think of. It's much safer to be working in an environment where others are there.

Later on you had panic buttons in some of the rooms. I think a lot of us back in the early days were more aware, you looked out for each other more. If somebody was in a room with someone she was a little bit uncomfortable with, we'd hover around the door and make sure that things were OK. It was a comradeship that was quite strong. Of course in a way you are competing to get that client, but once you got the client and you're in that room that competition stopped there. It was like the safety and the wellbeing overrode that, you made sure your comrade or colleague was OK.

There were times that you did enjoy your time with a client. I always used to say to girls, 'If you actually enjoy a session, don't be horrified. Your body can't take that amount of touching and intimacy without a release, and it doesn't mean to say that you've fallen in love with this person – this is a physical release, not a mental thing.'

It's a business transaction, but I still believe it's important to have physical pleasure from time to time. It's a good release for the body, it's a good release for the mind. You can get to the point sometimes where you're thinking, don't touch me, I can't cope with this anymore. You're giving so much of yourself mentally, physically, and I think it's really important to have that physical release. People are horrified or they feel dirty. It's important not to feel that. It's a body release. If you didn't have a man in your life, like I didn't, you thought, oh whoopee!

Sometimes you make believe you have been physically pleased when you haven't. I'd fake orgasms – but I've been married, that's no different from being married. There are times that as a wife you don't want to or can't be bothered but you do, you've gone with the flow and said it was fabulous when it maybe had not done a thing for you. Women are the best actors, no matter whether they're charging or not.

You're an actress in many ways. You're there for a purpose, you're going through the routine. You're not choosing them, this person's choosing you, so of course there are boundaries. Even if I had five, six, seven showers a day, I would always go home and shower again, and I'd have my own soap, my own deodorant, my own personalised things at home. The things I had at work in my little carry-around bag were for the industry. I had a different deodorant. Underwear that I would buy for work was for work – I wouldn't wear that underwear if I was going out. I always kept things quite separate – it just made me be able to come back to being who I am. I was no longer the actress, the sex worker – I was Kelly Reid again. I wasn't Jan Wilson [her working name], I was Kelly Reid. I separated the two people.

I was just as giving as Jan Wilson – Jan and Kelly could still have the same empathy, seeing clients who had certain disabilities. This person may have had bowel cancer or something, they've got the bag. I used to see one man that had the bag. That wouldn't put me off caring about somebody in my personal life, and it didn't deter me from seeing him as a client. That never bothered me. Those people always found that they couldn't go and meet somebody and indulge in the sexual side of life, they felt embarrassed, they felt rejected. For him and others alike to come in and pay for that intimate side, for sex and companionship, worked very well.

When I was working in the brothel scene I never took private clients and saw them at my house or their house, because that's crossing the boundaries.

You're not working in a fish-and-chip bar or selling Fisher and Paykel whiteware – you are selling your body, don't sell your soul. There's a big difference, and once you start mixing the two – I'll socialise with you, I'll see you as a client – it's very jumbled and you can become vulnerable. It's the same for a lot of professional people, like doctors. To socialise with patients you're changing the roles and you're overstepping the boundaries.

Clients sometimes wanted to meet out of work – you might get some client that's lost his wife or come out of a relationship and they get attached to you. I'm not saying it's wrong, but I didn't meet anyone that I wanted to have as a lover. I've known women who have met somebody in the industry and had a wonderful life. That's fine, it's like people meeting on dating sites, that happens and that's great. If I'd met somebody that switched me on like that, I would have stopped the work and gone with him. I met some really interesting, wonderful people, but not somebody I wanted to spend my life with. I've never been an insecure woman where I've had to have a man in my world to make it full.

Sometimes clients fell in love with me, and I had to stop seeing them when it got to that level. One comes to mind. Sadly, his son was killed in a car accident, and it was very traumatic for him. I probably played a comfort role – we'd talk about his loss, and he started to tell me he loved me. I've had to stop seeing them when it's got to that level for my own sake. That's too much for me. I think most workers have experienced that, where they want to put you on that white horse and save you. They may have been going through some vulnerable time themselves.

I would never see ones that were much younger, because I had a son that age and it didn't fit with me. If I had a daughter it might have been different, but if they were my son's age, I don't think so. I was strong-minded, I always made those things clear. This is my life – this was my journey, this was my body and I wasn't about to sell it under somebody else's rules.

I think you've got to have that control. If you don't, it will sweep you up and spit you out, if you allow people to railroad you in that industry. There are people that don't give a shit about you; you are a machine to make money for them. That can destroy you if you don't have a grip on that, and I will sit there and say this to any girl that enters the industry if I ever get the chance. The same words will come out of my mouth until the day I die – the industry's fine if that's where you want to be, but keep your boundaries and don't sell your soul to anybody.

I know women that have done things in the industry to please the bosses and the clients because they've been told they have to. If you tell an 18-year-old girl in a brothel that she has to have two men in that room, she has to do this and do that, that's what she believes she has to do. And she's scared to have an opinion of her own. After 20-odd years of working in the industry I saw that many times.

It can have a mental impact on workers. Some who have been sexually abused in their childhood have got into the industry. They're not empowered – they've been controlled and they're still controlled by people. That's the side of the industry I'd like to monitor. If you're going in blindly then somebody in there can blind you more, because you are selling your body. You're not selling a washing machine, you're not selling fish and chips – it's a whole different ball game.

Women who have been abused – sure, they're there; they're also in offices, they're in every kind of job in the world. But there are a shitload of women in the industry who have not been sexually abused, and I am one of them. I was never sexually abused; I had a very safe upbringing. There are a lot of women in that industry who have not been down that road. What I'm saying is some that do come in are not empowered. They've had that taken from them through their abuse, so if they're left to their own devices that could happen again.

A friend of mine was a counsellor, and I used to take girls who had been sexually abused to her. Twenty years ago I trained to be a counsellor at Manukau Polytech, but I never finished it. My plan was that I was going to become a counsellor for sex workers, not to come out of the industry, but to cope with it while they're there, empowering them while they're in the industry.

Then my father became very ill. He had cancer, and I spent a lot of time helping my mother nurse him, so that kind of went by the wayside. I should have gone back and finished it, but I never did. I wasn't doing any other work, that was my sole income. I regret not finishing the training. I put that into things I do today, I use the skills I learnt then, but I can't take it to the complete journey because I'm not qualified. I do regret that I didn't continue it. I think it's good if people can do some studies while they're working.

I had a couple of relationships in Australia. One in particular, we came close to getting married. He was OK with my work, but I had difficulties with him being OK. I'm thinking, if you could accept me working then what kind of a man are you? And he's thinking, I accepted her knowing she was working, how can I tell her that she has to stop? So there was a lack of communication. I think probably in the end I won that argument. I walked away – 'You've accepted where I am, so I'm going to move on.' In hindsight if he'd said I had to give it up, I would have said no, so there's no happy halfway.

I had concerns going to his company Christmas party. I said, 'Do you realise there could be somebody there that I might have entertained?' And he said, 'That's just too bad.' He was actually quite wonderful when I look back. So we went and it was fine. I don't know whether there was someone there, I was too scared to have a look around.

He was my lover, he was the one that I wanted to be intimate with. He was the one that I didn't have to put the boundaries there with, that I could be me with. Work was a mental and physical robot. He was getting Kelly Reid, work was getting Jan Wilson. I was very physically and mentally attracted to him, so there was no 'God, I've done all this today, I can't be bothered doing this tonight.' I was making love – it's a whole different ball game.

It's harder as you get older. I would have to tell a man that I was once a sex worker, and because I've been on my own so long now, that's a part of my life that I don't know whether I want to share. It's not about embarrassment, it's that it's really none of your business, take me as I am. But you'd still have to say in case somebody else did. I've been out of it now for some years, but that stigma is still there. It doesn't matter that you're a good person, that you've been a good mother or a good daughter or community person.

So you have to meet somebody that's very understanding, and that's not always the easiest to find. I did have that with the person in Australia, but wrong time, wrong place. At my age now I'm likely to say, 'If you don't like it, go.' I'm not about to sit there and make excuses for it.

When I came to Auckland, I worked at Geisha, downtown, for a couple of years, and then I went to work for a lovely lady that had managed one of the Geisha brothels. She opened a place in Newton and I worked with her for over a year. She had cancer and she passed away, and a few of us decided we'd go and do our own thing, because we didn't want to go back into a parlour situation. I decided to do an all-inclusive price, rather than charging so much at the door and the ladies negotiating extras in the room. I was one of the first to make that change in Auckland. It could have been detrimental to us – we could have been done for brothel-keeping or all sorts of things.

We had a lovely little place, a nice three-bedroom apartment in Newmarket, all private parking at the back. And then when our lease ran out we went to Newton and worked by day in a more commercial-type zone. Business was great back then, money-wise and business-wise and client-wise. We pretty much only worked through the day – the latest would probably be about eight o'clock at night. And most of us had lives, we had kids or whatever.

I preferred working privately – there was nobody controlling you, telling you how you should be doing things. I think a lot of the brothels were training them how to please a man at any cost, it didn't matter whether it was something you were uncomfortable with. So working privately you just don't have that – it's your rules.

We always had somebody else in the house – none of us were in that apartment on our own. That was a rule we made. I'm not a great lover of women working on their own because I think that can be dangerous. At least there should be two working together.

While we were in Newmarket a man had a heart attack, we had to get the ambulance. He was an elderly gentleman, he was in the room with one of the girls. I was in the lounge reading the paper and next thing she lets out this 'Whoa!', and he was on the bed and he'd had a heart attack. We had to give him a bit of heart massage to get him back. He had no clothes on so you can imagine trying to get the underwear back on this man that was like a dead body. You didn't need to be a rocket scientist to know where he was and what we were doing, so I asked the ambulance to be very discreet. I said, 'I don't know whether this elderly gentleman has a wife or not, but could you get the nurse or somebody to ring me because his car is here.'

To cut a long story short he lived, he was fine, his grandson came out and got the car. I said to him, 'Let's keep it discreet from your family.' And he said, 'Oh god, yes.'

I would not have gone to the police with any problems, not back then. The work was illegal and they had no empathy or sympathy for you. I knew women who were raped, mostly on outcalls. There was no empathy. The girls couldn't come to the brothel owner because all he would have to say was, 'It's an illegal industry, what do you expect me to do, go to the police? What you're doing is illegal.' They couldn't even go to the police – 'Well, you're a sex worker, you're a hooker, you're a prostitute – what do you expect?'

Some went to Rape Crisis; some just got on with it. Some didn't feel they could get help because of the stigma around their work, so you tried everything yourself to support that person. If you went to court there's media in there, it was always 'Jan Wilson, prostitute, was raped'. They like to sensationalise things, put 'prostitute'. Whether you're a sex worker, whether you're a private accountant, whatever, you've been raped, for heaven's sake.

Police entrapment was certainly a thing that happened – they would come in and have their sexual moment with you and then bust you. Or as soon as you talked about having extras they would bust you. You've got those that would have the sex and then bust you. Nobody is going to take that to court. You're fighting a losing battle because people would not believe you – they would not think the police would possibly do anything like that. Yes they could, and yes they did.

I asked one if he was a cop – I really had this bad feeling that he might have been. If you've worked the industry for that long you kind of have a sense. I asked him, 'Are you a cop?' And he said, 'No, no.' There was just something about it, and I said to him, 'I'm sorry, I don't believe you. Well, the session's over, I've got nothing to offer you.'

In the massage parlours, we had to register our real names in the police book. The police said they used to use it if something ever went wrong, or if anything happened to you. But I think it was really to keep an eye on the girls, maybe busting them at their homes. It was just an excuse so they had control over who was doing what and where. When I left Geisha, I tore that page out. I took that page that my name was on.

Later I had a three-bedroom apartment on K Road, a perfect place to work from – it was private, it was discreet. I lived upstairs, and we used downstairs as a working arena. I wasn't working this day actually, I was upstairs. Anyway the doorbell went and I came down and answered the door. When I let him in I saw the shoes, and I knew they were cop shoes. He came inside and I just knew it. Within seconds there's four cops walking in the door.

I just knew, those shoes were a giveaway, coppers' shoes. They came in and started questioning the girls that were working. It was a month before the law changed. It was scare tactics. They started asking all these questions and I said, 'Hang on a minute.' I said to the girls, 'You only need to give them your name and address, you don't have to answer these questions.' They wanted to go through the bags, and I said, 'No, you produce a warrant, there's no drugs in this house. You damn well know that I don't do the drug scene.' Then they had a look through the room and they tried to say there's tissues, and I said, 'Well, go upstairs, that's where I live, there's tissues in my room too, and so what?'

They eventually left, and they said, 'You've got 24 hours to close your doors.' And I said, 'No, I won't be', and I shut the door on them.

I was working with [Labour MP] Tim Barnett on prostitution law reform, and I made my complaint that there was intimidation a month before this was to go through. I spoke to Tim Barnett in parliament, and I know that the police were rapped on the knuckles.

I used to get flown down to parliament pre-law reform to talk with different politicians. I was advocating as a sex worker, I was strongly advocating for decriminalisation. I'm very proud that I can say I was part of making a law change in this country. That's something I always said to my son – one day you can say your mother was instrumental in making a law change. And my son was the very first person I rang when we got out of the gallery. I was there on the night. He was in Auckland, and I called him and said, 'Your mother's legal.' He went, 'Yes, good on you, Mum.' He was so proud that I was able to do that.

I worked for a couple of years after law reform. That whole weight had been taken off your shoulders in many ways – you could negotiate prices over the phone, you could negotiate that they had to use condoms. You could set the boundaries. That was huge – you didn't have to worry about an undercover cop knocking at your door trying to entrap you.

I just wish that the previous 20 years had been like that. Because you were constantly living in that little arena of fear. You just got on with it, but you always knew at the back of your mind that there was that possibility. I wasn't raped in the industry, but had I been raped I probably wouldn't have taken that to the police. After law reform, I would have. They have to comply by the laws too now and treat you not as a prostitute, but as a human being.

I don't believe that legislation, signing a bit of paper, is going to change people's mindset. It's like gay law reform, that went through 20 years ago and people still stigmatise that. It's up to the individual to walk with their head high and say, 'This is who I am and I'm OK with it.' I remember saying, 'Don't be in judgement, because everybody in the sex industry has a father, a mother, a sister, a brother, and one of those children out there could be yours.' Always remember that no matter where you come from, who you are, that could be your child out there.

I worked up to my early fifties. There's a lot of men out there that do like the mature ladies and feel like they can have a conversation with them, and you get the young guys that want an older woman. It was never an issue with me working later in life. I had a regular clientele – some of them I had seen for 20 years, so it was never an issue, I sort of grew old with them.

I started my menopause in my late forties. It was an actress job, lots of lubricant. They don't know you've got the lube there so they think they're doing a great job. That didn't faze me too much. Wise women in the industry always had a knack about timing and how they did things so that the physical side of it wasn't too long, too strenuous. You would lengthen out the massage, you would chat away – you would leave that side of it until the end, and if you worked your work right most men can be satisfied quite quickly. You don't want to be battered and bruised, you don't want an hour of sex – it's way too hard on you and you've got other clients to see. You'd get the odd one that would want to pound away at you from the time they come in, but that was rare, if you were wise.

In many ways, I think the sex industry trained men up. There were times when men would actually send their sons in to be taught how to fulfil the needs of a female. So many men go, 'This is what works for a woman – penetration.' I've taught guys throughout the years that that's not quite how it is. Men have come in, and said their wives have gone to bed with headaches, and I can see why, because they really are not educated around a woman's body. It's a matter of just educating them that there's a few other buttons that you need to push.

The industry is quite difficult to get out of, because what do you put on a CV? What do you say you've been doing for the last 10, 15, 20 years? It's very difficult. The most important thing today is what you put on a CV. You need a degree for sweeping floors. It's different if people are using it as a part-time job to up their income a bit, you've still got something else to put forward. But when you've used it as your main income, it locks you there.

I was lucky because I was open with my journey of sex work. I have been involved with the gay, lesbian, transgender community for more than 20 years, and I have been supporting people with HIV for all those years, because it could have easily been me who contracted the virus in the 80s. I love the gay community. I love the versatility of it all. And they were the ones that accepted me working in the sex industry. It was always, back 20, 30 years ago, 'What do you do, Kelly?' 'Oh I work in the sex industry.' "Good on you, girl.' If you were to say that in the heterosexual world it was like, 'Oh my god, you do what?' That stigma has always come from the straight community, not from the gay, lesbian, transgendered. The thing that connects me into the gay community is that I understand stigmatisation because I've been there, done that. So the voluntary work that I do is to give something back for how accepted I was into their world. Some of the drag queens call my son their brother. They call me Mother or Aunty. I love it, it's great fun.

So the people at the AIDS Foundation knew me and I managed to secure a job working for them. Where I am now, in sexual health, they also know I'm an ex-sex worker. So I've been working in areas that work hand in hand with the sex industry and the wider community. And the knowledge that I have around being an ex-sex worker, it works for me in the jobs I've had. I run a support group for under-35s living with HIV. A lot of these younger ones can't tell their families that they're gay, let alone they're HIV, so I play a loving, caring, aunty, motherly role and give them the support and help them on their journey of accepting who they are. And I work for a district health board.

I've never been ashamed of my journey. The only reason a lot of us hold back what we've done is because you're protecting family members from the stigma. I protect my grandchildren now. They don't know. They will know when I'm ready to tell them, or their father is ready to tell them and they're old enough to understand.

I think the industry has made a better person of me. It's taught me not to be judgemental. It's opened my eyes to life more. It's made me more compassionate to people, for the journey that people face in life, whether they be disabled, whether they be marginalised. It's allowed me to be a voice and speak for people that can't, and I still do that today. I think it's given me a lot more than just general nine-to-five office work would have done. It's opened my eyes to life.

The thing I'm most proud of is my son, his acceptance of me. His words were, 'You're still my Mum, no matter what.' Very proud of how he's been able to handle that. My family, for again being accepting, allowing me to take my journey in life without being judged. Certainly proud of the fact that I was involved in changing a law around prostitution. That's really important for me, because I have lived through the pre- and post-law reform. I can see the differences that it's made for workers, for their human rights and their safety and health and their general wellbeing. I can see that those laws are in place for them to use if they need to. That was a good way to end my journey of sex work.

Kelly was interviewed in Auckland in February 2012.

CATHERINE HEALY

CATHERINE HEALY

I WAS BORN in 1956, and I grew up in a little suburb in Wellington, a little bay. My father and mother built the house, and currently I own it, so it's nice, the place I grew up in is the place I'm now living in. My father was a public servant and my mother a shorthand typist, and they had four children; I'm the third.

My father was Catholic; my mother wasn't at all. We weren't wealthy, we were middle class. There was an edge in our bay, with gentle individualists, boat builders, artists and people like that. I loved it – I still feel it's a very special place. Great playground for kids – we'd have forts, and trees, that kind of classic 50s, 60s upbringing, where kids were skating and had dinghies and canoes. Sounds idyllic, and it was in so many ways. We were all readers, I loved to read. I used to write a bit, send things off to competitions, that kind of thing. Academically I was strong on language and English, but I was a bit dreamy. If I didn't want to do it I wouldn't do it.

We were all expected to go to university. And I was a 15-year-old coming into my own in the 70s – that feminist kind of stuff. Germaine Greer came down in 1970, when I was in the fourth form – though she's no hero of mine now, she's hostile to sex workers and transmisogynist. If you had an older sister, as I did, hooked up into the protest movement, the anti-apartheid movement – you had these role models, so you could sit at home and read *Salient*, and be aware of debates. I was very conscious of that.

I went to teachers' college in 1974, and to university. It was a very good time, and it was very liberal, teachers' college. There was a group of us who were selected and given freedom to decide what would be relevant to us as individuals to learn, which was extraordinary. So instead of having the imposition of a model of learning on us, we had the freedom to sit and think, what do we want to know, what excites us? It was a really happy time. I said I was interested in photography, so that became one of the things I did a lot of. In my third year I spent three weeks on a study tour in China.

I would work in the woolstores through the holidays. There were lots of students there, so you had lots of friends, had a really good social time. I also came into contact with Māori properly for the first time. I had not been aware of Māori at all – that was a big intersection for me, to run into people who were living very differently.

The reality of going teaching was a bit scary at 20, so I did full-time university to delay that. I had moved into a flat of mountaineers. They were really inspirational – they were older than me, and they were doing exciting things like climbing in the Himalayas and South America. And then I was a young teacher – juggling different lives.

I taught for nine long years. At the end of that time, I was travelling a lot in school holidays, and I started to become really fed up with teaching. I was really keen to get out and do something else. I saw a job as a receptionist in a massage parlour, and I answered the ad and got the job, to work on weekends. And that's how I became connected to the sex industry.

I was a receptionist for two and a half months. I was reliable, of course – I still didn't smoke or drink or have any habits. It was July 1986 when I answered that advert, so I was 30. I became the receptionist – the reliable receptionist for Friday, Saturday, Sunday. And then sometimes they'd ring me on a Wednesday, because I was reliable.

It had been the House of Ladies, and it had just gone through a name change and was called Number 12. It was in Boulcott Street, it was a very old house, and it had about three or four floors. A wonderful stairwell, and you'd run up and down. It was a very healthy, fit place to work in for a receptionist, and I enjoyed that – I was still part of a tramping club.

The massage parlour work was a very closeted world. I didn't even know a massage parlour was a brothel. I knew they had to massage topless, because

I'd had a flatmate who talked about that, but I thought they were paid wages. When I took the reception job, I didn't know until the second night. I thought they were massaging. The job was explained, you'd introduce Julie to John, take John and Julie to the room, make sure you remember how long they're in there for. After forty minutes, half an hour or whatever, go and tap on the door and say, 'Time!' That's what I did, diligently. And I didn't understand until one woman said to me on the second night, 'I've just had a straight!' We had straight/gay by then, and I remember thinking, what's the issue, what do you mean? She said, 'He didn't have any money!' I didn't even understand that. I said, 'How much do you get paid an hour?' And she said, 'We don't. We're prostitutes.' My big hullo moment.

Then after about two and a half months I jumped the desk, as they say, and worked. The clients would say things like, 'When are you going to go through, Catherine?' And the manager as well would sometimes say, 'Have you thought about it yourself?' She was good though, because she was always saying, 'Keep your day job, don't give up your day job.'

I was the receptionist, and then they were short one night. I was interested in being with the crowd, being one of the girls, not expected to be apart from them and bossing them around. So I had that kind of worker solidarity issue, and I became a sex worker. My money as a receptionist, $60 a night for eight hours, was fine, and I was still earning money as a teacher. I wasn't motivated by the money, but of course when you started to earn big money it was amazing – $2000 a week in 1986 was huge. Very empowering.

Another crowd, their parlour had closed down for renovations, the Lily of the Valley, and they came across and joined with us at Number 12, the House of Ladies. So we merged for a few months while their parlour was being put together. They were very stroppy and strident, and very on top of their game. They had a lot of lines: 'Well, why did you come to see a prostitute if you've got no money?' was one of the lines I remember. They'd give the clients telling-offs, which was a revelation to me, it was great. It felt more empowered, they seemed very empowered. They were a tight bunch, and they'd worked together for years.

The women I was working with at that time were interesting as well, but they didn't seem as cohesive. The Lily people came as a group who seemed to flat and shop and eat and talk – they had a lot of social relationships going on with each other. They had a lot of ideas, and seemed to be free to discuss them.

They dressed like they'd come out of *Dallas*, they were really amazing dressers. They were astounding – very glamorous. Over the top. Gowns, full evening gowns, I kid you not. I remember going out to buy my full evening gown, and it cost me $400. It was a black velvet thing, but I wore it for years and years. Up till then I had been wearing synthetic things, cheapish clothes. But then when these people came over they were really wearing designer clothes that cost a lot. Long dresses. And everyone wore heels. When I became more politicised I started to wear trousers. But they were expensive clothes, always expensive.

I had to be taught how to do makeup because it hadn't entered my life before then, I'd been anti-makeup. So I had to go and have a lesson. Makeup, green eye shadow. Girl-next-door look. And I got skinnier. I took up cigarette smoking and coffee drinking. I was 30 and became thin and went for a bob. Dyed my hair, that was a bit fast.

A lot of us became good friends, so we lived and worked together as well – we became flatmates and friends, and had Christmas together. I started to pull away from my other life. The other bits I was keeping going, like the tramping, it became a bit hard to keep those worlds going.

I quit teaching, took a year's leave. There had been a crossover with teaching for six months. I must have been a terrible worry for the principal. My clothes started getting fancier and fancier, and my cars, too. I bought a really exotic Fiat that cost a lot of money.

When the Lily opened again the girls left en masse, and I felt quite sad. Then I got a message to come and join them. I was very flattered. So I went over to the Lily.

It was 1987, when the share market crashed. The clientele dropped away significantly, and I became concerned about my income. I'd taken a year's leave of absence from teaching, and that year had come and gone, and I'd resigned formally. I was now dependent on sex work. So when I saw the income was dropping – I was still curious about sex work in other places, and somebody suggested that I work at Bill Crowe's, which was a place up in the hills at Oriental Bay. It had a kind of exclusive tag around it – the clients would talk it up and say they were clients of Bill Crowe's, and they'd say it with this appreciation for the finer things.

So I was interviewed and met Bill, and I began working there. It was a very social and interesting place to work, and you certainly had a room with a view. You could look out at the night sky, or you could just swan around in the lounge in a long velvet frock, thinking life doesn't get much better. It was a very old house – it had kind of a formal elegance and a run-down feel to it. It took on a lovely ambience at night.

Bill wasn't bossy, and I liked that. It truly was a working environment where you felt you could govern yourself. He was a character. Quietly alert, not opinionated, not forceful, but certainly a presence. He could be very amusing, and a little bit cutting. I think he appreciated being the ears for the town, and hearing all that was going on. I wasn't particularly aware of people, so it didn't matter to me who they were. That was the interesting thing, because Bill would always formally introduce you, and you'd hear their whole name. It wouldn't be, John wants to see you, it would be John So-and-so, and it would be the whole name. Most of us were unaware, really, of who they were. We had our own busy lives. Probably a lot of those people's anonymity was well protected because we really didn't have an appreciation of who they were. I do remember some job descriptions that were fairly strong.

There was a very strong safe-sex culture. The clients wouldn't offer more money for sex without a condom, they'd just want sex without a condom. 'Do we have to use this?' It would be a kind of plaintive statement. And the safe-sex culture is constantly battered by those sorts of comments. Not quite that the client is stupid, not quite that the client is disrespectful – he's just probably thinking more that this is a love affair in the moment, or whatever. So all of those sorts of nuances, and stupidly saying, 'Let's do it without a condom', like he would to his partner or girlfriend.

I wasn't there in that sexual way. I was there as a person talking, thinking, aware of them. I was functioning, making sure they were having sex with me. It didn't matter which shape or form they came in, outstanding, articulate, intelligent people, it didn't matter. I still had the same template, and I'd apply it to them. They would have sex, I'd allow them to have sex with me.

There were certainly attractive people, and you had good sex with them.

But it just was an honourable thing not to go over into real sex – and sometimes you were tired, you were below par. You knew you had to perform, do things, be present, you couldn't float right off and be distant. You could work the formula, but you had to have an authentic kind of role as much as possible, without getting caught out.

I think the clients were looking for the feeling I have when I sit down in a hairdresser's chair and someone just pays attention to my head and gives me a nice massage on top. I think, oh, I'm in a cocoon here, a wee bubble in time. There were those who were definitely not having sex with anyone else, so that intimacy and contact was important, and we became the sexual fixture, the person who would hug and have sex. But also people who weren't looking to bring you into their life. People who may forget you completely, not looking for anything to stick or stay on, just an encounter to lie down, collapse, have a spa, shower, massage, sex, and leave without a backward thought.

I think there were people who were thrown by the intimacy of the contact, who didn't expect that there would be a real human being on the end of the sex provider. And for me occasionally too there would be people who leapt out and would impact on me as a person. That was something I was susceptible to in the first year or two.

Shortly after I started working as a receptionist I remember these guys coming in and asking to meet the manager. I later found out that they were the vice, and they would come round to do regular but semi-friendly check-ups. They'd sit in the lounge and chat and guffaw, sort of 'Ho ho, how are you, girls?' It didn't feel ominous, but it felt a bit odd.

And I remember coming to work one night, and a woman had been arrested, and the girls were doing a collection for her. So the story was whispered and told – she'd massaged someone, then done the usual kind of 'Is there anything else you'd like?', and the police had come back and arrested her for soliciting. That was very scary. And so everyone was on high alert. That was my first experience. And of course I ran into it myself head-on, four years later in 91.

I remember very strident people saying things like 'We need rights!' I'd come from a teaching background, and I thought, where's our NZEI [New Zealand Educational Institute]? I was very conscious that sex work was work, and I felt very strong and empowered and happy and stimulated and all those things that you associate with a good job. It felt great, and why isn't there an organisation?

In terms of setting up the [New Zealand Prostitutes'] Collective, the fact that sex work was a crime was a big motivating factor, and the idea that people didn't accept sex workers. That sex work felt like work, was work, and needed to be recognised as work. That was all mixed in with the times, of course. We had HIV coming, and it was a scary, threatening thing for being a sex worker. So, lots of overlapping themes. Also, you would hear people say, we don't get any sick pay, and we don't get any holiday pay and so on. So there was that kind of discussion as well, about management practices.

Labour, management, stigma, recognising sex work as work, equal rights, equal protections, public health, HIV and Aids were the major themes – and of course the fact that sex workers were criminalised, and there would be these police raids where they'd come in undercover and entrap sex workers for soliciting. Then there would be this reality of going to court and being prosecuted, and that was pretty horrific.

In the early stages we met in our flats – my flat, usually. I think it was October 87. And I had a contact in the Department of Health. She was working in the AIDS Taskforce, setting up contacts for government to engage with at-risk communities. The AIDS Foundation was up and running. The needle exchange was just getting going. So this woman from the Department of Health invited me to a meeting they were having. I went, and I talked quite frankly about sex work. They said, there may be some money available and you could run a programme.

Then they wrote to us and said, 'We've got $35,000, think about how you could use it.' So we thought, do we want formalisation? Do we want to be in a contract with the government? I was really enjoying this kind of work where you could just come and go – there weren't any kinds of strings attached, it was a fabulous feeling. But I also had a lot of curiosity and a lot of disquiet – in the first year I'd added up a few things and thought, there's a cause here, there's something that's not right.

Also, we felt that if we let government off the hook, we may not get another chance to hold them into a relationship with us and talk about the things that bothered us. We didn't have any formal relationship with government on matters that affected sex workers, apart from that which we were reluctantly rolled into, which was the relationship with the police.

We had the idea of a little community base in Wellington and Auckland, that we put together a magazine, that we could give out condoms. We typed up our points on an A4 and sent this back to the Department of Health. We asked for $50,000, and they gave us $50,000. We received that money in October 1988, so it took some time.

We were all equals together in the collective, and we didn't have any titles, we didn't have anything like that. But when it came to the media, we needed someone to speak. We thought about how to play it – not to speak about our personal lives, to speak about the issues, keep media focused on the issues. We are the New Zealand Prostitutes' Collective, don't ask me if we're sex workers or prostitutes, I'm here to speak about the issues.

We went to look for premises, but we had to pretend we were nurses. And we got the police to organise a meeting, because we didn't feel that we would have the pull to get every massage-parlour owner to come. They all came to the space that we'd found, 282 Cuba Street, and sat around, and the police were there too. I led the meeting, which was daunting. People from the AIDS Foundation spoke about the importance of Aids. It was one of the few meetings we ever had with the police and the massage-parlour owners and sex workers.

So we kicked off. We had the little community base – it was a sweet little place. It had little pink cushions, a little mezzanine floor. It was set up quite beautifully. It was fairly run down, and we had a guy who came in and planted the garden for us out the back. He later became a male sex worker and a very strong sex-worker activist in Sydney.

We had gone round the country knocking on parlour doors, trying to get into places to say we're doing this, come and join us. Also I went out to the street and approached the transgendered people. I said, 'Hi, my name's Catherine Healy and I'm from the New Zealand Prostitutes' Collective. We're setting up an organisation and I'd like you to join us and come and be part of it. We're going to try and stop Aids, and it's really important' – you know, that kind of thing. They said, 'Oh yeah, OK, that could be interesting.'

I remember them looking at me. I really felt comfortable in Māori circles, but I thought, gosh, I haven't met anyone who's transsexual. They had very little to say to me as I tried to talk with them on the streets, and I thought, they're really wasted, and this is going to be really hard. But when I came to know them they weren't wasted at all.

They arrived and they kept arriving – I just loved it. These transgender Māori – the whole place just started to come alive with them. The very early founding members put their hands up and packed it in. People that weren't able to cope with transgender street-based sex workers and had this vision of the Prostitutes' Collective being a nice white middle-class scene didn't stay around.

I went around Auckland to meet people, to tell them about the collective. I remember being quite shocked. I had been doing a lot of travelling in Thailand and had been into the red light area in Patpong. I saw things in Auckland where I thought – gosh, bare floorboards, this is really rough. And I was affected as well. I remember sitting there with the Māori owner, and he was rubbing one of the girls' backs, he said, 'Are you sore?' And it was such a human scene. It always stuck in my head, sitting in this shabby, rough parlour on Fort Street. I was looking through middle-class eyes at a really impoverished part of the sex industry, and seeing that as quite sentimental and gentle. I remember standing on K Road in a strip club. It was a little place, and the woman just standing there with nothing on, talking to me about the collective. She was just right there with nothing on.

We had an argument about the magazine's name, which started out as *Fallen Angel*. Somebody had written to say they hated the name *Fallen Angel*, and why did we choose such a disempowering name. It was meant to be ironic. So halfway through the production of that issue, which was done on the photocopier with collage, cutting out, pasting, we had a debate about the name. That would have been 89. And we came up with the name *Siren*. Sex Industry Rights and Education Network.

We went to Australia in October 88, had a look at their group, the Prostitutes' Collective of Victoria. I remember saying, 'We need legalisation', and them saying, 'No you don't, love, you need decriminalisation.' My understanding of what it was came into being, really. Melbourne had just legalised, and that was a very restrictive model. Brothels were allowed, and it favoured the state to have undue control over sex workers, where most would be locked out from that system. The sex workers even to this day must have mandatory checks on a three-monthly basis.

There was a conference in New Zealand, our first national conference on Aids, in 1989. I remember getting nine transgendered street-based sex workers to that conference. It was great. By then the collective was swinging – the original members were scarcely active, so it really was almost just me and the street-based trans workers.

And we made our first submission. They were trying to criminalise escorting. The police wanted to contain and control the sex industry into the massage parlours, but inherent in that was the contradiction that if you were caught for soliciting you were kicked out. So escort agencies had emerged in response to that difficulty of having nowhere to work from. And they would have a telephone operator and a driver, so people would be taken out to see clients.

Anyway we did this submission to a parliamentary select committee. The submission still today is a very strong piece. It was a very grand room – they sat up, looked at us. There were three of us there, and they were really interested. [Labour MP] Trevor de Cleene was on the committee and he started to shake his stick. I'd described the collective and said, we're volunteers but we have one who's waged. And he wanted to know who the waged one was, because in his mind I guess it meant that person wasn't a real ho. We were very dressed up, too.

The Department of Health didn't tell the police that they were going to contract with us, so it was up to us to bring it to their attention. I did that on a day when they visited, as per usual, visiting the massage parlours. I remember saying, 'Look, this is what we're thinking of doing, and here's the letter from the Department of Health.' The reaction was spontaneously positive – it was, 'Great! Good on you, girls, I've always wondered when you were going to do this.'

The role of the vice squad was to keep the names of the sex workers on file, so they would go out there and approve whether people could work in the massage parlours. There was this contradiction – everyone knew massage parlours were really about commercial sex, but that was against the law. So the squad would come round and meet people. And sometimes they'd go out to your home and check that you really lived there. If people had convictions for drugs and things like that, they would be made to leave the parlour. And the police would approve receptionists and massage-parlour owners and their licences.

I worked with a woman who was arrested and charged with having a roach of marijuana. The parlour came together, and everyone said, 'What can we do? She can't possibly leave.' The sex work was her work, we couldn't see her surviving in any other place. Her name was Katie. So people said, 'I'll call myself Katie.' We had three Katies, and we hid her. We told the police that she'd left, and when they'd ring up to see who was on, we had three Katies.

The police announced that they were going to go round and check that people were who they said they were. I was living with my mother, and I hadn't told her at that point that I was a sex worker. So I told her that they would be coming out to visit, and it was all to do with this nightclub I worked in. And the thought of them driving into our lovely little neighbourhood and parking their police car in our leafy suburb, and coming up to knock on the door to check that I was there – quite intrusive, isn't it? It was appalling.

Then the vice went in undercover, and someone at the Lily was charged with soliciting. She was a bank officer five days a week, and she worked a Friday night there. By the time her case got to court, we'd built this relationship with the police officer, and he had seen the error of his ways, and had said, 'Look, I'm really sorry.' I think he'd seen us as people and realised the impact on people's lives of a conviction. I remember him saying when we went into court with our friend, that he wished us luck. It got biffed out on some kind of technicality. But it was horrific, horrible.

I felt really sure of my ground around the law – actually I was deluded, I have to say, but at the time I thought I was well within my rights. The client would come in, and you had to wait for them to be proactive and request sex, and then you could accept it. The offence was to offer yourself, offer sex for money. And the client could certainly offer money for sex and not break any law. So I would say what the law was as a kind of strategy for circumventing soliciting. I'd say, 'The law in New Zealand is, you can offer me money for sex and I can't offer you sex for money. Don't you think that's unfair?'

But being involved in cases after the fact, and realising just how vulnerable we all were, it wouldn't have mattered what we'd said, actually. I think we were all sitting ducks. Generally the massages were nude, so just describing that, saying, 'I'm in a darkened room, and she had no clothes on, and she was obviously offering herself to me for the purposes of prostitution,' even though she didn't say anything. That would have been enough. The police officer stands up and reads out the charge sheet and the summary of facts, and the picture's painted. This woman's faceless, almost, and voiceless – but she's nude.

Typically people would plead guilty. You would get diversion if you pleaded guilty, then you'd be let off with a warning and get a diversion. Which in fact wasn't a warning, it was something that sat on your record, and if it happened again you got convicted.

They came in on a Friday night, at the Lily of the Valley. It was seven o'clock, and these two fresh-faced cops popped up. They were well-dressed as clients – we didn't know they were undercover cops. They were saying, 'Oh, we've never been here before.' And nobody liked to do newbies, for the reason that they didn't usually have money. They were booking a half-hour massage, which was a good sign that they probably didn't have any money.

So, a week later, I was at home, and I was rung up by my boss at the massage parlour, who told me that the police had come in and all the girls had been arrested for soliciting from three different parlours, the Lily, CJ's and the Pink Palace. They had come back to get me. They'd arrested nine women in total across Wellington. I was really scared. I thought, oh god, they're going to send me to prison.

May Day I was acquitted; the case took five hours. The police gave evidence, and I spoke for myself. The effect of the charges were ongoing, and I worried all the time that it would happen again. It attacked my integrity – I felt vulnerable.

It sharpened me up emotionally. To know the arguments in your head intellectually was one thing – to know it deep inside, to feel it through emotionally was another. It really steeled my determination. I was really determined on the law and sex-worker rights and so on, but it gave me another tier. It was quite tough. It was interesting to think it through, and think, I'm 30-something, I'm not 18. Poor kids who were 18, how would it be, those kids that get convicted?

The police held a meeting afterwards, and I had to go along as the collective's spokesperson and sit there and watch these wretched massage-parlour owners put their heads down while these two guys who had come in undercover introduced themselves, and said, 'We're the new vice.' They just lectured these people, who were twice their age at least. It was so rude. I said a few things.

I was public and I was speaking out. The industry was used to living in a grey space, very cowardly in some ways but very courageous in others. It was everyone's inclination to shut up, put up. So this was very new and different, to be consistently speaking out. It did make people vulnerable. I was very involved with NZPC and it was becoming more and more complex and more and more time-consuming. So I was really torn. I realised I could be very effective if I was outside the industry, and didn't have the anxiety of worrying about being caught out. I also had a very serious relationship. I had a partner chipping away, who was very uncomfortable with my being a sex worker. So there were those different factors lining up, and I stopped work.

But I missed it. I certainly missed it. I still to this day reflect on the merriment, the naturalness – just lots of things, like standing there at the kitchen sink, making a cup of coffee, and the chats. Stretching out on the couch, waving at the clients. Just being comfortable in a place where I enjoyed for the most part working. The friendships have continued, but the physicality of that place – it was very warm and closed in. It didn't have a lot of personality, but it had a lot of elements that I liked. The floods – we'd turn the spas on, and we'd forget, because we'd be smoking, lying back on the couches fagging away, one more fag. And we inevitably had put a client in the room and had forgotten about him, because the interesting things happened amongst ourselves, talking. We'd go down and there'd be a foot-high flood. So we'd have to kick our shoes off and get the orange towels and soak up all this mess.

I remember feeling relaxed and comfortable with my body. I was thinner. Turning the shower on. Having yaks with the clients. I mean, the clients used to fade into the background, but sometimes you'd see them in sharper relief, and there'd be quite cool talks and discussions. I think sometimes I liked driving home at three in the morning. It was very still, and the world was asleep, and I was awake. I liked those sorts of contrasts. Being self-employed, too, was interesting. That gives you a sense you are freer, provided the money's there. But in my latter years I was on a bit of a treadmill, because I had a lot of financial commitments.

In late 1991 there was a concentrated operation and the police went round many massage parlours in a sustained way for two weeks. I was on the phone to the Ministry of Health, and said, 'We've got massage-parlour proprietors ringing us, they're really up in arms.' We even had one saying that our outreach workers were not to come into their parlour, because it was putting them at risk. I said, 'That's it. We are seriously considering giving our funding back. We will go back underground, unless you look at this law and the impediment it's providing to us being effective in this HIV prevention work.' I'd discussed it with people in the organisation, and we were deadly serious, there was no question. We were going to give our money back and go back underground. I had to ask the waged workers how they felt about that, because they would lose their jobs.

People were really on board. They felt it was an intense time and we had to call it, and that's what we did. The Ministry of Health was funding us to distribute condoms to the sex industry, which we were doing, and we were cutting some of the enormous anxiety massage-parlour owners had about holding condoms on the premises. That was a huge breakthrough. Everyone was getting behind this whole safe-sex culture, people were recognising their responsibilities. But the police were taking these condoms, they were using our condoms as evidence.

And Maurice Williamson, associate minister of health in 1991, 92, had been commenting very forcefully about how crazy it was to have this conflict of trying to run an HIV prevention programme with the law the way it was. He was the first political advocate for a change in the law from the National side. There had been comments from Trevor de Cleene, who was with Labour, prior to that. But Maurice was from the Nats and consistently spoke out.

There wasn't actually a campaign for decriminalisation – there was just a series of rolling events. We met with politicians – critically, we met with Maurice Williamson and Katherine O'Regan. I was on the National Council on AIDS.

For me it was a thing of always trying to think about who would be important to support decriminalising sex work, and trying to hook in to different kinds of things. There was also a forum where a number of different national women's organisations met and discussed issues in common. It was a very important forum, and I was invited.

And I spoke at Rotary clubs. I did a lot of those, right throughout the greater Wellington area, and sometimes even clubs in Auckland and so on. We had kind of an approach to always say yes – we felt it was important to go and speak and build that public idea.

There wasn't a strategy. There wasn't an idea of writing down a plan to see it all unfold. And after it happened I remember people saying, well, can you share your ideas on your strategy? And that wasn't what happened at all. It was just a constant chip, chip, chip, chip, you know, almost obsessive. And using every situation that presented an opportunity to nudge it forward.

Then Labour MP Tim Barnett agreed to sponsor the bill. We started to have regular meetings, and we formed a committee to go and meet with Tim on a regular basis to get the legislation down. So we had to argue over every kind of word. Then it had to go off to the parliamentary legal drafters.

The bill was a private member's bill, and it had to be drawn, out of a biscuit tin, actually. It came straight up, so that meant it got read by the whole of the parliament. Then it had to be voted on. Should it be sent to a select committee, or should it be ditched? I think about 100 voted for it to go to the select committee, which was a good indication of huge support there at that time, but later it was whittled down.

The arguments against were scarcely developed at that point. I'd try and engage, because you've got to listen to what people are afraid of, and when people bring up arguments, you've got to try and listen to the elements. You have to think, OK, what will it really mean for young people growing up in New Zealand, knowing that sex work is there and you can become a sex worker? And I thought, it's a bit ridiculous, because right through literature and in movies, we've had that visibility. Society has all sorts of issues that are captured in film and coming into lounges every night. So the idea that sex work would be something new to contemplate for a young person, the idea that the law would make it more of a risk for a young person, was ridiculous.

The big supporters were the women's organisations, and all of the public health groups. Sexual health, the doctors, the venereologists – great supporters.

Youth groups – once again, connecting in through the public health vein. We had a group of Catholic nuns who were really in favour of it, and their social justice network. And individuals as well.

The act – it was an evening, it was winter, June the 25th. 2003. We had people from the collective who'd come from around the country, and supporters as well, and we went into parliament. It was absolutely jam-packed. We'd been involved in media throughout the day, and had been stopped on the steps of parliament and so on, going up. So it had that momentum, that wonderful sort of build-up. I was terrified, of course. A lot depended on it. I had my partner come as well – it was a momentous night. He came with my step-grandson, and he wasn't allowed to sit with me because he didn't have a tie on – I didn't realise that was the rule.

All these impassioned debates went down, and different politicians spoke from the heart. Georgina Beyer spoke very strongly about having been a sex worker and how when she was raped, she had to sort it out herself although she wanted to go to the police, and that there should have been no barriers to her being able to do that. So that was a very powerful speech. Winnie Laban spoke about her constituents being religious. She had changed her point of view, because she recognised different things that sex workers needed – human rights and so on.[1]

So, yeah, it was really electric. And then they had this cry, you know, 'Unlock the doors, unlock the doors!' The politicians had to file out, whichever way they were voting. It was really funny looking down and thinking, god, which way, which door are they going to go through, is it the ayes or the noes? And some played around and joked and talked and laughed. We were sitting there thinking, hurry up, decide.

The moment when it was called, we just leapt up and cheered, and it was fantastic. It was just fantastic, it was a fantastic rush. It was so close. One abstention. Fifty-nine against, 60 for. Right down to the wire.

---

1. Georgina Beyer, a Labour MP from 1999 to 2007, was the world's first openly transgender MP. Luamanuvao Winnie Laban, a Labour MP from 1999 to 2010, was New Zealand's first Pacific Island woman MP. She was made a dame alongside Catherine Healy in the 2018 Queen's Birthday honours.

I had no preparation in my brain for a loss at all. It had to go through. I had not prepared myself for a loss at all. I just hadn't allowed that kind of thinking.

So we went off and the media was all lined up in this big room. It was pretty busy, and I couldn't have a celebratory drink either, I had to stay sober and drive home. Then I had to get up at six in the morning. They came out to my home and interviewed me. And of course the sex workers and everyone had a wonderful time, and I had to pull away from that because I knew I had this round of interviews and couldn't celebrate to the full. But we went over to Bar Bodega – very nice, very lovely. And you had that kind of nice feeling, horns were tooting, stuff like that. I mean, it was a momentous thing for us. Fantastic.

And the next day I did that interview, and came in to work at our community base, and people poured through, just kept coming through, and flowers and balloons and sex workers. The woman on our 1989 poster came in, I hadn't seen her for ages, with a helium balloon. So it was just so lovely, and a reporter was sitting there from the *Dom* [*Dominion*] *Post*. People were buzzing.

It was weird, too, because after that we had to change our language. You know, the whole complaint tone. It was a weird vacuum. I was very curious for the sex workers working through that change. They really couldn't believe that they could relax and say anything they liked. There was a brothel – and even just being able to say you're a brothel was different – on Victoria Street, CJ's. They rang, and they just couldn't comprehend that they could talk freely, because they'd lived through police arrests and so on.

We had a sex worker who was up on a soliciting charge and had to go back to court. So here she was on one side of that law with a soliciting charge, and had to go back to court after the law was repealed and have it acknowledged by the judge that there was now no longer any case. So that was thrown out.

The minute the law changed, then other changes happened too. I'd imagined there would be a settling-in period, and things would relax. That didn't happen at all. We had to continue to defend the law, to talk about its attributes, to explain errors. We went into a very intense time with city councils. The lobbying groups moved their attention away from the MPs and started to lobby the city councils and say, now you're charged with the zoning of brothels. What are you going to do? And so city councils started to draft bylaws, and we had to lobby again, on a different kind of level, with councils. Some councils came through with terrible bylaws that really recriminalised everyone again, effectively.

When we began, we looked outwards internationally, but we were restricted by technology and distance. We had no idea that further along, we would be recognised internationally, in terms of decriminalisation in particular.

After the law change, gradually the invitations started to come in, the curiosity about what had happened and the realisation that New Zealand had done something really big – the first country to decriminalise sex work. People started to arrive from overseas – we've had researchers from countries like Japan, we're written up in a Japanese book. Namibia, another book, it's written up as a model. Europe, Canada, the UK, film crews arrived, like the CBC – the Canadians. International media ring a lot, the Irish. In 1995 I did a short-term consultancy for the World Health Organization, working with the Ministry of Health in Vietnam to develop a program for sex workers based on our community peer model. Of course we have our own researchers here, Gillian Abel, Mike Roguski, Calum Bennachie, cutting-edge stuff.

Vietnam has sent high-ranking officials to look closely at what we're doing here with decriminalisation, and they had a conference in Hanoi to discuss our model. There was also a formal discussion in Beijing. It was really gratifying to speak to these audiences. So it's gratifying to know that the law change and the work that we do is recognised in other parts of the world. It's referred to as the New Zealand Model.

I spoke at the international Aids conference in Toronto in 2006. There were 26,000 delegates, 4000 speakers. Bill Clinton was there, and we were on the same page in the programme, which was the size of a telephone book of old. The rooms we were speaking in were cavernous, and I was speaking in the room next to his, at the same time. Both rooms were packed. It does say something about the interest, internationally. But then again, I may have just got Bill Clinton's overflow, without the dry-cleaning bill.

Then the Oxford Union debate came along. In 2009, December, I opened an email and screamed – it was, 'Dear Ms Healy, I would be very honoured if you would come and speak to the Oxford Union debate.' It was about, we've had President So-and-so here, we've had famous movie stars, and I thought it was a joke. I wrote back and said, 'I've received this email and I just want to clarify if it's for real or not.' They replied, and laboured on their credibility, as if they needed to convince me that the Oxford Union was an OK thing to deal with. So that was February 2010, and they asked if I would like to be a speaker or if I would like to have a debate. So I said I'd like to have a debate, and then thought, shit, what do I do?

I took my step-grandson, Kyle. My sister Patricia and my niece Jessie came – they live in Europe. We arrived in Oxford. It was winter, and it was just rich with all that you would have imagined. The students were youthful and beautiful and gleaming, and wearing morning suits – it was very formal. The audience was there, and the ancient old hall and so on. I said the world thinks we're all at it down under with Viagra on our breath. That sailed over the heads of most of the audience, although one woman came up after the debate and said she'd heard David Lange 25 years before when he'd made his uranium quip.[2] And the vote – yes, it was a bit over the top. It was fun. And we won.

And of course, Baroness [Vivien] Stern is a great champion. She hosted a big meeting in the House of Lords, in conjunction with Niki Adams and the English Collective of Prostitutes, who are relentless in pushing for rights. I spoke at that meeting as well.

Sex-worker movements around the world look for good, positive examples. I think we're recognised as a good sort of example in that narrow niche of law reform. And sex-worker movements want a lot more than repealing little bits of law – there's a whole other thing that goes deeper, like anti-discrimination and the end of stigma. The recognition of rights right across the spectrum. I know we are identified as the best practice at the moment in terms of law related to sex-work law and decriminalisation. We have an integrative approach to sex workers and sex work. And we are the organisation with the longest-standing contract with government.

---

2   Labour Prime Minister David Lange famously quipped that he could smell uranium on the breath of an opponent when he debated the moral defensibility of nuclear weapons at the Oxford Union in 1985.

The stigma hasn't gone away. You still have that little thing in the law that says that government doesn't morally endorse prostitution, and that means that if a sex worker wanted to become a police officer, organisations like that can say, well, morally we don't think you're up for the job. And the same for teaching, too. Governing bodies related to these occupations have said it's inappropriate to be a sex worker as well as a nurse or teacher. So that tells me there's still a long way to go.

One thing I'd still like to see is the recognition of sex workers as ordinary, sometimes rather extraordinary, people. So people aren't fearful of saying that you're a sex worker, have been a sex worker. What we need is people coming out, the diversity of people coming out – which puts it on the sex workers, which is quite hard.

Hate crimes are another issue. I think sex workers are victims of hate crimes, and it's important that people see that. Sometimes I think it's difficult for people to see just how hostile some cartoons can be against groups of people, how some people might laugh when they see a cartoon depicting a sex worker in a negative way. If you changed certain elements and tried to do that to another group of people, people would say, oh no, that's really terrible, that's racist, you can't do that. But sex workers seem to be still fair game.

I've been the national coordinator of NZPC for years now. I found it very difficult after the law changed. I had imagined that I would leave some time after the law had changed, because that was always the pinnacle to get to. Then I thought, well, I can get on and have a life. But of course it didn't work that way at all, it became very intense, lots of bylaw stuff. The law changed but even so, years on, we are still fighting to hold on to what we have.

I really feel very strongly about sex workers' rights – I don't feel like I'm coming to work, I feel like I'm coming to do something that's important for everyone. There are wonderful people I work with in the organisation, Annah Pickering, Ahi Wi-Hongi, Chanel Hati, Tracy McKenzie, Anna Reed, Ange, Karen, Pam, Dana, Renee … gorgeous people. Founding members like Sharon Harris, Sue Forbes, who are all long stayers. Many others as well. And some great allies. Our nurse, Joy Brown-Douglas, has been with us for almost the whole journey. Loyal and strong people.

At times it's been quite hard. I'm quite cocooned, though. It is easy to move with liberal friends and family, and not ever rub up against some of that hostility that's out there.

And I'm still in the bay. I live in the house, I sleep in the bedroom I was probably conceived in. My partner Darryl and I. My brother Peter and his family live next door. And I will always live there. I have other countries I love, but it's my little bay – that house, that particular place. Family, friends, and people I've grown up with as well, so it's kind of a nestling effect. It's nestled me through profound grief in recent years, after deaths in our immediate family. Nestled in. It just is, it's just there, and it's always been.

There are little pebbles on the beach. It's a little beach, little rocky beach, and when you go into the water, it's a little sandy bottom. You don't have to go out very far, you can just lie on your back and look. You can look at the bush, you can look at the sky, or you can look out to the island. Just lie there. I might be in Spain, I might be in India, and having a cruisy lovely time. I can be in lots of places, I love lots of places. But it's that little place – I don't think I could live without it for that long.

Catherine was interviewed at the New Zealand Prostitutes' Collective offices in Wellington between May 2011 and August 2012.

STEVIE

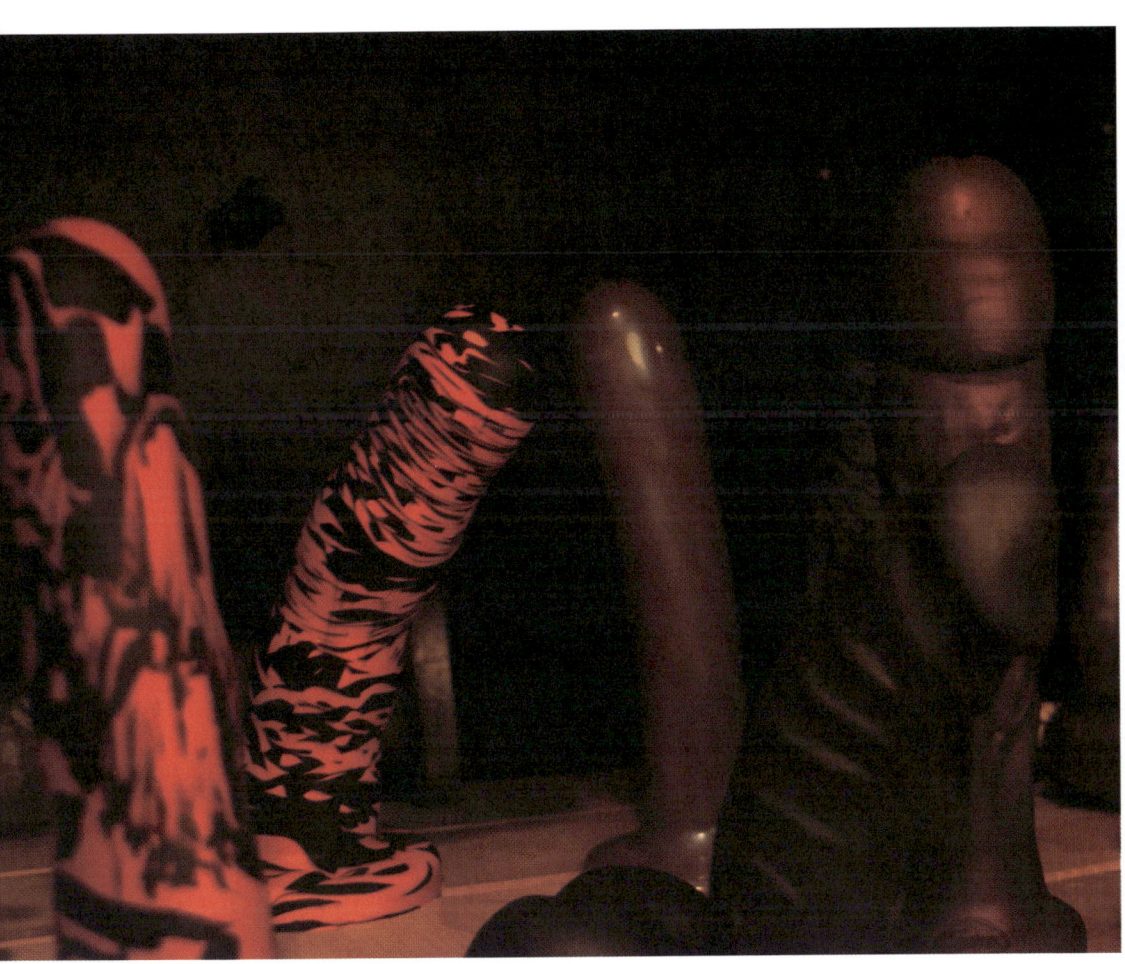

STEVIE

I WAS BORN in a housebus in the early 1980s. On Dad's side I'm Ngāpuhi, and on Mum's side Ngāti Maniapoto, in the King Country. We travelled around lots when I was little, and we moved from South Auckland to the West Coast of the South Island when I was about two or three, so I grew up there. Mostly we lived in the Southern Alps, with only a few neighbours.

My parents were both designers who made leather clothes and shoes to order, and sold them at the markets. But they didn't have any regular employment when I was little, so we were really poor. I've got four older sisters, two little sisters and a little brother. We didn't have much to do with any of our extended whānau – both of my parents had sort of cut ties with their families.

There was a lot of stress – I guess that's always the case when you're really poor and you don't have a lot of resources. Also, a really, really white area, and my parents had quite a separate social scene. They had friends from out of town who would come and visit sometimes, who were mostly from the Mongrel Mob in Auckland. They were really cool – I liked them. We had a housebus, and we used to go and stay at friends' places. We'd stay on the beach, and we'd light fires and get mussels off the rocks. They would drink crates of beer, we had lots of dogs – so it was quite fun, that aspect of it. Their community – people were so outrageous. They partied a lot. We did stuff that was really fun, like gathering food – there was a watercress patch.

I did correspondence school until I was 12. Then I went to school, and I was really far ahead in a lot of subjects, though I was really far behind in math. I was like, oh, I feel like we're not learning anything. It wasn't challenging at all. But it was nice to get to hang out with kids and do sports.

I went to high school briefly, and I was put in the A-stream class. And they rated our IQ, and I was like the second-highest IQ in our year. It was the same thing at that school – I was always like, 'This isn't challenging enough. And why can't we learn more useful things?' I was very staunch, and when other kids were getting bullied, I would be the one who's like, 'What's your problem?', and punches over the bully. And I had this relationship with the teachers where I would challenge them all the time. I saw most of what was taught in school as being a waste of time – like it didn't change anything, didn't fix any problems in the world, wasn't useful in my daily life.

I would often miss class for most of the week, and then come in on the last day and catch up. I'd still get the same marks as everyone else – so I was like, 'What's the point of coming to school, if I can just come to school a couple of days, and I could be getting stoned and hanging out at the beach with my friends?'

Plus, I was always out at school. I remember when I was about three, kissing the TV when pretty girls would come on. When I was about 13 I said to my friends, 'So, I think I'm fluid – like, bisexual.' But I never felt bad about not being heterosexual. My parents had quite a disregard for authority, and I think I just picked up that who I was was OK, and if other people had a problem with it, that was their problem.

I was out, but no one else was, and when I did hook up with girls it was really secret. A lot of the people who I crushed on or dated were feminine boys. Some were also into boys, and some liked to wear women's clothes in private. So I was always like, 'Oh yeah, sometimes I feel like I'm a boy.' They were like, 'That's cool, that makes sense.' I never thought, oh, I'm transgender. I don't think I knew that that was a thing that existed.

I've always known people who didn't fit into gender norms, but they just weren't talking about it as being trans. For example, my dad – he's a guy as far as I know, but he's always worn women's shirts and sometimes skirts as his ordinary clothes. I didn't realise a person could be recognised as a different gender to what they had been assigned as, but I knew you could wear what you wanted and be however you wanted to be.

I remember times when I was little when I'd say, 'I'm a boy,' and Mum would be like, 'You're not a boy.' It was less of an issue whether I was called a boy or a girl and more of an issue of how I experienced myself. I was always really high-fashion when I was little – I liked dressing up and having beautiful hair. I liked femininity, but I didn't feel like I was a girl. Everyone would be like 'You're a girl', and most of the time I was like, oh yeah, I guess. You can't change that. Everyone says you're a girl, so you just are one, even if you don't want to be one.

In fourth form I almost never went to school, and I left halfway through the year. One of my older sisters had moved to a nearby town, so she said that I could move in with her and her friend. So I moved in with them and I got a job in a factory. That was just after I turned 15.

Then I met a guy who was lots older than me, and I moved in with him. We got a housebus, and we lived in the forest for a while. Later we moved to Nelson. He was 28 and I was 15. We had no money. I remember once we stole a huge pumpkin, and lived on pumpkin soup for two weeks. I was used to stealing food, but this was a new town and I had no social support. It was really shit, it was really hard.

There was a house where some of his friends were squatting – an awful fucking dive. We lived there for a little while. I was trying to get on the independent youth benefit, and it was really, really difficult. I tried to get a food box from the food bank, and they were like, 'You need to have an address.' They wouldn't give me a food box, and WINZ wouldn't give me money for food because I had to be on a benefit to get money from them. It was really, really, really hard to survive. It was cold – all those things that are a problem when you're homeless. We didn't have a kitchen. We had to wash our dishes in the bathtub. There were none of the things that make it easy to make yourself presentable. I didn't have clothes, so I couldn't get work.

Sometimes I went to Christchurch to stay with one of my sisters. I was like, 'Oh, maybe I should go and get a job in a massage parlour.' I think I was 16, so this was before sex work was decriminalised. I went to Felicity's – they had an ad in the paper that was something like 'Massage, ladies wanted.' I thought, oh yeah, I could do that. I had walked past the neon lights on Lichfield Street, and I knew it wasn't just massage. I went in there, and I was like, wow, it's like another world in here. It's the middle of the day, and down these stairs there's a big dark room with a pool table. There were ladies dressed in red evening gowns. It was like a soap opera, like *Days of Our Lives* or something. I was scruffy, jeans falling off my hips and a beanie.

I sat down with the receptionist and she said, 'Cool. Do you know that you have to be 18 to work here?' I said, 'Yep.' She said, 'How old are you?' and I said, 'Eighteen.' But when I went to bars I would say that I was 23. When they asked if I had ID, I'd laugh, and I'd say, 'Honey, I'm 23.' Then they'd say, 'What's your date of birth?' and I'd give them the date of birth that meant I was 23.

She was like, 'Cool.' She gave me a piece of paper – I wasn't really planning on a piece of paper. I can't count. She said, 'Write down what size you are and your date of birth.' I didn't want to look like I was counting, so I wrote down what I thought would be right. She looked at it, and she was like, 'You're not 18, are you?' And I was like, 'No.' 'How old are you?' 'Sixteen.' 'You need to be 18 to work here, or you need to be able to lie about being 18.' So I didn't get that job.

Later, back in Nelson, I moved into a house with some friends. I was on the dole, and it was nice just to have a chilled-out life, have a bit of stability and live in a house with people who I liked. Not have a boyfriend and not have any drama – just have enough money to live in a place and eat. I was just hanging out – I got really into yoga and meditation. I was doing weaving – I was doing heaps of gardening. I got into organics. That was cool. Then I got pregnant, and started living in a housetruck.

When my baby was born, I had just turned 20, and most of my friends had moved to Wellington to go to university. My neighbours were cool, and they had children, but they were 15 or 20 years older than me, and married, and owned their houses. I got depressed a lot – I don't know how people who live away from their whānau can have babies and not get depressed, because it's so isolating.

I decided to move to Whanganui, because I wanted to live in a commune, and it was cheap to buy land. I found this cool property that was owned by some anarchists who had a little community. I didn't know what anarchism was – everyone I knew who was like 'Yeah, anarchy!' got drunk at 10 in the morning and had fights with the cops. At the time, I half believed what the media said about 'radicals'. These people were like, 'No! Well, yeah, maybe. But it's also about building communities, organising together to meet everyone's needs,' and all this cool radical nice stuff that people do for each other. And they were really cool. I loved how they did their social relationships – active listening and taking turns speaking, not making assumptions.

Later, when I had moved to Wellington, I read this book of feminist essays. The book was talking about patriarchy and oppressive systems, and I was like, 'Oh, right! It's not just in my social scene that the guys talk over the top of women, or it's not just coincidence that the boys are outside playing hacky sack while the women are cleaning up after dinner. Oh my gods, there are other people who think like me, and they're called feminists. I have to find feminists.' Then I was like, 'I'm done with guys.'

About a year later I joined an anarchist collective. I was also involved in Anarchist Black Cross, the prisoner support group. And I went to an anarcha-feminist conference, and met heaps of really cool women. I became heavily involved in radical left political activism, especially women's rights, queer rights and sexual-violence survivor support. The anarchist community had its problems, but for me it was revolutionary – I learned that organising collectively meant it was possible to change the unfair circumstances people were living in.

When my son started school I had to find work that I could do between 9am and 3pm, but there wasn't a lot out there, and all parents want those jobs, so that's how I started doing sex work. I thought, if it makes me feel bad, then I'll stop doing it and find another way. I looked on the internet for how much places were charging, and I thought I'd find the place that charges the most and go and work there. So I did that.

It's funny, because a lot of sex workers that I meet think the girls who work at those expensive places must be really beautiful, 'skinnier than me, prettier than me,' that kind of thing. But I didn't think that – I was just like, oh yeah, I could do that. I've got stretch marks, though. And I didn't want to shave my legs or my armpits.

I went in and met the manager, and she explained the on-call service – that I would tell them what days I'm available, and they would text me if there were any clients that want to make a booking. I wore something a little bit understated, and some mascara. She was like, 'What you're wearing is fine, and we have clothes and shoes that you can wear when you come in. So if you're around and get a text you can just pop in.' I said, 'I don't like shaving my legs, do I have to shave my legs?' And she was like, 'You probably do. You'll definitely need to shave your armpits.'

The first client I saw was terrible in that he was 'Oh, can you do it without a condom? You get really good tips.' And I was like, 'That might not be all that you're going to get.' 'Oh, I've had a test, blah blah blah.' Also, I hadn't had sex with a guy for two years, so I was like, fuck, I don't know if I remember – how does that go?

He kept asking personal questions – the sort of things people often ask each other in chit-chat. I was very out about everything in my little queer anarcha-feminist community, so I wasn't really used to people asking me questions that I didn't want to answer. I had to not answer him in a way that was cute and funny so he didn't get upset. He asked, 'What do you do for fun?' and I didn't want to say, 'Party with a bunch of dykes and plot the revolution.' I was like, 'Ummm …'

Now if they ask I say I like going to the beach. And it's true. Or I like camping. If they're like, 'What have you been doing?' I say, 'Oh, I ate a really good pizza the other day,' and I can tell a great story about this amazing pizza. You know, the point of talking with clients isn't exchanging information, it's just so they can feel comfortable or connected.

I didn't stay at that brothel for very long – it wasn't really me. I decided to try and work independently. I knew this trans girl who was working from an apartment, and she said, 'You can come and work at my place for a while.' I was like, 'Fuck men, I'm going to work as a lesbian escort! I'm going to get so much money because no one else is doing it.' And it turns out the reason no one else is doing it is because there's not much market. I got heaps of calls from guys, and I'm like, 'Why are you calling me? Are you a lesbian? No.' There's not a lot of female clients out there. I was like, oh, this sucks. I thought it would be fun – I'll have sex with girls, get paid.

Not so much.

So after that I went to work in a massage place. I decided I didn't feel like having sex with guys, so I thought I'd just do massage. I worked there for about a year, and I really liked it. The workers would go in and hang out on the days we were on call. It was just hot oil massage and hand jobs, technically.

Sometimes other things. I really liked working that way because the clients didn't expect anything else. So if they were trying to touch your bum, you could let them or you could be like, 'No touching.' For the most part they expected you to say 'No touching.' If they wanted you to be nude, you would charge extra. I really liked that – they had no expectation of more, so if you didn't feel like doing anything else you would still be able to do the work and get paid.

Plus there was a bit more art to selling it – you've done the sensual, exciting massage and you're doing the hand job. You could at a completely unfair moment be like, 'Oh, I know it's totally unfair to ask you this now, but if you want me to give you a blow job it's X amount extra,' and they're going to say yes because they're halfway to coming and you're really hot and they're really turned on. So, if you were good at selling extras you could make twice the money.

In other brothels, if they come in and they've paid top dollar to see you, then they really want to get as much as they can. So for some of them it means they want to have some kind of intellectual discussion on top of the sexy stuff. It's extra work. I'm not about extra work! The sex is all good, but I'm not here to educate men. I would charge a much higher fee for that.

When I worked at this other expensive place, this one annoying guy would try and talk politics with me, and I felt like, I will intellectually fucking smash you. Don't even start with me. He'd be like, 'Oh, the new National Budget's just come out, isn't it amazing?' And I know that the government has cut funding to education, health care, sexual-violence support services. It's hard to have sex with a National voter! Change the subject! So I'd say, 'Politics is so boring' in a cute voice, and bounce my boobs. Like I said, not here to educate men.

After the massage place, I had a break for a while, then I worked at another really expensive appointment-only place. I saw a couple of clients there who I had seen at the massage place – so they went from paying X amount to paying twice that at least. I'm the same person. I'm a few months older, the towels are newer, the bed is a bit bigger, twice the money please.

Some of those places only hire thin, white, cisgender women, mostly in their early twenties and inexperienced in the industry. Women who they think pass as middle class. They say it's not racist, or classist, or discriminatory, it's just business. They say that's who the client wants to see. But that's what systemic racism, classism and transphobia look like. I'm not saying 'Call it a duck', but it does look like a duck.

For me, putting across a middle-class image wasn't difficult, but saying 'we are high class' is a marketing strategy that relies on and reinforces a hierarchy. I don't dig that aspect.

I think there's two ways they promote women in the boutique, appointment-only places, and one is the sweet young flower who just wants to experience the world, and can you show her, can you make her a woman? They don't say she's a sex worker, they say she's a courtesan, or basically your girlfriend. They use the language like it's an exciting affair. Or sometimes they promote the sex workers as sharp, savvy, highly educated and travelled women of the world. They pretty much say, 'We are different to other places – all our girls are middle-class girls and none of them are doing it for the money.' In reality, no one does any kind of paid work just for fun – everyone's doing it for the money. Pretending it's not work is a distancing tool that reinforces stigma about having sex for money. And it's an insult to the clients' intelligence – these guys aren't stupid, they know they're paying to have sex. There's no shame in the game.

Lots of the appointment-only places will only take workers who haven't worked in brothels before. They say that if clients have seen you before and paid X amount, then they're not going to want to pay twice the price, which isn't really true. And they don't explicitly say it's about class, but they say they can't get bookings for former brothel girls because they're too loud, they're not well-mannered enough, they've learnt terrible habits.

So you might have a whole lot of women who are quite young and haven't worked before, and they've just got this one boss who tells them how it is. The boss can be telling all the sex workers that everyone does kissing, or that it's OK to let the client come on your face, or whatever. They might also tell new workers that women in other brothels have to sit around for 23-hour shifts and see 170 clients in a night, and theirs is the only ethical one that lets you choose. Because they care about you. The boss might position herself as your aunty, and the workers don't usually get space away from her to talk to each other. It's a bit suffocating, and it obscures the employer–worker relationship.

I had one of those madams try to stand over me when I stopped working at her place. She was pressuring me to work when I didn't want to, and saying I would owe her money if I turned down a client, so I quit. I told her to run her business within the law. Then she said I didn't make the grade, tried to keep my lingerie and toys, threatened to sue me for slander, called me a butch dyke, and said maybe I fancied her. I said she had excellent powers of observation, but I liked smart people. But, yeah, you have to remember that your boss is not your mum and you don't need to share your personal life with her.

When you work in a walk-in brothel, it has its own problems – it's loud and there are often annoying drunk people, clients come in and hang out with no intention to pay, if you put your bag down stuff will go missing, and like any job the boss is still out to make money from your labour. But at least you can complain about it with the other workers and share stories about the clients and tips on how you handle them. And you know that none of your colleagues will run and tell tales to the boss.

Realistically, different brothels work for different people, and all types of workplaces have their good and bad points.

After that last place, I went and worked in an expensive fantasy salon. It was a dungeon, and they had BDSM bookings, dominatrixy bookings or fetish bookings. I do lots of fetish stuff in my personal life, so I was like, yeah, I could do that, seems like I could get paid more for doing that, and you don't have to actually have sex with clients.

I thought that clients would come in asking for all sorts of weird stuff – but then what people asked for was mostly really boring. I was like, oh, right, my personal life is way more interesting. A lot of them just wanted you to look scary – just wear PVC and do what you always do in a bedroom. They wanted you to be a bit sassy and give them orgasms.

I remember one guy who was kind of cool. He was in his eighties, and when he showed up, first he said, 'Now I must ask you something. Am I too old for you?' It was really sweet, and I was like, 'Oh, no, I like mature gentlemen.' Then he said, 'Do you like kiwifruit?' 'Yeah, I do.' He had an orchard, and he went to the car and brought me back a box of kiwifruit. And he brought me a present – some jewellery that I would never wear, but I was like, 'Oh, that's really cute.' He said he would have ideally liked to take me out for lunch before having a booking, because that's the proper way to treat a 'lady'. Before that booking my boss warned me I'd have to bite my tongue about gender roles, and she was right, he had some pretty old-fashioned ideas. Sweet though.

Anyway I had this girlfriend, and she took me to this movie, *Boy I Am*. It's about trans guys, and she was like, 'You have to come to this movie with me.' We watched it and I was like, 'Oh, right, I didn't know that existed.' She was like, 'Huh? Huh?' I was like, 'Interesting.' I wasn't like, 'Oh, that's me!' Yeah, I get it, I feel kind of like that. Cool. But there was no big moment.

And then one day I was at work, and the client went and got in the shower, and I was sitting on this big wooden bed in front of this big gilded mirror, on the white sheets. I was wearing really high heels and stockings and lacy lingerie, and hair extensions and makeup. I looked at myself in the mirror, and I was just like, oh my god, that is not me. I had this moment – whoa, that's how the world sees me, and that's not who I am, and I'm not all right with that. That was my moment of, I think I'm done with trying to be a girl.

I had a few months of intensively thinking about that stuff and having talks with people before I decided to transition. I was lucky because I already knew lots of trans people, mostly trans women. I had one really good friend who was a trans guy, and we'd talked quite a bit. I understood the basics. I also understood that a lot of trans guys wanted to be really masculine. People I knew were like, 'Yes! I'm getting hairy! Yay, I look like a guy.' I was like, 'That's great for them, but it's not where I'm at. I like being feminine, I just feel like I'm a feminine boy.' I didn't want to get hairy, I didn't want to get masculine, I just wanted to have a dick.

When I started to physically transition, I was fairly involved in trans communities and I had stopped dating cisgender people. I sort of didn't want to take hormones, but to be allowed to get surgery I had to take hormones. I talked to surgeons overseas and they said, you can't get a penis unless you have hormones and top surgery first. But I don't want to be a masculine man, I'm not a man or a woman. Western frameworks for gender are so far behind they think they're first. I'm a non-binary takatāpui transsexual, and I like being feminine, and I want a dick, and I don't see why I shouldn't.

You don't have to be a guy to have a dick – half of my closest friends and lovers are women who have a dick, and some of my friends are guys who don't. There needs to be a shift in the way we categorise people and their body parts as gendered. Unfortunately at the moment, though, our health-care system is a mess in terms of trans health-care, and if a trans person says something that providers don't understand, then it's very hard to get the medical care they need.

When I went to the endocrinologist, I guess you know what gives you your A-plus for getting hormones. So I shaved off all my pink hair, and I wore a rugby jersey and a binder. And I'd heard that a lot of trans guys had gone in there and that particular endo had said, 'No, you're such a pretty girl, why would you want to become a boy? You'll get hairy and bald, and end up being an ugly old man.' He would try and discourage them, then put them on pills that don't do very much. So I butched up and went in there, and said the A-plus answers. I said [deep voice], 'Yep, I always felt like a boy. I always liked girls. I always knew I should be a boy, I just want my body to reflect how I feel on the inside.' So I ticked all the boxes. It was really easy – I didn't get any of the 'you're a pretty girl' business.

I was really lucky, I got onto a pretty decent dose of T – testosterone – pretty quickly. So my body started changing really quickly, especially my smell. I kept thinking there were boys in my room. Oh, it's me. OK. I didn't really like smelling like a boy, and I didn't like getting hairy. And I've always been able to deal with heaps of people's emotional stuff, but when I was on a lot of T I couldn't deal with as much. I couldn't just read people any more. It was really, really hard. That was the thing that I wasn't expecting. But I did get new junk! Hormones often make dicks more like clits over time, and clits more like dicks. It's all the same thing really.

I hadn't realised how much hormones affect you. Like getting turned on at the drop of a hat. I had just thought this was socialisation, that men are taught that you can look at a body part of any woman, it doesn't matter who she is, whether you're attracted to her, you can see a random sexualised body part and get an erection. But that's actually hormones. A lot of things that I thought of as being just about socialisation – it's not just about socialisation. I mean, how you choose to respond to that is a whole different question, but yeah, hormones. Wild times.

So I started working as a trans boy. It was interesting, because my clients didn't know what to expect. Most of them hadn't ever been with someone who was transmasculine before. Some of them had been with trans girls, some hadn't been with anyone who was trans. I started advertising in the paper and online, and clients would come see me, and they wouldn't really know what to expect. Sometimes they'd be like, 'Oh, awesome, you're quite boyish,' or sometimes,

'Awesome, quite girly.' There was one guy I'd talked to on the phone, and when he came round, he was like, 'Oh, I really liked your boy voice better.' And I was like [deep voice], 'Ah, right,' because my voice changes a lot.

Some of them usually saw trans women and were like, 'You're like a trans woman, and that's what I'm into, but also you've got a vagina, so that's different.' And others were like, 'I usually see boys, and you're kind of like a boy, but you've got a vagina, so that's different.' Others were like, 'I usually see girls, but I've always been a bit curious about seeing a guy. But I'm not gay!' I was like, 'Mmm hmm, that's cool, you be whatever you want.'

I also started doing lots of doubles with trans girls. From a sex-worker perspective, whatever your niche is, you want to upsell. And also, my friends are all broke – everyone's in a similar basket. So I'm like, 'Do you know what would be really hot? Have you ever had sex with a trans woman? You should book me for a double with my friend.'

Out in the world, many people are too chicken-shit to admit they're attracted to trans women, but in the world of sex work it's a lot more OK to just say what you want. The sex industry is beautifully sex-positive and practical in ways that very few other spaces are.

So I started doing lots of doubles, and that worked really well for me. Probably half the work I do now is doubles with trans girls. It's nice being able to get other people work, and it's also a drawcard in that not many people do that. It's fun working with friends too – you get to have a giggle about the booking afterwards, and it's not boring, sitting around waiting for the phone to ring.

When I worked before as a girl, lots of the clients were just coming along to have a sexy time with a girl. They know what they're after, and they know the general kind of experience they're going to get. They're imagining they're going to have a similar experience to what they've had before. Whereas when they come to me now as a client, especially if they're coming to have a double booking, they've got an idea in their mind of what they want to do, sort of, but usually it's based on porn, and it's probably not something they've ever done before.

A couple of weeks ago me and my friend had a half-hour booking. The hilariousness of this guy – he's got like eight different complicated positions that he wants us to try and do in half an hour. I'm thinking, 'Dude, maybe you get two.' You've got to factor in having two showers, and getting dressed at the end, so you've probably got at the most 20 minutes of interactive time, and they think they're going to do eight or nine high-impact porn positions. It's pretty funny. Honestly, you get halfway through doing the first thing, and they're ready to come, and you have to try really hard to stretch it out for a bit longer!

For me it's heaps more comfortable and productive working independently, and as trans. I think the biggest thing is that I can do my own marketing. If I work in a brothel, the receptionist might say on the phone, 'She's pretty, but she's very alternative.' That doesn't sell. You want to be like, 'She's a hot suicide girl', or however you want to sell it. But you don't want to be like, 'She's *unusual*.'

So now I have my own website, and I do all my business through that. So by the time they make a booking with me, they've been to my website and they've seen my photos. I have a frequently asked questions page, so they can go on there and it answers all their questions. There are links to people like me doing porn, and doing porn with trans women, so I'm like, 'This is the kind of thing. You want to get in the middle of that? Hit me up.'

My work persona is very down to earth – I'm not into overperformance. I think it's unnecessary to be Super Hooker, and I really don't need to prove anything. So I like to be like, 'The experience you get from me is that I'm casual and genuine and I give amazing head.' I keep my personal life private, but they do get a pretty authentic experience.

My perception is that there is definitely lots of stigma and discrimination around sex work, so I'm careful about who I tell. I would imagine that if I told a landlord that I was a sex worker, I don't think that they would give me a house, so I wouldn't tell them. Lots of times I haven't experienced discrimination, but it's just because I've managed the situation.

Some people think if you're a sex worker then you want to have sex with everyone. When I was younger, it was always, 'You're bisexual, so you must want to have sex with everyone.' People also think that about sex workers – you must love having sex all the time, you must want to have sex with me. Which is interesting, because if you're having sex as a job, then what you want to get from your personal life isn't just mediocre sex – you get enough of that from your work. What you want from your relationships is other things, and maybe that includes sex, but you probably don't just want to have random sex that's not particularly intimate with random guys that aren't really your cup of tea. Because you're already doing it, and you can get money for that.

I try really hard to keep things separate. I have a working name, a separate phone number and separate email address. It's a little bit tricky sometimes, because lots of my friends are sex workers, sometimes my lovers are sex workers, and then everybody has their extended social scenes, and everybody has their clients. People have long-term clients, and maybe they even have relationships with that client at times, or the client-relationship lines are blurry, which is interesting, because that's not at all how I work. I work with really, really clear lines.

I know older trans – and cis – women who have clients they've been seeing for the last 20 or 30 years, and they might even be like, 'I don't do sex work any more but I have a couple of old regular clients who come around now and then.' I don't know very many people at all who have been involved with the same person for the last 30 years, but I know quite a few sex workers who have had relationships with clients for 30 years. And I have no doubt that if one of those women got really sick and needed someone to look after them, those guys they've been sleeping with for the last 30 years would come and do that. I think that's quite cool. In fact I even know sex workers who have married their clients. It's not common but it happens.

I don't allow those lines to blur though. Probably it's mostly because I have a kid. It's not that the clients are at all risky, but there's a risk of society's perception being that you have sex work happening around your kid, or you have lots of strange men around your child. There's a lot of stigma about parents being sex workers. In reality, sex workers are very regular people and have a regular amount of concern about their children. People are generally good parents that go off to work just like anyone else.

I think part of it is because there's a lot of stigma on clients – people think clients are dodgy, weird, or sad and lonely, or abusive, or can't have a girlfriend because they're horrible people who want to dominate women. And it's totally not reality. Most of your clients are just very normal people. In fact some of them don't have time for relationships and feel more comfortable paying a sex worker than going to bars and hitting on people who might not want to be hit on. I think some clients just see it as more ethical and less complicated.

I have, over the years, done lots of different community work. Lots of feminist and anarchist activism. Running a community centre, setting up an animal sanctuary, doing lots of fundraising, organising conferences about indigenous feminisms, and lots of transgender and queer stuff.

I kind of imagine that I'll always do sex work in some form, but who knows. For one thing, I'm really into informal economies. I think it's nice being able to not necessarily work all the time. It's also nice to have a regular job where you have regular hours and regular income, but even if you have a job like that it's still good being able to get some extra money if you need some extra money.

And I just enjoy sex-worker culture. I find sex-worker culture really affirming, and really practical around serious issues. The sex-worker communities are so diverse. In some other areas of activism that I'm involved in, the demographics of the people are very homogeneous. I don't find that at all with sex work – sex-worker activism is so broad. You've got people from all backgrounds, different cultures and different genders and different ways of living. You've got working-class people and middle-class people – it's very cool.

I was watching this TED talk with Juno Mac from the English Collective of Prostitutes. She was talking about how she started sex work because always at the end of the pay cycle she was just replenishing the overdraft. And I thought, that's exactly what sex work has done for me as well. Before doing sex work I was always overdrawn. I was good at getting my bills paid, but that often meant that I wasn't able to buy good food that I wanted to eat. We regularly went dumpster-diving. Some of my friends would go and they would drop food off to all the single parents. Or I would pay for some things and my flatmate could dumpster-dive – you can get lots of vegetables and bread out of dumpsters but you can't get soymilk and you can't get sugar.

So, a big dance around how to get your basic needs met, and the overdraft was never paid off, and I couldn't afford to buy a fridge or a washing machine, so I had to rent them, which was cheap by the month, but you rent a washing machine for three years and you've bought a dozen washing machines.

Then when I started doing sex work I could pay back my overdraft. And I'd had that overdraft since I was 18. I'd had this thousand-dollar debt sitting there, and then I could pay that off. And I could have more food in the pantry than I would eat in a week. If I didn't get to the shops at the end of the week it was OK, because there was food there. And you didn't have to eat the vegetables quickly because they were damaged produce from the bins.

When you never quite have enough resources to just cover your daily needs, you definitely don't have enough to accumulate resources. So, being able to save. Prior to starting sex work I could never ever save. It means feeling like you've got security, and being able to have plans for the future. I remember planning to go on holiday. I was like, wow, I've never planned a holiday in my life. Being able to just plan to do something in the future for a holiday – not something that I would ever have done before doing sex work. I feel like, once a year being able to go away for a couple of weeks and have a holiday is such luxury.

I grew up poor, and as an adult, completely without foundation most of the time, I worry about food. So for me, having cupboards with food, with canned goods and dried goods, makes me feel stable and not frantic.

When you don't have your needs met, you can feel really frantic and chaotic, because you're always trying to get something that you need that you don't have – especially when that's something real basic like housing and food. So doing sex work for me, besides being able to pay my overdraft and have food, or buy new blankets, or have clothes that don't have rips in them or didn't come from the free box outside the op shop – besides how that materially is really amazing, also psychologically it's amazing. It just made me feel a lot more calm, and like I had more say over my day-to-day life. I think it's real big stuff.

Stevie was interviewed in Wellington in March and April 2015 and June 2016.

DANA DE MILO

DANA DE MILO

I WAS BORN in 1946 in Auckland, and I was the only one of my mother's 13 pregnancies that survived. She had a lot of miscarriages – most before me, and one after me.

I grew up in Grey Lynn. Dad was a boat builder by trade, but after the war he became a builder – he had to start as a chippy, an apprentice. He was sick through my childhood, but he never complained. Later they found he had Hodgkin's disease. He was a wonderful man.

We were quite poor, although we lived in a middle-class area. No one knew we were poor, because Mum said you didn't have to act poor. Dad got a pension for being sick – seven pounds a week to feed three people, pay for your house, pay your gas and electricity and go to the hospital. And as soon as he was out of hospital he'd go back to work.

My parents absolutely adored one another. We were very close, the three of us. From the moment I can remember, I knew that my dad might pass away, that he had a disease that was incurable. So I was always ready for it. He died when I was 11.

My first knowing about myself was when I was about three. I was the apple of my grandfather's eye. I don't know if it was Christmas or a birthday, he gave me this car, which was cast iron and bright red with lovely black shiny wheels. I remember being quite disgusted because this thing was so pretty but it was clumsy and heavy. I remember my granddad – he was Scottish – saying, 'He didnae like it, mither!' He said, 'Mither, I told you. He's different.'

That's stuck in my brain – it came back to me when I was in my teens. It didn't stop him from loving me or cuddling me or anything, but he knew I was different. He'd brought up two sons. He knew I was attracted to different things – I was attracted to beauty and pretty things. I'd sit in front of the china cabinet and look at the china.

I dressed in my mum's clothes in secret. Mum wouldn't allow me to – I used to get a hiding every time. So I couldn't wait for her to get out the door. I'd have to clean the house or something, and whoosh! Into the clothes. Radiogram on, and I'd be dancing round the house, dusting and vacuuming and spinning round.

My grandmother allowed me to dress up, my aunty allowed me to dress up. My mum's friend Aunty Peggy had a wardrobe for me, full of old wedding gowns and ball gowns that she couldn't fit, and I used to parade up and down in them.

I was the tallest kid in the school, and I was rather precocious, because I was an only child and I was clever. I could read and write and recite poetry and everything before I went to school. I could talk before I was one, apparently, and I've never stopped since.

I hated school in the end. I got teased, because I was a sissy. I sort of liked it, because they were calling me 'she' and 'Suzy'. It wasn't till Form 1 that I started getting bashed, but I always got teased. And the teachers weren't much better, aiding and abetting those kids.

I remember the first time I lied about my sexuality. I was about seven. The kids had scratched 'Suzy' on my pencil case and ruler. My mother's saying to me, 'I want to know, who's Suzy? Scratched all over your pencil case.' I went bright red from the toes up, trying to think, what am I going to say? She said, 'Oh, I know. You've got yourself a girlfriend.' I went, 'Yes!' Sort of phew, thank goodness for that. That was the first time I really lied.

One day my mother asked me to set the fire. So I had the paper, and on the front it had 'GI swaps sex', and it had Christine Jorgensen in one photo wearing a hat – she had been a marine or something – and in another photo with finger waves. I remember tearing it out, folding it up and putting it in my pocket, and taking it into my room. I'm in bed with the torch reading about Christine Jorgensen and thinking, that's what I want. That's me, I know that's me.

I became very religious. A lot of gay people or trans people, especially from my era, will tell you that they took up religion. I prayed to God every night and every morning. I used to cry at night, begging him to change me. 'Make me a man or make me a woman. Don't make me feel like I feel. I don't want to feel like I'm in between. I want to be one or the other.'

I wanted to be an actress. I used to dream every night that I would come home in a red topless sports car, with three black poodles and three white poodles, and I'd look like Jayne Mansfield. And I'd mince down the path and strut up to the door and say to my mother, 'Do you know who it is?' and she wouldn't know. That was my dream as a child – I'd always dream about being a woman. But I'd wake up the next morning and I'd be still the same.

I did know another queen in my area. She used to call herself Marilyn. She was a little bit older than me, chubby, Māori, quite pretty. We used to dress up in her sister's clothes, and she got stuck in a dress and we couldn't get it off. We got caught, and her father gave me a boot up the arse and told me not to come back again. I think he thought it was my fault, but it wasn't, really. We both wanted to do it.

I always felt that I was in the wrong body, somehow. And at 11, my own breasts started to grow. I had sore nipples, and I got these little puffy things. Then the kids started teasing me when I went swimming in the summer. 'Suzy's got tits, look at Suzy.' And pinching me, pinching them. I was upset. I told my mother, and she took me to Dr Jack. He said, 'I advise you to send him to the Johns Hopkins clinic in America.' My mother said, 'What with? My husband's just died, I've got two pounds two and six in the bank. How can I send Darryl?' He said, 'I'm sure that he is different – he should have been born a girl.'

Dr Jack kept me sane, because he understood me. He read about me. He said that through me he learnt about people like me. He knew that it wasn't mental, and it wasn't my surroundings. I was born like it. He was very understanding. And it was through him that I first heard the word 'transsexual', in 1972, when he went to court for me.

I found out very early how to get money and get things by sex with boys and men. I'd do hand relief or oral and charge them one and threepence. Then I'd go down to Herne Bay, to the fish and chip shop, and get potato fritters and chips with all this money I had. I used to buy heaps, and I'd go back to school. They'd say, 'Come on Suzy, give us some,' and I'd say, 'Well, you give me that fountain pen, or this or that.' I was trading what I knew at an early age.

In Freemans Bay there was a milk bar owned by an Indian man. The Indians used to go out in their vans with all the veges, and go around the suburbs and sell them to the housewives. And they all used to go there afterwards and share their takings and drink, and go behind the dairy and have a mimi. I'd go and grab hold of their ure, and con them into giving me money. Then my friends and I would go off to the movies and get lollies.

So I was sexually active very early. I enjoyed it with boys. The men, nah. The boys a bit older than me, yeah – especially the Māori boys. Pākehā boys, it was just for the money.

When I was 12½, I got permission to leave school. I went to work as a French polisher for a guy called Doug, and he helped me. He said I reminded him of his daughter. I'd go home to their place and play with the girls, and was quite happy playing with the dolls with them, making stories up and trying to fit into their dress-up clothes.

About that time Mum had met Angus, from the Isle of Lewis. At first he was an absolute gentleman, perfect, divine. He was coming to Mum's for about a year, and Mum said how did I think it would be if he lived with us? Did I like him? And I said, yes, that would be fine, because I thought he was lovely. Two months later he was a completely different person – horrible, beat my mother. I hated him from that moment on. He used to call me a sissy, a queer and a poofter, behind my mother's back. He tried to get me to masturbate him, show me what was what. I said, 'I know what's what,' and I fled. I never told my mother that he did that. I knew it would hurt her. She would think that was what caused me to be like this.

So I ran away. It was a long weekend. I was supposed to be staying with my boss, and I told him I wanted to run away. He helped me. I was supposed to go home after work on the Tuesday, and I never went. Instead I went and stayed with some friends.

I already had seen people similar to me. Mum used to give me money sometimes to go to the movies. I'd go in to the Civic Theatre, and walk around

Queen Street looking at the clothes and the furniture. And I came across Vulcan Lane. All of a sudden, out of a taxi came these four – Aunty Maime, Moana, Gina Grace and Frieda. Gina Grace and Moana used to wear boys' clothes, but with all the makeup on and their hair done. Aunty Maime used to wear tights with blue and black stripes. She had Samoan shoes on – wooden soles with a clear plastic heel with a flower in it – and a man's shirt over the top. She was Rarotongan. She used to have about three wigs, one on top of each other. But she was the only one that looked girly.

One night I followed them, and they went to Gleesons Hotel in Hobson Street. It was quite rough – it was a seamen's pub. I became friendly with them, went to parties with them. For two weeks I tried to be a boy, with a suit. I didn't look ugly, I was well groomed, but I was a sissy. Everyone picked it, they laughed at me, so I thought, well, if you're going to laugh at me, I'll give you something to laugh at, I'm going to dress the way I feel comfortable.

Of course that brought up all its own problems.

I was still 13, and I was cracking it. I'd already been doing it at school – it was no different, really. I'd meet the guys at the Queens Ferry, which was the seamen's pub. And Gleesons. We used to go to the public bar, which would be swimming with beer, you sat on beer crates. It wasn't the nicest pub. Guys would buy me a drink – I was sort of cracking it and sort of not. If I had no money, and somebody wanted to go with me, and he was a Pākehā, then I'd ask for money. 'OK, it'll cost you, though.' And then you'd make them take you for a dinner, and buy you cigarettes, and get money off them. Give them a head job and it was over. But if it was a Māori or a black guy, someone I liked, nah, I didn't. Charity! Charity girl – that's what we used to say.

I got picked up by the police all the time, for nothing, just because they wanted to. I was only 13, but they thought I was 18 or something. So they picked me up for being underage, but there's nothing they could do. They'd hold you in the cells for a while, then throw you out. The police were just smartarses. 'What do you fucking think you are, you're sick.' They said we were sex fiends, freaks and fetish people – all the things we weren't. It was them that were like that, not us.

I used to go on the ships with some of the girls. They were queens, butch queens. We were called drag queens because we lived as women. The ones that worked as boys and did drag on the weekends or now and then were classed as butch queens.

So I went on the ships with these queens – they were stewards on the ships. International and New Zealand ships – but you didn't go on the New Zealand ships unless there was no other ship. You'd go on the Pommie ships and all the other ships from round the world. I always made friends with the Pommie queens, butch queens. I met them in the pubs. You'd go back on the ship, next thing they'd be in drag. The guys just loved them, because, like most gay and trans people, they were good at cracking jokes, and they've always got an answer for something. They're a bit of entertainment.

So the queens would hide me on the ship, on the top bunk with all their stuff in front of me. I'd live on the ship – I went to Australia on a ship before I ever went legally on a plane. I've been all round the South Island, Invercargill. We used to come in and out of Wellington, as well. We used to get a taxi straight to the Sorrento from the wharf – we'd be in drag. It was fabulous.

The ship girls used back slang to talk to one another, so the guys didn't know what they were talking about. And we picked that up mixing with them, and we had our own kind of back slang, so the client and the boyfriend didn't know what you were saying about the guy that just walked in the room or something. We used back slang – 'You're nurragy urragy down the rurragy' – 'durragy rurragy'. You'd roll it all in, really quick, flat out, putting the Ns in among the words, like 'gnirl', 'rnoad', 'crnacking it'. That's all died out, because ships are all automated now and there's no such thing as ship molls any more. We still use it now, some of us, because we still know it from back then. And the younger ones have picked that up from us, but it is no longer a language.

I used Māori words because I mixed with Māori a lot. I was very lucky – I was always accepted by Māori. I could call them a black bitch and get away with it, because they knew I didn't mean it nasty. They could call me a white maggot – it's true, it's stating the bleeding obvious. It's not meant to be nasty.

I came to Wellington about 63, on the train. I had nowhere to live when I first came – I lived in the railway station ladies' toilets. Used to put my bag in in the day – it cost nothing to have your suitcase in the baggage department, but it cost to leave it overnight, so I'd take it out every night. I used to go to the Sorrento every night, stand on the street. 'Could you lend me two and six, please?' You'd get two and six to get into the Sorrento. Or you'd get money off one of the guys who'd come out. I'd wait for somebody to come out the side door to go to the toilet, and I'd get money off them and go in. If I was with the seamen, they'd pay for me. You'd get someone to buy you cigarettes, buy you drinks. Someone would pick you up or something.

It was difficult when I came to Wellington, because I knew nobody and had no one to live with. It was very difficult to get work, because if you even had a Beatle haircut, even if you were a straight guy, you were classed as a poofter. We were so backward. In those days if you went to town you still wore hats and gloves.

I lived as a woman all the time in Wellington. That's why I had no work – no one would employ you. Most of us had to crack it, or roll, because we had to survive. If they couldn't crack it, they'd try and get his wallet – that's what they called rolling. I've done that in my time. But as soon as I got a job all of those things stopped. It was about survival – either live or die. And if you're starving, you'll do nearly anything.

They had crates of bread outside the dairies, and crates of milk. We used to knock them off. It's awful, but it was about surviving. I lived in Rolleston Street for a while, me and two real girls. We used to go on the ships. I stole a cabbage from the front yard of the house next door to the dairy. The dirt was going all the way up the street and they traced the dirt. We were having cabbage soup – we were so hungry. That was my first time in trouble – for stealing a cabbage.

I was the first Pākehā to go out during the day – there was really nobody that went out in drag during the day, only at night time. You were too scared – you thought you'd get sprung. People would stand and stare and talk about you like you were a mental patient. 'Look, Joe! What the fuck's that?' 'Oh, look at that! Hey!' People in their forties and fifties who you'd think would have better manners were absolutely appalling. I used to think, how could you be so ignorant and so rude? You feel like filth, the way you've been treated. In the end, you think you're a bad person. I used to think, I would never do that to anybody, stare and talk about them. Where's your manners?

I also got in trouble for pinching to survive – stockings or hairspray or food. Or moonlighting – snowdropping – taking clothes off clothes lines. You'd go and get your drag off the clothes line. Terrible when you think about it, but you had nothing. You wouldn't take it all from one clothes line – bra from there, pants from there, then you'd go home and wash them all again.

Cracking it slowly came into my life, because I had no job. You lived from hand to mouth, and some days you never got a crack.

There were a lot of construction sites in the 60s. I'd go past, and there'd always be guys working late. You'd go in and ask if they wanted sex or a head job. You'd get the money, and you'd be off and get pissed. Forget it, push it out of your head.

I'd go in a park, behind a building, anywhere. I mostly used to pick them up in the club. You'd go to coffee bars and hook up with somebody, and whether or not you got money, you'd get cigarettes, you'd get fed, you'd get drinks. You might go home with nothing in your pocket except a couple of shillings, enough to not get done.

I noticed in the club that guys would come and talk to me, but when I stood up they'd faint, because I was so tall. But if I walked across the floor and a guy called me, then I would get one. I thought, well, maybe I should walk on the street? I seem to pick them up all right when I'm walking along from the pub.

So that's when I started doing the streets. That'd be about 64. I used to do from Dixon Street up, once everybody was in the clubs and the streets were more empty. It was early closing in those days, six o'clock. The streets were usually bare by 9.30, 10 o'clock. There were other girls working too – not queens. I was the first Pākehā queen to be working the streets. There were two Māori – Tammy and Carla – who worked down by the bus depot in Courtenay Place.

The other girls didn't come on the street – they got picked up from the clubs. They were all much shorter than me. I did better because I was on the street and guys would see my legs. Then when the miniskirt came out, I had good legs for that. I was never sprung – I don't know how I got away with it. By then I'd learnt the art of getting them aroused, and I'd take them up Mt Victoria to the lookout. I used to get them all excited, feeling them up. Then all of a sudden they'd say, 'No, no more!' And you'd know you'd got them. So I'd just rub their thigh and nibble their ear and keep them aroused. By the time they stopped the car and turned the lights off, you'd open the zip and it'd be all over, Beethoven, by the time you put your hand or your mouth there. And I'd go, 'Oh! And I did want you to fuck me!'

I got away with that for years. Guys didn't know the score – they didn't know what I was. And that's why it was easier out in the open. 'Oh, you're a tall girl, you're a big girl.' And you'd pounce on their crutch. They'd give you the money and you'd go up there.

Cracking it was all self-taught, nobody was there to teach me. I knew about tucking in a way, because I'd read about the Greek athletes, how they used to put their testes up into the sockets. I never let anybody see me down there. I'd do trick sex – that's when you're either doing it in the cheeks of your bottom, or you're having anal sex and they think they're in the vagina. What most guys thought was a vagina wasn't at all. They'd say, 'Could I give you some more money? Do you think I could have anal?' I'd say, 'Oh yes! That's extra!' You'd wipe off the lube and go, 'Ooh, ow,' when all the time they'd been in there in the first place. That's how dumb they are.

I remember once I picked up this guy. The babydoll look was out then – the empire line. I had this beautiful magenta satin one, and I used to wear balloons in my bra, with water in them, because they were warm and soft. Because we were poor, we kept them in as long as we could, but they would start to rot. I'd been with this guy up the hill, and we were coming back down to drop me at the Sunset. Once I'd cracked it once or twice, that was it, no more for the night, you just wanted to get away, get pissed and have a good night. Anyway he gives me a squeeze on the breast after we'd finished, and it started getting all wet. He went, 'Oh, what's happened to you?' He'd asked me what a lovely girl like me was doing doing that, and I'd said, 'My boyfriend left me, I've got no money, la la la.' You know the number. So when I started leaking, I said, 'I didn't tell you! I'm pregnant, I'm lactating, he left me pregnant.' And he said, 'Here's five quid for a pram.' I thought I was in heaven – 'Thank you very much!' I could pay the rent for two weeks and get pissed.

They didn't really know. And the very feminine look and the wigs and everything was just coming in around 64, 65. It was like when I went to Melbourne, they didn't have a clue. In Sydney they did, because they had Les Girls. Wellington never really liked all-male revues. Yet they'd go to Carmen's because they'd heard that there were drag queens working there. They'd go, 'Is that one there?' It would be poor old Carlotta, she'd had about six kids and she used to do everything under strobe light because she had saggy boobs.

It was friendly on the street – you'd call out to one another. We were all mates. Tracy-Lee would be always pregnant, and she'd work right up till she had her baby, god love her. All her money used to go for her kids. There weren't a lot of girl street walkers – girls used to pick up from nightclubs and dances and things like that.

I never got in a car if I didn't feel safe. First impressions – you could usually tell. Guys, when they're wanting to do something they shouldn't be doing, they get dry mouths and they're nervous. If they're not, you're a little bit wary of them. I always made them drive on, and talked to them while they were driving. And if they wanted something I didn't do, or I didn't like them, I'd make them drop me off again. I went on senses – that's why I'm good at judging people straight off. I've never wanted to risk anything much for money. So I've always been pretty lucky.

I'd get extra out of them – I was always called Miss Extra. Everything was extra. I only gave a price for one thing, and if they wanted anything else it was all extra. I used to just pull the wallet out – 'I'll have that, thank you, and that.' And of course they're in a position where they can't really say no, because they're willing and able. It's all ready to do its little number, and I'm plucking money out of the wallet at the same time. They can't say no till it's over – too late, I'm out of the car. That's how I got all my money.

We got away with it, because a lot of clients didn't have a clue, they just thought we were glamorous girls. I know girls who got sprung, but they didn't get beaten up or anything – I think the guy'd be too shocked. This queen, Frieda, was staying with us. She went up Mt Victoria, because she had to learn to crack it. She's pashing up this guy. She's feeling him up and he starts to feel her up, and she's got a hard-on. He gets such a fright, he screams. She had to jump out of the car and hide in the bushes till he went away.

In 1964 I went to the psychiatry department at Wellington Hospital. It didn't matter how embarrassing it was, I asked to see a psychiatrist, because I wanted to have a sex change. That was more or less unheard of. I used to have to lie on a table nude with a sheet on top of me. The guy would examine me and talk to me, and record himself talking on these great big tapes. Every man and his dog would come in and lift the sheet and look at me, and I'd be lying there with tears rolling down, because I loathed people looking at me like that. I'm thinking it's going to help me, and all they'd say is, 'Go home and put on your men's clothes, you'll never be any use to a society. You'll never be a woman.' It was so stressful, but it made me more determined than ever.

I started hormones when I was 19; it was 1965. There were three trans girls that came from Australia to be strippers at the Purple Onion for my friend Pasi – Etepasi Daniels. He's 76 this year, and he opened the first strip club in Wellington, the Purple Onion, in Vivian Street. The girls came over to work – they all knew him from Sydney, where he had worked at the Purple Onion in the Cross. He had girls working for him, but he wanted these queens, because queens are so much more glamorous.

I was sitting in the Sorrento with some of my friends, and those three girls walked in. One had a green see-through frilled blouse on and I could see the little titties bouncing. We would put bird seed in our bras, or water in balloons, and they moved like breasts move.

I went up and said to Natalie, 'How did you get those?' I was quite shy but I couldn't help myself. She said, 'From hormones.' So I went to her place with her and got the name. When I left Natalie's place, I said to myself, the first doctor's surgery I come to I'm going into. I'd never been to a doctor in Wellington – the way you get picked on, he could have thrown me out for all I knew. They used to say 'Get out!' in shops. 'Get out or I'll call the police!' They wouldn't let you try on clothes, like you were some diseased creature.

And the first one was Dr Ongley. I sat down and told him I wanted Stilbestrol, 30 milligrams. He said, 'And do you know what these do?' I said, 'Yes, they give you breasts.' He said, 'Do you know what else they can do? They can cause thrombosis and heart problems.' I said, 'Yeah, yeah, yeah.' So that's how I started my hormones. And then I sent all the other girls to him.

I told him I wanted to have a sex change. I was the first – I don't know why, I was the blimming scaredest. But I always used to be the first to go to all sorts of places. Soon as I found they treated me well, I'd send the other girls. All of them went there, went to him.

My Auckland doctor, Dr Jack, had told me that until you're 21, your parents can commit you to an asylum. I didn't want to be committed, because I knew I wasn't mental. I'd asked Dr Jack if I was mental and he said, no, you're not. He'd studied it because of me.

Once I was over 21 I thought, my mother can't put me in the loony bin now. It was seven years since I'd seen her. So I wrote to her, saying, 'You know, Mum, that I've always been a sissy. Well, ever since I've left home I've lived, dressed and worked as a woman, and one day I would like to have a sex change. If you don't understand that and don't want to know me I will understand, if you don't want to speak to me ever again. But I wanted you to know.'

She sent me a letter back – I've still got that letter – saying, 'Dear Darryl, so good to hear from you after all this time. I was shocked about your news, but as I've always said, you're big enough and ugly enough to look after yourself. It is your life, you can live it as you see fit.' Then at the bottom she put, 'Don't forget there's always a home here for you. Your loving mum.'

A month later she arrived on my doorstep in Adelaide Road. She looked lovely, but she looked very drawn and oldish. She'd just driven eight hours from Auckland. I felt like an absolute arsehole – my mother looked like I had worn her out. I fell on my knees and put my head on her knee. I was howling and saying, 'I'm so sorry for you to see me like this.' She's patting my head. 'It's all right, darling. We've talked about it. It's your life, live it as you see fit. I want to be part of it.'

I had to go to work, so I said the girls would pick her up and take her down to the Doodle Inn, the topless restaurant where I was the hostess. She said, 'I don't think I could eat dinner with bare breasts.' She'd never seen that sort of thing. I said, 'You come for dinner and I'll pay for it.'

I had on an emerald green short A-line skirt. I had a cape jacket, and underneath a magenta pink low-necked top. I had navy blue shoes with a chain on them and a navy blue bag, and I had my hair pulled back with a band, and flicked up at the sides. She said, 'Stand up! Go over there!' She said, 'You look absolutely beautiful. If I had a daughter I couldn't wish for my daughter to look better. That's all I needed to see.'

She was really, really accepting of everything. She fell in love with all the queens – the boy queens, the drag queens, everything. She used to say to them, 'Any of you girls want to come to my place, there's always a bed, if you come to Auckland.'

I met Chrissy Witoko when I was 14 and she was 16. I had met her in Auckland briefly through Aunty Maime. Then I came to Wellington and she was here. We were best friends, right up until she died. She never cracked it in her life – she always worked. Always. She worked on the wharf in leather pants, and she was a manager and owner of clubs from about 1967 onwards.

Chrissy's parents were fabulous to me. That always happened with the Māori queens' parents. It was always all right for me – 'Oh yes, Dana can have a sex change, but with you it's just a phase you're going through.' I'd explain to the parents that they were exactly the same as me. The parents were different about me because I wasn't theirs.

I can see why a lot of girls went back into men's clothes, because it was so very, very hard. For me there was no going back. I got picked on as a boy, so being picked on as a girl wasn't that hard. At least I was happy – I was never happy as a boy.

When girls met me and said they wanted to be trannies, I'd say, 'Go back to your job and transition on your job. Go home, tell your parents, doesn't matter whether they accept it or not, then come back to me.' I always said to those young girls that prostitution isn't all it's cracked up to be. It looks glamorous, because you're all dressed up, and you have money, but it can be the absolute pits. Yes, it's fun in the beginning, but once the fun and the glamour wears off, if it's your everyday job and the only way you can get money, it can be very very hard. But because they wouldn't go back to their jobs, I'd have to teach them how to be hookers. Which killed me.

Nowadays there's not that many girls go on to prostitution like there used to be. They used to think it was glamorous – they've got nice clothes, they look lovely, but they don't see the other side. Having to drink or take drugs to cope. The shame. I said to my mother, 'I did everything you taught me not to. A liar, a thief and a fucking prostitute. The whole bloody three of them. I never wanted to do any of them. Life made me do that.' I never wanted to steal things. I didn't want to tell lies. I didn't want to be a hooker.

You lived in run-down places, because they were the only people that would take you. When you got a nice flat, the rest of the girls would end up being kicked out and come and live with you, and you'd get kicked out. Or I'd have a husband – a boyfriend – who would go and rent the flat.

I had quite a few relationships, up till I was in my late forties. Two different ones of seven years. One-night stands, one month, one year, one minute. Crying over one, dabbing the eyes, and fluttering the eyelashes two hours later for another one. It was about trying to be normal. Society made you feel that you were abnormal, so it's normal to get a husband and a house, be a housewife, clean his clothes and his shoes and cook for him, be subservient.

I never had one man call me a he or a bloke – yet I'd seen other queens, drop-dead-gorgeous queens, having their boyfriends say, 'You're nothing but a fucking man' when they're fighting. I never had that. And I think that's because I was very careful. They never saw me down there, never felt a hair on my body.

Carmen was the first transsexual that I had ever seen on the street in my life, and that was probably about 1959, 60, in Auckland. I met her again when she came to Wellington, and I worked at the Balcony from the second week it was open. I was one of her first waitresses, with Mystyne and Gypsy. I changed my name when I went to work for Carmen. She was putting my name at the bottom of the ad, and she wouldn't let me use Darryl. I used to use Tabou perfume, by Dana. And I always loved the Venus de Milo – I loved the name, but I didn't want to change my name to it, because it was too queeny, too sissy. Too gay. I was going to be Dana de Winter, but Carol de Winter stole it. So I became known as Dana de Milo, though I never changed it officially until 72.

Carmen conned me into going on stage after a year or so. I went on stage for a month and did 'Goldfinger'. I used to mime the song. I was all in gold, inside a gold net coming from a hoop on the ceiling. You could just see my shadow, and my hand would come out with the gold glove, beckoning – the web of sin and all that, you know. Then I would come out and strip to the music. But I only lasted a month. Didn't like what went on behind the stage. Everyone was very catty, all wanting to be the best on stage. They'd damage each other's costumes, all sorts of things. I couldn't wait to go back out and be a waitress. I loved being a waitress.

We used to all drink in the Bistro Bar at the Royal Oak – the hookers, the seamen, the trannies and the lesbians, and the gay Māori kids. The front bar was all white gay guys. They had good jobs. If we were walking along the road in drag and they saw us, they'd duck into a shop. They'd hide behind their men's kākahu – men's clothes. They never admitted they were gay openly like we did. We were the face of gayness, even though we weren't gay. We were the ones that got beaten up. They really learnt how to hide it. And they didn't like us, because they thought we were after their trade. Well, we weren't after their trade – we weren't after a gay man. I didn't want to have gay sex.

The lesbians lived itinerant kind of lives too. You were either a butch lesbian or a fairy lesbian, a bitch lesbian. Often the one in the suit was the one that got pregnant to a Jap or something. But they were great to us. And a lot of them fancied the queens. I used to say, 'Why?' And they'd say, 'You're the epitome of femininity. The most feminine things we've ever met. Just what a lesbian dreams of having – this beautiful doll.' And they always stuck up for us. We were great mates, especially with the Māori lesbians. We used to party together. We didn't have any problems.

We were the bottom of the gay heap, even though we were the face of it. We were the ones that were getting beaten and put in jail. If I can say anything good about the HIV virus, it's that it brought our communities together as one. Most of those gay guys didn't like lesbians – they were very misogynist. They didn't like Māoris, unless you were a corporate Māori, which was very rare in those days. You didn't get into their club, the Dorian Society. There was a great divide.

The Royal Oak was another world. When you walked through those doors of the Bistro Bar, the music playing, the smell of lovely perfume, and all these beautiful girls – and I'm talking real girls as well. Everybody went there that was in what society called 'the seedier side of life'. Really we were the better side. We were much more genuine, more honest and more caring about one another than society really was.

When my mum came down to meet me, she fell in love with all the girls and all the gay guys. Everybody really loved Mum as well. So when she died, everybody came to Auckland, to her funeral. Karen and them hitchhiked from the South Island to get there. When they did the service in the funeral home, it was nearly all queens. And no one knew. They were all from Mojo's, everywhere – they all came. Mum had flowers out the door and down the road in Symonds Street.

Some of the girls stayed in Auckland. Cracking it up there was bloody good, because there was no queens up there. Everybody had come to Wellington to try their tranny wheels. You know when you have a bike with the little wheels for the kids? They call Auckland the queen city, but we were the queen city.

Everyone came to Wellington, because that's where the queens were and where you got help.

Then we went to Auckland, and of course clients knew nothing about queens up there. All these lovely girls, so they're all making a bit of money, and a lot of them decided to stay. Well, Auckland had never had such an influx. Money was good up there – I remember when I used to go and visit Mum, I could make a fortune.

Anyway the police got a bit angry and started raiding all the houses. A lot of the girls used false names for the Stilbestrol. Mine said Miss D Pickering, which was my name. They busted into our houses. They smashed my mother's picture. They beat me up in my mother's bedroom. We all got done. They found the pills, and the charge was using a false name to obtain a prescription poison. What were you going to do with hormones? It was just ludicrous. They don't even get you high. It's still on my record – it still comes up as fraud.

They all got fined and I got fined – even though it wasn't me that said to put 'miss', it was my doctor. Dr Jack stood up in court for me and everything – that's when I first heard the word 'transsexual'. He said that he brought me into the world, and that he had treated me for a transsexual problem since I'd been a young child. He'd been my saviour. He said he put 'miss' in front of my name so that it wouldn't embarrass me and it wouldn't embarrass the issuing chemist. He said, 'She presents and looks like a woman, why wouldn't I put Miss?'

I paid the fine straight away, went to the lawyer and changed my name by deed poll. So when the police used to ask me what was my real name, I'd say, 'It's Dana de Milo.' 'No, what's your real name?' I said, 'Dana de Milo.' They tried to arrest me for it, but I proved them wrong.

My friend Cherie – a real girl – had been backwards and forwards to Melbourne, to the parlours, because she was a prostitute. She said to me – this is at three o'clock in the afternoon – 'I'm going back to Melbourne tonight. I've had enough of this. The money's brilliant in Australia.' She said, 'I'm going, are you coming?' I said, 'Yes.' Just like that – spur of the moment. Only did three or four spur-of-the-moment things in my life – one was leaving home, one was going to Aussie, and coming back. Bang! Just like that. I said yes – we left at half past eleven that night.

It was the 1st of March 1976. I was hoping to have my change in Australia. That's why I went, was to have my change. I thought the only way I could do it would be to go and work in a parlour. I knew that even though I was tall, I was just as passable as the girls that were working there. Some of them weren't that pretty. I never thought I was pretty, but I knew I scrubbed up all right. That's the reason I went. Plus, Muldoon just got in and everything was going downhill in a big way.

The day after I arrived I went to the White House, which was a parlour. They were illegal, but they were everywhere. And there was my old friend Hine, a Māori lady. An Indian guy came in, and he didn't want Hine, because she was dark-skinned. She said to me, 'You're a prostitute, you've come here to work – away you go.' So I just did what I always did with the Japanese guys and my boyfriends. I used to hide it in the crack of my leg and put my hand there. Put my leg up over their back, and it's in the crack of my leg, it's hidden. So that's what I did with him.

I ended up doing three that night. Thought I was bloody heaven on a pogo stick. I had walked through Richmond Road three times, never got sprung once. All the Greeks and wogs were out there whistling at me, guys on construction sites – 'Hullo girlie!' I was wearing yellow Cherry Tree trousers, and a halter-neck backless top. I had long hair. I just walked down Richmond Road, and honestly, they were running out of their houses. It was all Greeks and Italians in those days. They didn't have a clue, they were all out there whistling. 'Signorina!'

So I got a job at the Room at the Top. Before decriminalisation, queens got jobs just like that in brothels. They pulled all the money in, because they were the most glamorous. Especially Kiwi queens, we were fabulous prostitutes. So were Kiwi girls. They were well-known in Australia as good workers. Honest and reliable – very good hookers, Kiwis. We all worked as real girls – none of the clients knew, unless you were like one girl who'd get out of it, fall asleep and come untucked. The client would come screaming out of the room.

Cherie and I decided we'd go and work in another parlour. We go to this parlour in South Yarra, and the guy said, 'If you girls want to take over the lease and work, it's $300 a week.' So we did. I lived there. I used the bedroom as a work room – we both worked there. Then Cherie got a flat upstairs, and called it 'Ma Cherie'.

We had quite a good clientele after two or three months. I worked by myself, and I'd have one client in the lounge, one in the bathroom, one in the bedroom, one in the kitchen and one in the hallway. I'd offer them all coffee and everything – I wouldn't let them out the door, because it was all dollar signs to me. I was very dollar-oriented because I wanted my change and I wanted to have my boobs redone. So within six months I had $10,000 in the bank. I used to work from 10 in the morning till 4 in the morning. I was very busy – those doorbells went like mad.

All of a sudden, electricity and gas decided they wanted $600 deposit. We worked until our lease was up and our electricity got cut off. I still worked, by candlelight. Then the lease ran out and we had nowhere to go.

Cherie went downstairs to Eve, who was from Wellington. Eve gave her a job, and Cherie asked if she would take me on. Eve said, 'She's a transsexual, isn't she?' Cherie said, 'Yes, but her clients don't know that.' I ended up doing all of her clients as well. And they'd come back and they didn't want a girl, they wanted me. She said, 'I don't know what you do in that room but you must be bloody good, because they don't want my top girls, they want you.' I said, 'Darling, they're kings. Every one of them is a king.' I used to say, I should get an Oscar – I'm the best mattress actress in Victoria, because I made them feel like they were the only man on earth. They'd get on top of me and I'd be going, 'Ohhh.' They thought I was enjoying it, but it was my way of going, 'Eugh, get off.' I made all those sounds that sounded like you were getting off, which was just my way of letting the stress out of my body. I learnt to channel it into panting.

I was one of the few prostitutes that would kiss, I was one of the few prostitutes that would do a fat man. I did fat men, I did handicapped people – I did anything. To me, that was my role. I was a prostitute, and you do people that no one else would have sex with. If you look like the back end of a bus, that's not what I see. I see dollars.

I could be in there with the most hideous guy and make him feel that he was God by the time I was finished with him. I felt that was my job. You poor darling, you're so bloody ugly and fat and vile that no one would give it to you for nothing. But my job is to do it, because I am a prostitute. Why wouldn't you do someone that was crippled or in a wheelchair or whatever? Where else is the poor darling going to get sex? He's paying for it, my god! I might be old-fashioned, but I think that's what you're there for. And if you can't do that, then you shouldn't be a prostitute.

I had a Greek couple that brought their son, who was a couple of kangaroos short in the top paddock. No problem whatsoever. You just had to be like a mother – 'Take your shirt off, darling, and put it over there. Now go and have a shower. Pull your skin back and give it a good scrub. I'll come and give you a wash.' I'd wash him and tickle him and blow bubbles on his belly under the shower. And I always massaged everybody – everybody got a massage unless it was a real quickie. Even then I'd give them a massage because I wanted to feel their wairua. By massaging you feel them relax, you feel their wairua. You can sense who they are. If they don't relax, then you're always on your guard. This guy could be a cop, this guy could have sprung you.

I had known before I went to Australia that there was a doctor in Egypt, but I wasn't aware this was where I would be going – I thought I would be having it in Australia. The government funded several changes a year, or HBA[1] would fund most of it.

I had made an appointment to see Professor Richard Ball, a psychiatrist at the Royal Melbourne Hospital. I went at eight in the morning – I don't think they wanted you to be sitting there amongst the other people. I did a test that day. The test is so ridiculous. They put these pictures in front of you, of two guys sitting on a park bench. One's got his arm behind the other one, resting on the bench. They must think you're an absolute idiot – they say, 'What do you think that's about?' I suppose they expect you to say, 'Two gay guys sitting together!' But you don't – that's exactly what you know they want you to say. Anybody with half a wit would know that. I said, 'Oh, it's just two friends sitting in the park.'

They show you photos of bananas, and ask, 'What kind of fruit do you prefer to eat?' I thought, well, I really do like the banana. But I said, 'Oh, I love plums.' All these stupid pictures. They were testing me. They'd send you out to ask someone where the toilet was, see where they directed you to.

I must have passed, but they told me I'd have to wait three years because I was a New Zealander. They didn't know I was working in a parlour – if you say

---

1   A health insurance company.

you're a prostitute they won't give you a sex change. They didn't agree with that kind of life.

I said, 'I don't want to wait any longer. I've been waiting 17 years.' He said, 'We only do two at Easter and two at Christmas.' I said, 'Is that right? Well, I'm off to Egypt.'

So I wrote to Professor Beheri.[2] The people who had seen him were all happy. Looked good, everything – you wouldn't know. I got my letter back, and he said he would be pleased to take me, any time in February. I asked my doctor for a referral, so I could give it to HBA and see if I got anything back. Well, lucky lucky me, I got all my money back.

I flew out to Cairo on the 26th of February 1977. I arrived on the 26th and had my change on the 27th. I always loved Egypt, always had an affinity with it. The only butch thing I ever did as a kid was put a sheet around my head and tie a pyjama cord round it, get the straw broom and pretend it was a camel and I was the Sheik of Araby. And apparently in one of my past lives, if you believe in that, I was Nefertiti's sister's daughter.

Everyone came to see me off. I could see my mother – she always seemed to come to me when I was going to have an operation. I turned back at the doors at the airport when people can't come any further – there was Hine, and by Hine was my mother, and Cherie, and all the girls that had had their changes. They all came to see me off. We always did that, and when they came home we all went and picked them up.

To me, Professor Beheri was a god – he was my saviour. He was a wonderful, wonderful man. I told him that if I died, he must finish it, because I have to be able to be buried as a woman. He said, 'No, no, nothing will go wrong.' I was absolutely over the moon – it was just the happiest day of my life. Whether I lived or died, I had achieved what I had always wanted.

It's 33 years ago now. It's made me complete – how I felt about my body and myself. It made me stronger as a person. I stopped feeling I was masquerading as something I wasn't, because this is what the public make you feel. Which is silly, because they don't know what's in your trou. They don't.

When you're younger, you think the sex change is going to change the world, how it looks at you. But it doesn't. It makes no difference, really. But as

---

2   Egyptian plastic surgeon Gamal El-din Beheri.

a person, for me, this is what makes me feel complete. I know I was born male, and this is my bad luck. But to me, I am a woman. I always felt like a woman. I always felt that genitalia did not belong to me. I never had a full-length mirror in my bathroom. Nobody touched me down there unless it was a doctor. No guy ever saw me like that. It was something that didn't belong to me. So for me, my change was a completion.

I slowly got stronger and stronger as a person. There were times when we got taken advantage of – well, I started not allowing that. In work, you got low wages and they made you feel like you should be grateful to have a job. When parlours were legalised, nobody wanted us as trans workers. They started hiring us as receptionists, but they were giving us bad wages. Then one day I said, 'I'm not working any more for this amount of money. I'll go and get a straight job.' So they bumped the wages up.

I would never have said that before. You used to be grateful to be hired. And you used to think that you were a dirty person, because society made you feel like an oddball, so you have low self-esteem. You go for jobs and you get knocked back and laughed at, go to a new doctor and get laughed at. If you're treated like shit, you feel like shit. It takes you a long time to say to yourself, I am a good person, I am as good as the next one. I'm kind, I care, I'm clean and tidy, I pay my bills. It takes you a long time to come to terms with that. And the change helped me a hell of a lot.

My first real love after my change, I thought, it'll be different. He's not going to go off with a woman – I've got a vagina, so I'm everything he could want. But men are men. I realised I wanted to finish it because I didn't need the hurt any more. I sent him home and I told him not to come back. I felt, I'm a complete person.

The hospital board said, you've got to get rid of all your friends. You must never tell anybody what you were, must deny it. You never admit that you were a man, and you get rid of all the people around you, the gay people, and live a life as a woman. I said, that's absolutely impossible. I can't do that. They're like my family. We've gone through thick and thin together, been beaten up together, all sorts of things. Spat on, thrown drinks at. All sorts of things you would think would never happen to a person, we've gone through together. How can you say I have to dump them?

I could never live a lie. I used to go to bed with guys, and if they didn't know, they didn't know. But if it was going to be serious and we started seeing each other, I'd have to tell them. I couldn't live that lie. I think you'd be a nervous wreck. You'd be frightened to run into somebody. One girl told me not to write to her – 'My boyfriend doesn't know.' I said to her, 'You be careful. You might be in a car accident, and they say, "How long since your wife had a sex change?"' It's not the fact that you're a sex change, it's that you never told him.

When I came back from Egypt I was flat broke, and I wanted to get a straight job. Two or three weeks later, Eve arrived at the house and begged me to go back. I was very grateful to her for giving me a job. I still had that thing, when someone gave you a job you thought, 'Oh, thank you very much, I'll never do anything wrong. You're the most wonderful person.' Because of what society made you feel, when you got a job you thought you owed them your fucking life, excuse my French.

I wanted to start a new life. I didn't want to be a prostitute any more. I really only wanted to be a prostitute to get my money. And I was hoping, once I'd had my change, I could live a normal life, get an ordinary job. Well. I wasn't so eager to get out there looking. When you think about it, I didn't have any skills, really, to show.

In the end I went back. My first client, I'll never forget this. I had never got feeling down there, I never got erect or anything. And I go in to do this Jewish man who was bigger than the massage table, and was a nasty piece of work. He put his hand on my vagina and started playing with it, and all of a sudden I started to get excited, and I had to leave the room because I was going to chuck up. I had to learn in that moment to switch off. And it made it very hard for me to switch back on in my private life.

Here I was getting all horny from this filthy old man playing with me. I thought, I don't want to be horny and excited for you. I want to pretend to be, but I don't want to be. I don't want to get my rocks off with you. Yuk. I had to learn how to turn those feelings off.

I reached a point where I was over it. Sometimes it makes you lose faith in men. You see so many and they're so phony. The good ones are few and far between. They're creeps, to be honest, when it comes to sex. It makes you think that all men are like that.

I finished working at the end of 85. HIV was rearing its ugly head, and this one guy used to be big bucks for me. He was an absolute sex addict, and he used to give me $100 to take the condom off. Then he came in one night and had four or five queens. I thought, 'My god! Just imagine. He might have been screwing gay guys and they might have Aids.' I thought, 'I've got to stop this. I can't keep doing this.' I was petrified. It took me years before I was tested, I was so scared I had it. It was so easy, $50 extra, $20 extra, off would come the condom – because all I ever saw in the room was dollar signs.

So I stopped. I went on the dole, though I didn't want to. Then I got a job back in the place where I first started. I became the receptionist in 87, and I worked there till 92 – then in others till I came home in 2003.

I never wanted to leave New Zealand in the first place. I went to Australia for my sex change. My girlfriend used to say, 'Come on, we've got enough money, we'll go home for a good kanikani at the old Sunset.' I'd say, 'Yes, yes,' then at the last minute I'd say no. I just knew I'd come home and I'd never go back. I came back for a holiday after 17 years. It was the early 90s. I wanted to come home, because all my friends were still here, my old, dear friends. People were different here, and the food – the kai moana's to die for.

In 2002 my dearest friend, Chrissy, died. I was home, staying with my friend Jenny in Lyall Bay. And you've got both bays, Lyall Bay on one side and Evans Bay on the other side. The wind was blowing my hair in front of me, and the fresh air is so beautiful. I love the smell of the sea. I thought, I want to come home. I wasn't planning to come home till I was 60. It was a pact I'd made with Chrissy, I would come home when I was 60, in 2006. She'd retire, she'd be 62, she'd do my 60th. And we would travel around New Zealand.

She died in November 2002. She'd had diabetes since I'd left for Australia, but never had anything done about it, being scared to go to the doctor. They have whakamā, they're embarrassed about who they are.

When she died, I decided I wasn't going to hang around any longer, I was coming home. I was losing people who were close to me – a lot of Māori die before they're 60, especially if they've been drinkers or smokers. So I thought, I don't want to stay away any longer. I want to come home and get a place, get it together before I'm too old to appreciate it.

I had done a lot of volunteer work in Aussie, talking about being transgender. It was cathartic, coming out more as I got older. I joined AIDS Line and Hepatitis C Line as a counsellor.

I thought, I want to come home because I'd like to do what I do in Australia here. I'd rather spend my last years at home doing things for my own. I belong to the Chrissy Witoko Trust, a trust for the gay, lesbian and transgender people in Wellington, to help if they're sick with Aids or anything. And I belong to the Drugs and Health Development Project – I volunteer with them and belong to their board. I give people hepatitis and sexual health advice.

I volunteer for the NZPC, for the doctor – we have a clinic on a Wednesday. I'm the receptionist, and I talk to the tranny girls and give them advice. I try to tell them not to be hookers. I tell them now we've got rights. Look at me, if I can do these things in life you can do it, against all adversity. It's fantastic for young transgender. I say to the girls, 'If you want to be a sex worker, if you enjoy that, do it part-time, but make sure you get a straight job that pays all the bills. Make that your pocket money. You don't need to do that kind of thing any more.'

I joined the Māori Party when it first started. I got a group of 10 of us and we went to a fundraiser. It was a mix of trans and trans-friendly people, and we were very welcomed when we went in. I go to lots of their things. These women got to know me and like me, and they asked me to come to a women's hui. I've been with the Māori Women's Welfare League ever since, and the Māori Party since 2004. I get in the kitchen and do my bit. I do fundraising and sell raffles for them. I love it – I might be one of the first trans women in the Māori Women's Welfare League for all I know.

Once upon a time I would have said, I wouldn't wish this life upon my worst enemy, because it was hard. Since I went to Australia, life was so different, and I never got sprung. I developed and became me, and had my change, and got stronger and stronger. I would still love to have been born a woman so I could have had children. But I'm glad I lived the life I lived. Take away the bad, there was a hell of a lot of fun. We were part of the movement of free love, the forerunners of bucking tradition, standing up for our rights. I've had a wonderful life, and I wouldn't have missed any of it for quids.

You can get wrapped up in your own little world. I used to think 'Woe is me' sometimes, but then you see some poor person that can't walk. We have a bad habit of picking on one another. Even in my day, queens picked on those that were weaker and belittled them. What does it get you in life, really? We should be awhi-ing one another. I've always picked up people along the way – 'Come with me, girl.'

Aunty Millie Witoko, Chrissy's mum, she whāngai'd me in the 80s when I was living in Aussie. She rang me up and said, 'We had a family hui, and I told everyone, you know I was Dana's special aunty, well, I want her to be part of our whānau, we've known her so long.' I said, 'You didn't have to do that, Aunty, I felt part of it anyway.' She said, 'No, but I wanted you to be part of it.' I'm very honoured to be so accepted by Māori.

I've been living in Strathmore for six years. I used to say, 'I'd love to come home and have a wee whare on the side of the hill, overlooking the moana.' And what did I get? Waited a year and got my beautiful little house. I've been doing it up, making it ready to enjoy in my old age. I love it. I've got the view of the sea, I've got the view of the Kaikōura mountains when they've got snow on. I see ships, and planes flying past, it's just beautiful. Very grateful. Love being home. I'm poorer, but I'm happy. And I've got my babies, my dog and cat, and all my wonderful friends that are always coming to visit and stay. It's wonderful to be home with my whānau.

Dana was interviewed at her Wellington home on a series of occasions between April and August 2010.

ALLAN

ALLAN

I WAS BORN in Takapuna in 1967. I was adopted – my birth mother was a young Māori woman who had got pregnant to an Englishman in Wellington, and didn't tell him. Her parents said that she had to adopt me out, which she did. I was adopted into a bicultural family – Mum was Māori, Dad was Pākehā. My birth mother is Ngāti Hine and Ngāpuhi, and my adopted whānau is Ngāti Kurī, Ngāti Whātua. So I was pleased when I found out who my birth family were – I was pleased that they're still from up north.

They were older parents – Dad had been to the war. He was really cool. He never ever hit us, not once, but Mum did, and quite horrible, really. Later in life, Mum told me she didn't want kids – 'Your father was the one that wanted children.' I felt that my whole life, but I didn't know it. But it really made sense when she told me.

I was brought up in Auckland city, in a predominantly European area. We went to tangi and stuff, and you knew that you took your shoes off and rubbed noses, but that was about it. Mum couldn't speak Māori. She could understand it, but she couldn't speak it. And I listened to the messages she gave us – they weren't very encouraging. All my Māori knowledge I started learning at 18, I went off and started learning myself. It was really powerful – it was like this missing link in my life. It gave me all this inner strength. I was adopted, and I always felt I never fitted anywhere.

As a child I would always speak out if there was any sense of injustice. I had to speak out, even if I knew I'd get a hiding for it. I just couldn't help myself. Adults didn't like children who spoke out, and I spoke out a lot. Even from about Standard 4, I was misbehaving in school. I was expelled in Form 2, then at the next school I was put straight into the special class with all the misbehaving kids.

But I believe a lot of my behaviour was because of the whole sexuality thing going on, and no one quite knowing what to do with me. I knew from young that I was attracted to men, to guys. But I knew that that wasn't normal – so that whole confusion around all of that, that all going on inside your head, and yet that's not what you're meant to be doing. And you're getting all these messages from religion and TV, from society, that that's not what you're meant to be doing.

So you've got the adoption thing going on, then you've got the sexuality thing going on, so you've got all this misbehaviour, and no one looking into, why is this child acting out? Today it'd be looked at totally differently.

I went to high school at 12. I didn't hang out with third formers – I found them very immature. I matured a lot faster than a lot of my peers, I was bigger than everyone else. I was already having male-to-male sex with cousins. I was hanging out with fifth and sixth formers, so they were all going to nightclubs in Auckland city. So here I am at 12 going off to these nightclubs. Then I started wagging school, and running away from home, going away for weekends and stuff.

That's when Mum brought in the police, the youth aid officers. So they put me in Ōwairaka Boys' Home. They put you in the secure unit, which was like a little jail, to begin with. They were like, 'Will you run away?' 'No, no, no.' So they put me in the open house part. As soon as I was there I was out, I ran away.

I went to the fun parlour in Avondale, met up with a girl I'd been to school with. She took me to her brother's over the North Shore, so I lived with him and his girlfriend and baby. Ended up getting a job in a factory – I lied about my age, and I looked older. You couldn't get the dole – plus I was on the run from the police. They had been about to make me a state ward, but I took off.

Dad was sick over this period, over those few years – he'd been in and out of hospital, more in than out. For whatever reason I looked in the death column in the paper and I saw his name there. By this stage my photo's in the *Herald*, it's on the radio – they're trying to find me. And somebody reported, yes, we've seen him, North Shore. Mum drove taxis, so she sent this big burly Māori taxi driver over to come and get me. So off we went to the funeral – they took me straight to the marae, which was out Ōtara. You go round and do the whole hongi thing, and I just totally skipped Mum. Then the kaumātuas are getting up, saying, 'Oh, it's so good you've come back, ra ra ra.' But the way they were talking was as if I ran away from home. I didn't like that, because it wasn't right, so I stood up and said, 'Actually, I didn't run away from home, I ran away from a boys' home, and she put me in there.'

They didn't charge me or anything – they let me get an exemption from the Education Board to leave school at 14. I went back home, lived there for a while, but I didn't like it – I didn't really like Mum, and Dad was gone. Then I went to help a cousin's girlfriend's mates move, two young solo mums. I ended up staying with them – they took me in.

One of their boyfriends was in Ponsonby, and one of his flatmates was at university, so there were some university people coming through the house. And one of them was a trans from Hawke's Bay, who was transitioning. That was the first time I'd met anyone like that. I remember her saying to me, 'Oh, are you camp?' I said, 'Hmm, what's that mean?' She said, 'Gay.' 'Oh, I think I might be.' So that was the first time ever meeting anybody that was openly anything else but straight.

She was really cool, Sheila. She was Māori, she was transitioning, she was at university. All her brothers and sisters were at university. They were the first Māori I'd ever met who were tertiary educated. She was telling me about working the streets. She said, 'I'll show you how.' 'Oh, OK!'

Sheila was big, she was over 6 foot. She kind of took me under her wing. A lot of those older queens were really scary, very stand-over, that kind of stuff. But she was like, 'Leave him alone. Don't yous dare touch him.' I was really lucky in that way, no one would do anything to me because of her. So that's when I started cracking it on the streets. It was like, oh my god, I can make money doing this. I was too young to be getting the dole, I wasn't really meant to be employed at that age, and it gave me a means to survive without hurting anybody, doing any crime – even though it was a crime in those days.

Even before Sheila showed me, I remember being in the bogs in Panmure, the area I grew up in. Our Friday night was, Dad would take us down to Panmure, we'd do our groceries, go to the library, get some books out. Then on the way home Dad might stop at the pub, and my sister and I would be outside in the car park with our chips and our drink. And I remember being in the bogs in Panmure, and there was a hole in the wall between the cubicles. I saw this eye through the hole. Then I looked through and they started jerking off. Oh my god. Then a bit of paper came through and he'd written a note on it, offering me a dollar or something. I can't even remember what it said, but it was basically offering me some money for some kind of sexual act. It wasn't much money – I think I would have done it for free, anyway. So it was like, OK. After that, that was me every Friday night. I'd be down into those bogs, into those cubicles, having sex with all these older guys. And not often for money – just that first time. I would have been 11, 12ish.

Then all of a sudden meeting all these Māori on the streets, all these trans workers. When I first met Sheila it was like, oh my god, it's not just me, I'm not the only one like this. It felt good – there's all these other people out here that are like me. Well, kind of like me – they were all trans. I knew that wasn't me, but I liked the sex work part of it. I liked that sense of whānau that you got with them. Even though some of them could be quite awful – you had to have your wits about you. They'd roll you or beat you up. But if you got beyond that there was still this sense of community. And you were moving in those circles with all the gang members and prostitutes, and in those days there were a lot of ship molls, because you had all the ships coming in. All these people, all this underbelly of Auckland, were all moving in the same circles and in the same bars. I was totally not doing anything with whānau by this stage, so they were like my whānau.

I wasn't trans, I was a gay guy, one of the few. The queens didn't really like poofters. And the gay scene was very anti the queens, especially the sex workers. The sex workers in Auckland were not allowed in the gay bars, though the ones I hung out with could get in because they were very unspring, they didn't look like queens, and they were nicer. I hung with the nicer ones that weren't the evil stand-over. There were a lot of those ones – they were horrible, they were just nasty.

I was the one of the few males that could work on the streets. In those days, if any of those queens saw male workers they would beat them up and kick them off the street. They'd be pushed into doing the bogs, and I didn't really like doing those sort of places. I worked from K Road and the top of Queen

Street, and as a male I could hang around outside the male toilets at the top of Howe Street. But I more hung out where all the trans workers were. There'd be one or two girls, not many girls, because they'd get beaten up too. Everyone had their designated areas where you worked. You'd have all the trans sex workers on one side of the street, then on the other side you had Mainstreet, which was the punk rockers' place, so you had all these full-on boot boys and all that kind of scene over there. It was hilarious, but it was fun too.

Safe sex didn't exist. Well, I'm sure it did, but we certainly didn't practise it. You talked about, oh, you could get VD, but you never really heard of anybody getting it. I never had any STD checks, ever. Aids hadn't come out then, actually. It just came out as I was finishing, and I was like, oh, holy fuck, I've been in this high-risk group.

That whole safety thing – you had to really suss out very fast, am I safe? And just work with your gut instinct every time. And often, you probably weren't, in reality. Here you are, this young 14, 15-year-old, and you're with this fully grown male. They could be taking you anywhere. But often it was in the Auckland Domain, or parks, or back of buildings. You're hopping into cars, hopping into strangers' cars. I remember Sheila saying, 'Watch them, they'll circle around, they'll drive around. You've got to learn to see – oh yeah, that's a client. They've been around the block, they're coming around again, here they come, looking. Then they pull up. Just go up and ask them, do you want business?'

She'd point out – OK, undercover police are in these type of cars. Most of the time I got arrested, I'd be so off my face I didn't even remember. I'd be so out of it on pills, I'd wake up in the central police station – oh my god, where am I? I've just had this whole blackout. And that was often the way – I'd start off in these bars on K Road, then hit the streets, the nightclubs, and then you'd take more pills and more alcohol, and then be totally blacked out and not know what's happening or what's going on. Often I would wake up in Central and think, oh my god. What am I here for? It'd be for prostitution, soliciting, whatever. Shoplifting. You'd be out of it during the day – a lot of them would go on these sprees into the city, rolling shops and shoplifting, clothes and stuff.

Then after a while the police get to know you. So you'd start off your night and go into these bars, and then all the police come in with their paddy wagon, and they're like, 'You. Out. You're under age,' because they know you, and they know that you're 16 and you shouldn't be in the bar. They're grabbing you before your night's even started. So that was another reason to get out of here and get to Wellington and be somewhere different.

I got sent back to the boys' home – you're doing all this minor crime, so you get remanded there before you get sentenced. They said, 'Will you run away?' and I went, 'No.' I got back from court, and that's when I out the window and left. By this stage I was cracking it – OK, where are the nearest bogs? Go there, there'll be some old fag there, which there was. 'Take me to town, take me to Ponsonby.' I got them to take me back to this old house. There was this old queen there, Rangi. She was cool, she used to take in a lot of the young queens. So, 'Dress me up – I need a disguise, I need to earn some money.' I dressed up for the first time that afternoon, went out, cracked it. Hooked up with a girl that worked the streets, she was one of the few that did. She took me back to another queen's house, who she was staying with. Then we jumped on the Silver Fern and went to Wellington.

The police were looking for me, so I did drag the whole time, and lived it 24/7. It was kind of fun, and kind of exciting. It blew me away that, just because I'm dressed like this, all of a sudden these straight guys want to have sex with me. No way would they want to have sex with me dressed as a guy, but because I've got women's attire on and a different demeanour, there were different guys you could have sex with. There were definitely more clients, more money, and a different type of client. Before, they were gay or bisexual, but these ones identified as being straight. I found that mind-blowing.

Some didn't know until it was very obvious – 'Oh my god. You're not a woman.' 'No. I'm not.' Some knew, and some didn't – you could get away with it. But when it came to between your legs, that made it very obvious. But by then, a lot of them were like, 'Oh. Well. I've come this far,' and sort of didn't mind so much, they just finished. Anyway a lot of the time I wouldn't be letting the clients do stuff to me – it'd be me doing stuff to them, more oral and stuff, so they never got that far to find out what you are anyway.

The queens in Wellington, they were the first ones I'd ever met that had day jobs, that worked in offices or worked for the council. I'd only ever met trans that were sex workers. They were accepted more in society, in the community.

I believe it was because Carmen was so out there in her time. The police were totally different – they treated you differently. They weren't like the Auckland police, who were just out to arrest you and get you into those police cells, get you off the streets. In Wellington they just wanted to know who you were, and they were fine. Once they knew who you were they left you alone, as long as you weren't committing any crime. Well, actually you were committing a crime by soliciting, but that obviously was OK with them. They knew why you were out there, what you were doing, but they obviously didn't mind so much. You had those coffee lounges – the Evergreen in those days. We didn't have places like that in Auckland.

When you're working the streets you get to interact with other workers, so there's definitely that camaraderie, and that banter, being able to discuss clients or whatever issues you may be facing. And it's like a social thing, as well. It's like a night out, you're dressed up, you go out, even though you're working. You can be drinking, you can stop at a bar in between, or a café. It's like having fun on the job, especially if you like the work, like what you're doing.

I definitely get how some people's preference is to work the streets. There's definitely a buzz. There's that edge thing – that excitement of not quite knowing how the night's going to be, or who you're going to be interacting with, or how the client's going to be. There's definitely that excitement of working on the street. And it's hard and fast work – it's quicker. It's not like working in a parlour, having to do the whole hour. Sit with them for the hour and entertain, do the whole massage.

A lot of the sex workers I know from my early days are dead. Lots of them overdosed, lots of them committed suicide in police cells. A lot of them are not around any more, and some of the ones that are around are very fried – they kept living that same lifestyle, kept taking the amount of drugs we were taking. Our lives were real sex, drugs and rock 'n' roll – probably sex, drugs and disco. It was nightclubs and partying and drugs – you lived for that, really. As much money as you were making, it was going out just as quick. You were living hand to mouth. Or living in motels, so your money's going on that kind of lifestyle, and you're eating out and that kind of stuff. I saw from when I left the industry, and I would be away from Auckland for 10 years, then I'd come back for some family thing, have a look around, bump into different ones on K Road. And I could just see, whoa, they don't have their looks any more, they've really aged, or they're really fried, too much drugs. You're not able to have conversations with them, which is really sad.

I first came across stripping in Wellington – no queens that I knew of stripped in Auckland. All the strip clubs – women strictly worked in those. Some of the older queens had spoken of being able to strip in clubs in Auckland in the earlier days, but way before my time. In Wellington a lot of queens stripped up at Club Exotique, on the corner of Cuba and Vivian. So that was a buzz. It supplemented working on the streets, because you worked out of the streets right outside there. So it was easy, if you were bored or there wasn't much work – oh well, let's go up there. Plus you could get a drink because they had a bar.

When I first visited Wellington I stripped as a male. I had gone down there with another queen, so her and I would do a double act – she stripped as a female, I stripped as a male. As a guy you stripped down to a G-string. Then we would simulate having sex.

Then later I was working dressed as a female, so I had to learn to tape. I remember one queen trying to show me how to tuck. Oh my god! It was like, *no*. Pulling your penis right up the back so from the front it doesn't look like you've got a penis, it's tucked right up the back between your arse cheeks, basically. A lot of them didn't even tape. I used to tape for stripping, but a lot of them didn't need to. I don't know how it stayed there.

I didn't have breasts, so I never took my top off. I left the top on, but stripped down to having nothing below. And because they can't see a penis, they just assume you're a woman. Plus you've got the wig, the clothes, the mannerisms and the ra ra ra – and the dim lighting, of course. Love dim lighting.

Then I heard they needed strippers up in New Plymouth. So a group of us – there were three queens, myself and a woman, who were all sex workers – the five of us went up to New Plymouth. We got to this little hick town, walked into this strip club-slash-massage parlour. We were able to stay there to begin with, in the back of the strip club. The guy needed strippers. And that was kind of buzzy. It was like, oh my god, there's all these straight redneck farmers sitting out there in the audience, and they all think we're women. It was cool, but it was such a boring little town. I think I lasted two months.

I wore drag for six months in Wellington, until the police got me. Once the police found me and fingerprinted me, and knew who I really was, that's when my true identity came out, and my real age. I was looking at jail, then somebody told me, 'You could go to drug rehab.' I was taking lots of drugs. I thought, drug rehab sounds a better option than going to jail. So I quickly went about trying to make that happen. Then the court put me under the A&D Act[1] and sent me to Masterton, to the Tōtara Trust. I only had drag clothes – I thought, well, you ain't going to be cracking it in Masterton. Oh well, I don't need to be dressing up like this any more. So they had to go and buy me some boy clothes. I stayed there for six months, then I asked to be transferred to Auckland, to Odyssey House.

I got up there, and that was just horrible. There were no letters, no phone calls – worse than jail. And they had all these rules. I didn't like being with all these under-age people – I was used to being with adults. I lasted two or three days, then I walked out. I started working at night – I would dress up at night. I dabbled in it, and I got a job at the marae, tried to straighten my life out.

Then when I was 18 I did six months in prison for aggravated robbery, for something that had happened one or two years earlier. The lawyer said, 'They could have charged you with something less than that,' because aggravated robbery sounds like a full-on robbery, guns and stuff involved, but it was nothing like that. The guy was getting rolled in the toilets at this bar – I was there and I knew it was happening.

But that was enough – that was my real wake-up call. Up until then I'd only been on remand in Mt Eden. So once I got sentenced, it was like, OK, you're finally here. Is this what you want in life? The queens I knew were in and out of jail. They were more in jail than out, and that was their whole life. They were very institutionalised. I think they were in for drugs, maybe even robbery.

In a way it was good, because it did really wake me up. I thought, mmm, fuck no, I don't want to be here. This isn't the life I want. So I got out, I tried to stay away from the scene. I got a job at Auckland Hospital as an orderly. Then I slowly found myself getting pulled back into the city. I thought, I need to leave Auckland, I need to get away from the influences and everyone I know. So I went up north and lived with my cousin's family. People only smoked pot up there, people didn't do pills and stuff. So that was good – it got me off the pills.

---

1   The Alcoholism and Drug Addiction Act 1966.

Started learning Māori. There was no work up there – there were some full-time Māori courses going at the time, so I thought, OK, I'll go and do that.

I started trying to sleep with women, because that was what you did. Plus I was really put off from what I saw of the gay scene as a young fella, didn't like it. I thought, oh god, I don't want to be like those dirty old men, having to pay for sex. So I tried to go that way. But that was pretty traumatic. It was like, oh no, I'm not very good at this.

I lived up north for two years. I learnt lots of Māori, got all this sense of self, this identity, which was really huge for me. It was really cool. Then I came back to Auckland at 20 and slowly found myself coming back into the city, hooking back up with everyone I knew from the streets. I thought, no, I'm going to Wellington. So I jumped on a plane and buggered off to Wellington. I got me a job at the hospital. And that's when I met the mother to my kids, who was a nurse.

We were together about five years, had two kids. Then we split. I started going back with men, then I met this other woman, who blew me away. We had a really powerful relationship – we were together really fast. We did lots of full-on self-development stuff, looking into all our shit and all that stuff. Then I thought, who am I kidding? Once I realised, no, I'm not meant to be with a woman – once I made that decision, then all the turmoil just went.

Then I started changing how I conducted myself in life, too, in terms of being more honest and more honouring and all that kind of stuff. I was getting older, too. I did some university when I was in Canterbury – a bachelor of arts in Māori. Did two and a half years then dropped out, then I went and did massage training in Christchurch. I've done massage ever since.

I've been with Pete for 17 and a half years. Traditionally he would not have been the kind of guy I would have gone for. But I was at this stage wanting that inner person – it wasn't about the shell. I needed depth – before it was just all about what you looked like, and that was it. By this stage, I wanted to be with somebody nice. I wanted that inner person, that core of a person. And it was great – the universe provided this amazing man.

We've brought up all these kids. I've got two big kids whose mum I was with, then I've got two donor ones with a lesbian couple. They live with their two mums. Then they know that we're their gay papas, they come and stay with us. They've also got their gay nanas – their mum's mum came out about 20 years ago. It's so cool. Everyone's been totally into them, and their whānau totally embraced us as well when they were born. They're just beautiful women, really really cool. I look at our two little ones, they're home schooled, their horses are grazed next door, they have organic veges that grow in the garden. They live this really wholesome, beautiful life. Their mums are artists. They're very solid within themselves and very secure – you just see it in their little beings, how they are and how they conduct themselves. It's really cool. Then they come and stay with us in the city, they get a dose of the city life. It's been a real blessing – we've become a really cool extended rainbow whānau.

I started sex work again about three years ago. I got to Auckland, set up my massage clinic, and said, 'Pete, I'm bored. I've done this shit for 17 years. I've set up clinics wherever we moved. I'm bored. I've been thinking about doing sex work, what do you think?' He said, 'That's fine, if that's what you want to do.' So I set up a website, launched it, and it just went boom. Oh my god, the phone went hot. I was like, yep, I knew it. Closed the clinic down and simplified life – brought everything home. Thought, OK, I'm going to work from home now.

I did that for a year, then thought, oh, I wonder if I can do it as a tranny as well? Just in those lull periods. I found a guy online who did makeovers and photo shoots, so he did me up. I thought, OK, yeah, I can do this. So, launched that website.

Now between the two, I totally get what I want. And it's so interesting doing it now – not having to be off your face, not having to stand on the street corner, and being able to work privately, and it's all legal. I have dabbled in it on and off over the years, just bits and pieces, but not on this scale. I would place ads every now and then and get a few clients. In Christchurch you had to go into the police station and register before you could place ads in the paper. It was horrible.

Now I hardly advertise any more, because everyone's online these days, and my websites pull them in. You get your bunch of regulars, and then I've got a lot of overseas clients – they're all finding you online. I find a lot of people want to do it when they're away from home, or they're here on business.

I promote myself as a male escort, and I also do a nude sensual massage thing. The escort part is really just sex, people just wanting sex. The sensual massage is nude to nude – that's male clients, female clients, couples. I love working with the couples, I think the couples are so cool. I really love seeing that they're exploring sexuality together as a couple, no one's being dishonoured in the process. Often it's the male that's doing all this stuff and she doesn't know about it, it's all being done behind her back. So I love it when I see couples exploring this stuff together. It's straight couples mainly. Gay couples, well, they've got apps and things and can pick up other people. You've got sex-on-site venues that hetero people don't have access to.

I find people are opening up sexually these days. I don't know whether it's because of the internet. They can just push that button and see this other stuff, and 'Oh my god, they look like they're having fun. Maybe I might try that.' I get lots of guys that might have done a bit of teenage exploration, never done anything else the rest of their lives, but they've held onto that, that's been in the back of their mind for 30, 40 years, and they want to try that again. I find a lot of it's not even about sex, it's not even about ejaculation, it's just intimacy. They just want to be intimate, they want that human-to-human, skin-to-skin contact. Or it's just being held, it's being hugged. They may not even be able to articulate that, but I know that's what it is. It's that intimacy. It's not always sex.

I've had women clients, but the majority of clients are definitely male. Guys that have this idea of being a male sex worker, they just want to deal with females, well, the reality is, the market isn't there for that. I can count how many women I've had coming in. You've got to be really brave as a female, to come in to a male sex worker by yourself. It takes a lot of courage. But the ones I've had – really cool, really nice.

Then the tranny one – these guys want to try it out. Or they want to try being dressed up. They might do it privately with their wife's gear when she's not home. So I'm the first time that they try it outside of the home or with somebody else. Some turn up with their own gear, but I have a whole lot of gear that's purely for clients. Mine is separate – my toys and my stuff is for me, then the work stuff is totally for work. My work space is like that, too – I never want a crossover of clients' energy and stuff getting into my home. They walk in that door, then they're in that room over there, then there's a toilet and bathroom downstairs. So they never come into the living space of the house. I don't even use the same bathroom as the clients.

Energetically I want that separation. I always have, even as a massage therapist. If I ever worked from home, they had their own entrance. When I work, I cleanse the space after energetically. I'll burn oil, and I'll have a process of cutting the energy between me and that client. And that's as a massage therapist, and I do it with my sex work as well.

So I will do a finishing process – in my head, not outwardly. I always sweep over their body when I finish, and finish on the solar plexus reflexology point on the bottom of the feet to help reground them. Then I'll always wash my hands after. Then I'll change the linen, I'll open the windows so the air changes, and I burn oil so it cleanses the space. And shower, so I'm cleansed, the area's cleansed, then you're all fresh and it's all good for the next person.

And it works – it just flows. I see it, I see it in the outcome of the clients and the work I get. I don't struggle. It flows – I get what I want and get what I need. And it's perfect – now I have the energy that I can be of service to my whānau and to friends. It's such a nice balance. And I can go and do some voluntary work with the [New Zealand Prostitutes'] Collective, and give back in that way as well. And that's been really cool too, it's been really awesome.

Everything I do in my work is hugely healing. I believe some clients are conscious of that, and a lot of them are not and wouldn't be able to articulate it. Most of us haven't been brought up to engage in our feelings. And when you do this sort of work, you're coming in from a feeling base. It's very primal – getting people to let go of all the religion, all the indoctrination we've been brought up with, to actually just come into their bodies and feel what's going on, and to be OK with that, to honour it. I know that's how they feel afterwards – I can tell in the shift in their energy, and how they are when they come back, what they tell me.

I like to think that my service is done in a real professional manner, delivered from a place of light and honouring. I have clean linen. The premises are clean and tidy. And just putting my face on my website and putting myself out there, and not being a headless body – most people in the industry are headless bodies. You'll get to see their body, but you're never going to see their face, or it's smudged. I thought, nah, I want my face on there, I want my real name on there. This is who I am, this is what I do, these are my qualifications and this is what I'm charging. And charge high end for it and get it. I feel that my early years as a street-based worker, my diploma in massage therapy and everything I've done was my training to get me to this point.

To me it's my most healing work. In my massage training, you've got these contra-indicated areas, you don't touch the private parts of the person, they're all covered. Everything's got to be totally draped and you just uncover the area you're going to work on. Well, all that training's out the door for me now. I'm nude, they're nude, they're uncovered. Sometimes with the women clients, they prefer to start off covered, and I totally get that. Then eventually get to being uncovered, if they're OK with it. It always depends on what they're OK with. They set the boundaries and I just work with that.

Because of decriminalisation, as a worker you're so much more empowered. You can work, it is legal – that changes the energy that you're working with. You're not having to work under this shadow of darkness and seediness, actually it can be done in a place of light. It doesn't have to be all dodgy. It changes the energy immediately of what you're doing, the whole process.

And if I got into some sort of difficulty with a client, I feel that I can ring the police, and that the police will actually action it. I've seen that on the streets doing outreach with the collective – 'We've had this car going round hassling, we've rung the police.' And then the police have come round – they've come and asked us, have you seen this vehicle? So they're following up, and they're actually listening to them. No way would that have happened in my day. You wouldn't have rung the police.

I know for a lot of people, me being Māori is the attraction. Everything I do – it's just me, I am Māori. Everything, how you live and what you do. I know that is the attraction for a lot of people. They see that you are Māori. Even in my delivery, I suppose – I decorate with Māori art, so they're coming into that environment. I can have Māori music on – not always, depending on the client. The foreigners that are booking in find me online, they're booking before they even arrive in the country. I'm giving them a different Māori welcome to New Zealand than the Tamaki brothers are giving them in Rotorua. It's just them being able to come closer to somebody within the culture in another way. I don't purposely do that, but that's how it is.

People either resonate with that or they don't. I know as a therapist you're never going to appeal to everybody. It's an energetic thing, you attract your own clientele, and there's enough out there for everybody. I think it's just getting into that flow, and I believe a lot of that all comes back to how you conduct yourself in life. If you conduct yourself in an honouring manner and an honest manner, you're going to attract good stuff. But if you conduct yourself in a dishonest manner – and I have, I've lived a dishonest life and not been very nice – with that comes all the drama, comes all the worry and what-have-you. It's like, OK, I get it now. We all have that aspect, we all have that dark and light of ourselves – what part of yourself do you want to honour?

And I've worked it out now – I want nice stuff in my life, I want good stuff happening. So conduct yourself like that and be nice to people, and it comes back to you as karma, as pagan law. That's how it works, it's universal law – it just takes some of us longer to figure it out, and some may never.

I have no plan. I certainly didn't think I'd be doing it at this stage in my life, but here I am. I think, well, while I can, and I enjoy it, I will. I don't know how long you can keep doing this sort of work. Although you see some sex workers come into the collective who are in their sixties – all sorts of ages, and I think, well, they're still out there doing it. Who knows? I don't know.

Allan was interviewed at his Auckland home in September 2016.

JEANIE

JEANIE

I WAS BORN in 1958 and I grew up at Eastbourne, which is a very lovely place to grow up. My mother was also born and raised at Eastbourne.

My father was a grand old working-class Australian, and there was quite a lot of sorrow and hardship in his family. It was not an easy life, so I think he felt when he met my mother, who was on her big OE in Australia, that there could be a promise of something better. They got married in a registry office in 1953, and she arrived back home with this husband in tow – 'Hullo Mum, Dad, this is my husband,' and they had to have another wedding.

My father never really developed a successful career. He mainly did factory work, and worked with another local man as an electrical contractor. We always struggled financially – we were poor but happy, basically. And they were very creative, that's definitely where it came from for me.

A lot of quite wealthy people live in Eastbourne, so I was quite aware of this class thing. Our neighbours' daughter was the same age as me, and her dad worked in some quite high-up position in a major company. She always had new clothes, new shoes, lived in a really nice house and went on holidays and did all these things that we'd never do.

Later I went to Wellington Girls' College, which had a very good reputation. They still had streaming, and so I was in a class that did Latin and French rather than home economics. Mum always had slightly higher aspirations for us, and she got me right in that way, that I'd be better with more academic, intellectual, thought-provoking kind of stuff. I enjoyed school once I got into my stride and gained a bit more confidence. I did all the school productions, and acting and singing and violin and art history and all the things I liked.

I remember having a bosom pal. We used to call ourselves bosom pals because we had big bosoms. I made great friends with this girl, and in the sixth form we became quite rebellious. We got quite stressed out by University Entrance, whether we would be accredited, because we'd been a bit naughty in some classes. And also then the question was, what's going to become of us, what are we going to do? And we didn't have any idea, except we didn't want to be nurses or secretaries. I was already displaying independent thinking. I would have been utterly miserable being a secretary or a nurse. Both of us got accredited UE, but we still didn't know. We just didn't really know what to do.

At the end of the sixth form I got glandular fever, and when I went back the two subjects I wanted to do, music and Latin, were at the same time in the schedule. I went for a few weeks and then, it was the first big decision that I had to make myself in my young life, I decided not to keep going. I'd met my first boyfriend and he was a few years older than me. I felt like I'd moved on from school. I just thought, no, I'm going, I'm deciding to move on and enter the world. And it wasn't long after that that I moved out of home as well.

I got a job at London Bookshop, and I moved in with my boyfriend. I was mixing with academic people and people who were quite creative, a little bit alternative. I got a job at Unity Books for a while. There was a woman there who was a lesbian, and she really developed the whole women's literature section, including lesbian books.

I was going to be an opera singer, so I was having singing lessons. I decided I would do part-time work so I had more time to do my singing, and try to build a career in that. I did some waitressing and some artist's modelling, so I got used to standing in front of strangers with no clothes on.

From the age of about 19 to 21, 22, when I met my first girlfriend, I slept around quite a bit. I met lots of guys and had lots of flings. I came into my first experience in the sex industry from that, so it wasn't that difficult.

When I was 21 I went up to Auckland, because I had a singing teacher who'd moved up there. I wanted a piano and I was trying to work out how I could buy one, and the thought came to me that I could go and work at a massage parlour.

There must have been someone that I met who gave me the idea, because that's usually the way. Obviously I had a conversation that I no longer recall with someone who said that you could make quite good money, and you work in the evenings so you've got your days free to do other things. It all seemed quite ideal. I was kind of single-minded about what I wanted to achieve; I saw that maybe it wouldn't be too much work for a good return.

In 1979 in Auckland life was a lot cheaper. You could get away with just doing massages and having the odd bit of extras, the odd hand job. I had long, blonde, straight hair. I was a pretty girl, very pretty, and I wore all those 1950s and 60s frocks, though most of the time we sat round with a towel or no clothes so it didn't really matter that much.

I only worked for a few months. The singing teacher's life turned to custard; her husband was killed in a car accident. She absolutely fell apart, and she had some kind of serious ear problem that affected her hearing and her balance. There was no point in staying up there, so I came back to Wellington.

I decided not to pursue the singing any further, so again things were kind of wide open in my life – well, now what do I do? And I'd got involved with the Women's Centre, and met the woman who was to be my first girlfriend, so I was getting more and more into an understanding of feminism and lesbianism. I remember being sexually involved with a woman, and then going, 'OK, am I going to call myself lesbian or not? Am I going to take this label on board and all that it means?' I went through a process of informing myself and putting down all the pros and cons, and I read all the books that I could get my hands on about lesbianism.

Several of us, a mixture of straight and gay women, we started a punk band. And all the lesbians, who liked this very nice US west-coast, guitar, singing, lyrical, tuneful, oh-how-beautiful-it-is-to-be-a-woman kind of music, they hated our band, which was called Red Rag. Our road into feminism wasn't even just about lesbianism, it was more of an angry kind of stand-up-and-be-heard, and the vehicle for that was punk because it was easy to play, usually two or three chords, very straightforward. We used that band as a mouthpiece for our passions about things. We wrote songs about how men treated women and stuff like that, and we got into this whole thing about Māori land. We were quite passionate.

My second stint in the industry was in Wellington, for a few months in late 82 or early 83. We'd needed another guitarist for the band and we found Nikki, who was a very creative and fiery individual, very political and an activist. She and I got together; the band fell apart and we started another one. And then Nikki and I decided to go to Australia, then to Europe.

I had some money saved, but Nikki was not very well organised with money. She was aware that I'd worked in the sex industry a little bit, and she decided that that would be a way for her to make more money. She had a paid job at Women's Refuge, so it was all a very odd combination of factors, working in the sex industry and working in the Women's Refuge.

We had a friend who had worked, which may have been part of what inspired us. She treated it like just a day job, doing quite a lot of afternoon shifts, rather than evening ones. She had this love-hate relationship with it, but she'd normalised it. We ended up working at the same establishment, the Sultan's Tent.

I didn't really need to, I was all right for money and I didn't really want to. But I decided to go and work there as a receptionist, just to be supportive. So I occasionally did outcalls, if they wanted a blonde or something. I went to hotel rooms a couple of times. The people who ran the parlour are pretty faceless. I don't remember any of those people. What I remember is the women – there was a real sense of solidarity.

There's a lot of waiting around, and that's where you have the most interesting conversations and find out these are just ordinary women. They happen to be doing sex work, but they're not necessarily labelling themselves sex workers or prostitutes. They're just doing this work, and they have real lives, and some of them have kids and are trying to make things work. There's a solidarity amongst the women. The street is a very different thing, it's every girl for herself, but in the establishments there's a solidarity.

There's that idea that guys want young women, but there were women who were a bit older, more like 40. Their skill was in their personalities and how they dealt with their clients. Then there was the likes of me and Nikki. We were pretty rough-and-ready-looking. These were not necessarily sophisticated women who worked in these places – they were just doing it because it suited them for various reasons.

You had to work without any clothes on, that was a thing that you've got to get used to. Since you've chosen to display yourself only to other women, you've got to make a bit of an adjustment and have a reasonable level of comfort in your own body to be able to work skin to skin, touching people. Later I worked in the film industry. I always worked in costume, so you're dealing with people's looks, but I could never get my head around doing hair and makeup, touching people's faces and hair. I found it a bit yukky.

The Sultan's Tent was in Willis Street, upstairs. In the light of day it was pretty shabby and gloomy, dark carpets and dark walls. There were lots of bean bags where people sat round wearing nothing but a towel. I was in the reception area, putting on my best manner and answering the phone. I learnt how to make bookings and who was available and what they did and what people liked. People would book for a massage, and there was this whole kind of double-speak. It was understood on both sides that they were coming for a massage but whatever else they got up to was up to them. You'd ask if they had a preference in terms of women, usually to do with what colour their hair was, and if they were regulars they would ask for a particular person.

It was all quite kind of cosy and down-home in a way, people who came there regularly, guys who knew the women. My other friend had been there a while and there were people who just quite liked her. I think she kept a very clear separation, but they wouldn't have minded going to the movies with her. And there's this whole other side to being a hooker, you were a bit of a social worker, and a lot of these guys were lonely or inadequate in some way, they weren't Casanovas at all. They were just pretty ordinary guys with quite a few inadequacies who wanted a bit of company.

For me it was about the slightly fascinating, slightly thrilling thing of going, 'I can do this because I'm free and I'm an anarchist and I'm all these things.' We didn't want to admit to there being any boundaries or limitations on our lives. I was 23, 24; Nikki was younger, 19 or 20. Rebellion was part and parcel of our lives – everything was about being rebellious. We would do graffiti campaigns against people who we thought were doing the wrong thing. The number of political slogans that would appear on walls around Wellington – I used to say to Nikki, 'You need to disguise your handwriting.' Everything we did was radical and rebellious. We were very earnest about class and race and this and that, and being lesbian and being separatist. Everything was categorised.

We brought the whole topic of sex work into our circle. These were women who, even if they hadn't been lesbians, came from the sort of family backgrounds where they probably wouldn't have even thought about it. Certain people in any group lead the way in certain ways, and we were doing that, presenting an idea that no one had really thought of. It breaks down a barrier of intolerance – people go, 'This thing exists, there's no need to judge it or judge my friends for doing this.' Then the next step for some was, well, I need to make some money for whatever reason, would I entertain the idea of it? And some do and some don't. There were a few that gave it a go, but most probably decided against it.

We were a bit nervous about what some of the radical lesbians would think about us working there, but our friends were amazingly supportive. One friend was into cooking really healthy food, so she'd bring all these healthy cooked meals for us. She was like, 'This is one thing I want to do to support you – there's a perception that if you're doing this sort of thing, you drink a lot and eat takeaways and you don't really look after yourselves. You've got to at least have good food.' Which was fantastically supportive. She was experimenting with vegetarian and vegan food, live food and lots of bean sprouts, very healthy. She'd come in and, 'Here's your dinner.'

Nikki had a problem with more radical separatist friends of hers, who found it very hard to forgive her for working in the sex industry. One woman basically slapped her in the face. 'How could you do this?' She was one of those very fierce scary little dykes, and she was very purist, she would have lived a pretty separatist life. I didn't have much sympathy for those women at the time, but now I can see it was completely shocking and distressing for them.

But you're not choosing to be degraded. From a feminist perspective you're choosing to be empowered, because you're saying, I can do this, it doesn't water down any of my other strong passionate feelings about women or anything. We were like, 'No, we're not being degraded, we're actually strong and powerful and proud.' This woman was like, 'You're supposed to be setting an example, because you're really bright and political and committed to the causes, and then you go off and do this.' It was the perfect example of the two worlds clashing, not mixing.

It wasn't a problem having a partner who was a sex worker, though it did become an issue later. In Wellington there were other problems that were more to the fore. The amount of alcohol coloured our lives in every aspect, right up until when we left. It was like this solid drink session that lasted about a week. All sorts of things went absolutely haywire because of that and because we were pretty immature as well.

So we went to Australia. In the meantime I'd got involved with someone else, which was all very tumultuous and messy. I left Nikki in Melbourne and went to Sydney to meet this other woman, Stacey, who'd been a sex worker and was also a drug addict. She'd worked in places like Coober Pedy, where they do the opal mining and there's a very big brothel.

When Stacey lived in Wellington she'd been on a methadone programme really she was still an addict, she hadn't confronted and dealt with the roots of her addiction. She had extensive experience in the drug world in Kings Cross, and worked to try and help drug-addicted people. I always felt a bit guilty because I said, let's meet in Sydney. It wasn't my fault, but she did get back into drugs, and I was so stupid and naive, I gave her all my money. It all got spent on drugs and it was all this stuff about how she would buy this heroin and on-sell it so she could make some more money. She wasn't on-selling it at all, she was just using it, but she did protect me from it. She said, 'I don't want to be a person who gives you heroin. I'm not having that on my conscience.'

To me she was a fascinating person, the stories she told, the drug raids in Kings Cross and all these addicts living in these houses and you'd come home and find somebody dead, which was really awful, but I had this morbid fascination with this world. A friend of hers was still in Coober Pedy, so she decided that she'd go there. I bought her a bus ticket, this huge big long trip, and she said she would get things sorted and then she'd let me know and I could go and meet her there. And I never heard from her again.

She didn't want me to get involved in that world, and I was protected – I've always been protected. She knew she was being drawn back into it. When I tried to call, I got the friend and got warned off. 'She'll let you know when you can come,' and she never did, and I had to let that go. Then I was like, oh shit, I haven't got any money. She had given me a little cardboard matchbox and it had the name of an establishment and the phone number, and so I rang them, went to visit and got a job. It was a brothel in Surry Hills, with no signage or anything, just a blue light. Then I contacted Nikki and she came to Sydney.

I'd got a little flat with Stacey in the wops of Sydney, a further-out suburb. Pretty promptly once Nikki and I started working in this brothel, we actually moved upstairs. It was one or maybe even two terrace houses. The top floor was empty, so we went and stayed up there with a mattress on the floor. We never properly got away from the place. We started going a bit stir crazy, so we used to make a big effort to go sightseeing during the day before we started work. There's pictures of us on the ferry cruising round the harbour and the Sydney Harbour Bridge, going to various beaches and having fish and chips, just trying to get out of the place because otherwise you felt like you were always there.

During the day there were a couple of women who worked there and did B&D, bondage and discipline stuff, which was a whole other territory. They were very experienced and skilled, and I was really envious because they had the most fabulous leather outfits. It was all streets ahead of anything in Wellington.

And then it would become a more straight brothel, and you'd sit round in this kind of little lounge area. It was a whole different kettle of fish compared to Wellington; we had to go and buy frocks, you had to be well presented. I remember sitting round knitting fingerless gloves, and then you'd hear the doorbell and I'd shove the knitting underneath the cushion and 'Hullo.' The guy would walk in and there was a 'pick me, pick me' sort of thing. It was quite competitive in a way, and I did well because I was always quite fresh-faced – I had short hair, blonde, a couple of pretty dresses.

But Nikki found it difficult, she was not doing well at all. She was not typical-looking, and it wasn't like in Wellington. In Sydney they would pick you on what you looked like. Actually Nikki had the most fabulous body, gorgeous, but she had this funny little face with a turned-up nose. And she was a jeans-and-singlets kind of girl. We had to get her to try and put on makeup and not look ridiculous and lurid. The thing was to find things she could wear that she looked OK in and felt comfortable wearing, and bring out her style in a way that some clients were attracted to.

She's quite friendly and warm, and she liked to talk with customers, so it was a case of finding the ones who liked that. I didn't want to make a relationship with them, I didn't want to get close. I think once or twice I had repeat clients, but I preferred to have a different guy every night and not get involved. Whereas for her, that was the only way it could work, that she made a connection. They ended up finding her quite lovable. Well, she was. One older Chinese man used to take us out to Chinatown; she'd say, 'I want my friend to come as well,' and we'd have these amazing big feasts. In the end he kind of wanted to marry her, but she didn't want to, funnily enough!

A Greek man owned the brothel, Con. He was good actually, he didn't want his workers on drugs. I remember one beautiful young Eastern European woman who was getting more and more into drugs and he was very concerned about her. There was another woman there who had worked in different sorts of establishments – she was quite a successful sex worker, more professional than I'd been used to. She gave us a lot of help – she'd teach us how to get men to get their rocks off quicker, you don't want them pumping away at you for ages.

It was really organised; you had to check the guys' dicks to make sure they were clean, you had to get them to wear a condom. If you weren't sure you could go and get Con to check the client, and the guy would be squirming. Guys of course would argue and argue and argue that they didn't need to wear a condom.

Some guys want all sorts of stuff, and you could create your own limits. I had a guy who wanted a golden shower, where you pee on them. I did that once, but it was messy and disgusting. We had to put plastic on the bed. A brown shower you poo on them, which is going a bit far for me.

We used the Dutch cap, diaphragm, as contraception. It always felt a little bit uncertain. You had to use spermicide, and you had to reapply it, but you couldn't take the cap out, so you just squirted more up there. It was always a bit kind of, oh my god, what if? The good thing about a diaphragm was that if you had your period it would contain the blood as well.

So dealing with that was all a bit messy, and there were things that Nikki was prepared to do that I felt very unhappy about. She was struggling to get clientele, so she said she would go in for being spanked or strapped or something. I was really uncomfortable with it, and things became difficult between us, being in a relationship and living upstairs, and having this slightly weird competitive thing.

We did experiment with selling ourselves as a lesbian couple. But most of the guys didn't want you to get too involved in each other – they were like, what about me? I remember one guy was a voyeur, he wanted to watch us. Actually we were more comfortable with just titillating each other a bit, but then going back to him. We were shy and awkward about fully getting into it with each other while he watched. So it pressed a lot of buttons, and the strain and tension between us got quite acute. And the Greek guy's business partner was this really sleazy Italian guy. He didn't think twice about, 'Oh, there's two lesbians living upstairs, I'll go and get into bed with them after hours.' That was really revolting, and we said, 'Look, this is not appropriate.' I think eventually Con sorted it out, but it was ridiculous. I was getting really stressed out, Nikki was getting pretty stressed out, and there was this other young woman slipping into drugs. It was a pretty crazy scene.

One woman was very kind; I remember when we got a bit over living in a brothel, she said, 'Just come and stay at our place at Bondi Beach and have a bit of light relief.' She was very experienced as a prostitute and she had a lot of wisdom and compassion for younger women. She'd say, 'Oh, you need a bit of a break.' She and her partner had this land up in the rainforest, it was just gorgeous. She had a little girl as well, and that's why she worked, because she was building this whole other life up in the rainforest. It was a really good perspective – I do this work because I can and I'm quite good at it and I don't mind it, and it helps me to build the life I want. It was a really good positive role model actually.

I decided to put a time limit on it. We were planning to move on to Alice Springs and then to Darwin. We had heard that you could get from Darwin to Bali really cheaply. I said, I'm going to leave, no matter how much or little money I've made, I'm leaving by this time in August. So that spurred us on to make as much money as we could.

I wanted a time limit partly to stick to our plan, and partly because there's a really seductive, beguiling side to that work, even if you don't like it much. You can end up getting hooked into it, if you are doing OK with it and making money – it's intriguing, there's a fascination. I could see that it wasn't overall or long-term beneficial for my life, and I didn't want to get caught up in it for an extended length of time. So a time limit meant we just carried on with our plans, and on a kind of self-preservation level we didn't get sidetracked or stuck in Sydney being hookers.

I didn't think it was a particularly healthy lifestyle. It wasn't just the sex, although there's always that little nervous apprehension about will I get pregnant or will I get sick. It's a lifestyle associated with staying up all night, drugs, alcohol. Although we tried to eat properly, you can get into some quite bad habits. And we were in Sydney, the food you could get, you could easily just live on all sorts of exotic takeaways and luscious cakes with cream. It was a whole new world for us.

We basically just went, we're going to work until August and then we'll hand in our notice and go. And, simple as that, we just stopped. We shed whatever things we couldn't carry, because we were hitchhiking, and off we went. We had this big meandering journey across land and sea. We decided that we would do the whole trip from Darwin to Thailand entirely by land and sea, no flying, that was quite adventurous. It took us a good part of a year to get all the way from Wellington to Europe.

We went to London and then to Amsterdam, and I went back and forward a bit. Nikki felt more comfortable in London, but I ended up staying in Amsterdam. I was an illegal immigrant, and that coloured everything that I then did, the whole life I lived.

It was a really quite extraordinary lifestyle. It was all squatting; I never paid for accommodation the whole time I lived in London and Amsterdam. There was a strong squatting culture, and a strong lesbian separatist culture – you could live completely separatist in Amsterdam and not feel you're missing out on anything. There was a great music and arts culture, and you could get anything you wanted on the street. You just had to go where the rubbish nights were in different areas. We used to go to the market and pick up the food off the ground at the end of Saturday.

Amsterdam was making a bid for the Olympic Games, so they were trying to clean up the inner city. There were these big invasions by the anti-squat police who'd try and break their way in. There were enormous gatherings protesting about them cleaning out the squats, because there was nowhere else to live for a lot of people. I couldn't really get involved, because I was an illegal immigrant, so I couldn't get caught.

The choice to go on the game in Amsterdam was totally about how to make enough money to survive. Again I really put limits on it. I didn't want to do it – I did it as little as I possibly could to make a bit of money.

In Amsterdam it's all canals with little bridges; there's very little car traffic in those streets, and it's very pretty. There were a couple of bridges where the sex workers would stand. The other phenomenon in Amsterdam was the girls in the windows. My friends and I considered that to be pretty demeaning, we had a sense of pity for those women who did that.

So I found out which bridges you could stand on, and if it was cold then there was a little bar, small and quite crowded, where you could pick up guys. My friends and lovers would come and support me, which really touched and surprised me. I know some of it was curiosity, but they were there, and they were looking out for me in a way that I was always really appreciative of.

So I used to just stand on the street and pick up guys that way, or sometimes through this bar. The guys knew where to go – there were these fuck hotels, cheap hotels. The guys would pay the proprietor, and some of the proprietors would look out for you a bit, make sure that if you went in there you came out again. They were pretty rough people, and obviously the number one interest was collecting the money, but it was probably in their best interest to make sure that no one was murdered in their establishment. They were very basic, slightly grubby, tawdry places, but it was definitely safer to go there than to go to someone's place. I would never have entertained that idea for a moment.

Then this battle invariably would ensue about getting the guy to put a condom on. You didn't have the protection of an establishment where anyone could reinforce anything; you had to use your own wits and wiles. Once they were aroused and then you were like, 'Here's the condom,' and they were like, 'No,' you'd start getting dressed again and they'd soon relent. They didn't want to wear condoms at all, guys were completely head-in-the-sand about that.

One of the things that became clear was that I was largely in control of my own business. There was no establishment, there was no framework supporting you, you had to make it work yourself, but I could decide for myself how little or how much. I didn't have to pay money to anybody. A couple of times guys, usually Arabic or dark-skinned, would approach you and offer you some sort of drugs, 'You want some hashish, you want some blah

blah,' and then they would start pressuring you. I realised very quickly that they wanted to control me, they wanted to be my pimp. Of course I didn't want that.

I got warned off a few times by the other workers. I must have been quite basic looking, I didn't dress up, mostly just tried to keep warm, but I looked really clean, I wasn't a drug addict. A couple of the other girls were rough as, they had sores on their faces, and they resented me. I was warned off: 'You shouldn't be here.' I was a foreigner as well, and I was like, whoa, that's quite heavy. It wasn't the guys that I felt threatened by, just the pimps and the other girls. Every time I went out there I was on guard – take a deep breath and just do it, but be really alert and watchful.

One time I was sure I was pregnant and I had to find out where to go to get tested. There were places for sex industry workers to go and get health tests, but I was paranoid that because I was an illegal immigrant they would ask me questions that I couldn't answer, so it was very fraught in that way.

I worked on and off for a few months. I remember saying to myself, I'll just go once or twice a week, if I can just earn enough money, because we really could live on very little. We were squatting and living in that urban survival mode, which was a fabulous way to live. My enduring memory of Amsterdam is these amazing raggle-taggle processions, women and dogs and stuff, off on whatever mission we were on, to perform somewhere or do something and collect some stuff on the way or the way back. We always had these missions and we were out there, bands of us. It was almost medieval in a way.

I'd always played music, and me and three or four other women started a street band, a busking band. I was on the piano accordion and singing, and somebody on a little electric guitar and an acoustic guitar with a mike, someone playing the bass and someone on percussion. It was actually a much more wholesome way to make some money. That took over, and I was like, yeah, I'll just leave this whole sex industry thing behind and move on.

The last part of my stay in Europe I was in London, because it was easier for me to get work there and get a work visa. Because I was able to work I didn't bother with the sex industry. Other friends were doing it, but I didn't. It was a different kind of environment from Amsterdam.

When I think about why I ended up doing this work, part of it was that whether I was in New Zealand or wherever I was, I was outside mainstream culture. I was always guided by some idea that we were anarchists, and anarchists just did things the way they saw fit. I wasn't really referring to any social norms or conventional ideas of what a young woman's trajectory in life was meant to be. A lot of choices in my life, including working in the sex industry, were taking being self-determined to absurd lengths.

It was a kind of idealism that allowed us to do it, and reconcile it with being strong feminists. We weren't completely separatist, but we had lots of separatist ideals and politics – and we really were passionate about the rights of women, lesbians being accepted in society. We had nothing to do with men except that we happened to fuck them for money, a quite bizarre mix of things. We would go, oh yeah I could fuck you and you can pay me money – it was based on an angry kind of attitude, like we can do this because we're radical dykes so we can do anything.

Any illusions about it being easy money were quickly dispelled. It's not easy money at all. It's neither physically nor emotionally particularly easy. I don't think I ever really got comfortable with the actual job of taking my clothes off and massaging some stranger who'd taken his clothes off and trying to get him to get his rocks off. It was kind of icky a lot of the time, messy, and you were on guard because guys were always very concerned that you were enjoying it. So you have to pretend, because in reality, not particularly. I only remember one guy in the whole time who actually knew how to fuck in such a way that you got really turned on and had an orgasm. Most of them didn't have the skill, that's probably partly why they were there.

I think some of them were emotionally involved, and that was awkward because you weren't going to give it to them. The most level playing field is where the guy just wants to have sex, wants to have a good time, there's no feeling coming from him that he wants anything more from you. He can isolate – this is sex, she's a nice-looking lady with nice tits and I'm going to pay her money, we're both going to have an OK time, I'm going to get my rocks off and then I'm gone, that's it.

My good instincts were that I would always put time limits on how long I'd stay involved. I was never interested in it being a career. I recall one woman in Sydney who actually liked it, it seemed to be kind of a vocation for her, she liked having sex. I never felt that about it, ever. The most I could say was I'd grit my teeth and do it because it served a purpose. I always had some other objective in my life that I felt strongly about, so I could go, I just have to do this, it's a means to an end.

I always tried to work out, well, is it OK that prostitution exists? In the end there's no black or white, right or wrong. We were coming from the feminist, lesbian, anarchist, alternative-type place, so we tried to make sense of the whole thing from those perspectives. That's different from your junkie on the bridge in Amsterdam, who's only concerned about staying out of trouble and where the next fix comes from.

Not that I ever came to any concrete final kind of conclusive statements. Ultimately I don't think there are any, because we're talking about so many deep things to do with sexual bonding. Not all guys who go to a brothel in Sydney are hopeless down-and-outs with no other options. They must be relatively successful to even afford to go to such an establishment – you can't tell me they're all single men who are shy of forming emotional bonds with women so they go and buy sex. There's a whole variety of different needs, there's no one motivation, so I don't think you can say there's one right or wrong.

I felt it was sad both that men needed to buy sex, and that there weren't jobs, there wasn't work I could do that involved a better use of my talents and skills. I don't even think I was particularly good at sex. There were other things I could do a hell of a lot better. Around that time I was reading Elizabeth Lynn, who wrote lesbian fantasy novels about this wonderful society. I always think about those more ideal societies or communities where there's absolutely no need on anybody's part to turn sex into a monetary transaction.

Sex for me comes out of a relationship and it's about a bond, so what was I trying to find out through allowing myself to go into this area where sex is a transaction? I don't know. I had never had a lot of casual sex, apart from earlier days when I had casual sex with men. I always preferred to get involved and have a relationship. With women I was always drawn towards the deeper, of which sex was a part. That possibly made it more awkward for me as a sex worker, that casual sex was actually not natural to me.

I didn't have a boyfriend anytime when I was doing sex work. I think in some heterosexual relationships it would be very difficult. Somehow in the lesbian world it was a whole step removed, because the ways we related to each other were removed from the heterosexual world. It distanced it somehow.

In my own life, in my personal relationships, it was difficult – the most difficult was when we were working in Sydney and were living upstairs. That was the most intensive sex, we're having sex every night, sometimes two or three times a night with customers, and so it definitely impacted our desire. At times I felt a bit unclean or soiled. For me there was always something quite pure about lesbian sex and so you didn't want to sully it. I couldn't easily go from being with men for money to being with my girlfriend, it wasn't an easy transition at all. It all got too close.

The way I think now, I try and live from the heart. The mind can do all sorts of things. It can go, 'Oh yeah, just compartmentalise, I'm doing this because I want to make money and it's a better return for my time than working in a bookshop or waitressing, it suits me because ABC.' So you do all those justifications, and then something that is deeply felt, to do with your own personal relationships, you just put that in a little protective box in your heart and you somehow keep them separate, with more or less success. Sometimes I could, sometimes not so well. I know there were times when I'd feel very vulnerable, and I was just like, 'Oh no, not today, I can't do this right now.'

I did entertain the idea again in the 90s, and I went to see the Prostitutes' Collective. It's good because it gives people the information and the options, it's all laid out, but for me it was too much. I've got to do this, I've got to do that. That's one way the world has really changed – you can Google anything now, you can find out. In this climate that we live in now every single thing is commercialised, you need to have your CV and the right wardrobe and the right marketing. Everything is covered, you can go onto some website and find out how to put a condom on your client properly or where to go if you need to get contraception or counselling or advice or your rights as a prostitute. I don't think I would have ever even entertained the idea if someone had told me all these things to do with the law and blah, blah, blah. I couldn't be bothered. I guess there's different personalities, those of us who read up about everything before and those who don't.

I'm a creative person, and nine out of 10 of us struggle financially. If we choose to be true to our creativity and try and make a living out of it then we invariably struggle. The last time that I entertained the idea of the sex industry would have been about five years ago – wouldn't it be nice if I could just make some money, and it wouldn't take up my whole life to do it. And look at me now, I work 30 hours a week at a costume hire company and don't make enough money to live on. It's no wonder it's sometimes an alluring idea, the hourly return is way better.

I had this idea that there must be guys out there who like mature women, not unattractive, just need to scrub up a bit, get my hair done, etcetera. I talked to a friend, and she went, 'Nah, you're dreaming, they want young ones. They want them in their twenties or younger, they don't want old girls like us.'

I had a look at this online escort agency and sure enough, there was nobody over about 35. They were all gorgeous. I don't know how much airbrushing goes on, but perfect skin, gorgeous hair, beautifully made up, lovely long fingernails. They were all skinny.

You never completely close the gate. If I met someone who I could stomach being with – but it would have to be more than just him getting his rocks off. I'd have to get taken out to dinner at the very least and probably to the opera or something. He'd have to be cultured, he'd have to be mature, worldly wise, and he'd have to pay me and pay me well. It would have to be discreet, and he'd have to like a mature woman who's got a few warty bits these days, not perfect any more, but still not too bad. Maybe that is more an ideal than an actual possibility. I don't know.

I would go with it, if I could get paid somewhere in the vicinity of $500 once every week or couple of weeks. Maybe I'm dreaming, I don't know, or maybe that's a blueprint for how the sex industry should operate, that it's not an industry so much, that you can make discreet arrangements.

I don't feel pushed into it, but I feel like there's lots of potential in life and that's just one potential solution. It's probably more likely that if I meet a man or a woman, and they're better off than me, they would naturally just feel happy to support me. I don't know whether this other thing is just a bit of a fantasy. I don't know if men even exist like that anymore. Probably not in my world anyway.

I don't really talk about it today. At work, and in the Buddhist organisation I'm involved in, I haven't even talked about being lesbian. It's not that I feel uncomfortable or that I'm hiding anything, it's just that there are parts of my life that are not relevant to that situation. I don't see the point of shocking and distressing people. Especially as you get older, there are so many different layers and facets to your life and things that you've experienced in the past that you really choose who you share that with.

It's deepened my understanding of life. I don't have any regrets, even if now I would have no interest whatsoever hanging out in some crowded little bar in the red-light district of Amsterdam. I think that all experiences have kind of added to me as a person. I haven't always felt entirely free and easy about it, it's perplexed and disturbed me at times, but I've never actually gone, 'I wish I'd never done that.'

Jeanie was interviewed at her Wellington home in February and March 2013.

MISTY

MISTY

I WAS BORN in Timaru in 1966, so I'm heading into my late forties. I've got three half-brothers and a half-sister, and Mum was Mum and Dad, all my life. I don't know who my father is. We moved around a bit, Christchurch and Timaru, back and forth.

I had a few things go down when I was younger, just normal stuff, older men interfering with you and that. A couple of foster homes I ended up in, I got messed with there, though not full penetration. Thirteen was when I lost my virginity. I also had gay interludes with the babysitter. And me and my cousin – she was also getting interfered with, so me and her used to do stuff when we were seven or eight. It was just normal, just the way it was. And lots of little things at school with boys – 'Show me yours and I'll show you mine!' Or 'Don't kill that snail!' 'Show me your hooey!' 'OK, give me that snail!' Yay, I saved a snail because I showed my pussy to a boy. Then the boys got onto that … In the end I cottoned on, and started bashing them.

I had trouble at school, because I had not very good spelling, reading, writing, the basic stuff. I had dyslexia as well, and they didn't pick it up for a long time. I was very good at art and running and sporty things. I had a hard time with educational stuff, and I was expelled at 13. Mum shipped me up to Christchurch because I was getting into a bad crowd, so she wanted me out of Timaru. I was boarding and working at Lane Walker Rudkin, packing socks. That was a cool wee job. I lied about my age, they thought I was 16, but I was quite mature for my age.

Then I worked at Tate Electronics, then I did waitressing and bar work. I wanted to go to England and do my big OE, so I had three jobs for about two years and saved up the money for my ticket. I headed to London; I had a one-way ticket and 100 pounds. I survived over there for a couple of years, and came home not as full of myself and arrogant as you are at 21. It was the best thing I ever done, was go and explore the world.

I had a few jobs when I got home, then I was working at Canterbury Sea Products in the oyster sheds, making big money. I enjoyed it, didn't mind offal and smelly fish and that. The boys were really good, we had a good crew. When I came back from London, I'd saved up hundreds of pounds, and back in the day 100 pounds was worth 300 New Zealand dollars. I had about four or five grand, I was rich. I went car-hunting and found this little Morris Minor convertible 1951, forest green. And that little car got me into a little bit of trouble with the law. I had no registration, I got fines – I got three or four grand's worth of debt with that little car.

I had been making good money, but then the place started going under. Our overtime stopped and we had short weeks. We noticed a shortage of teabags and toilet paper – signs of a place in trouble. I got court things for the fines, and Mum was getting bailiffs knocking on the door. It got out of control, and I had to find some money quickly. I didn't want to ask the family – none of my family have money, Mum was always struggling. I thought, what am I going to do? Prostitution! I'd always been fascinated by the industry anyway. I'd always loved sex, loved men, never had any issues with them.

I just opened the phone book and went, bang – it was a place called Femme Fatale. I went in, did the interview, got the job and got into parlour work. That was when I met Anna Reed [see page 39]. Anna was a great influence, and that parlour was really cool. It was run by a woman – I stuck to women operators because I thought men just want to try and fuck you as well.

The boss seemed OK, and they told you about all the safe sex stuff, condoms and that. I practised safe sex anyway, because I never wanted to get pregnant, that was my biggest fear in life. I still haven't, and I'm not going to, so that's good. It was a very high-class parlour, so I was lucky I didn't just fall into one – the universe guided me. I worked there for about five years, then I worked at Felicity's, another parlour, then I worked in Auckland and Wellington and Dunedin – I travelled all round. Then Mum got sick, and I came back to Christchurch and settled at Femme Fatale again.

In a place in Dunedin I got into a bit of B&D, which was interesting stuff. It was quite a specialised area. I went to Dunedin and got trained with a mistress down there. She had a parlour with a dungeon and she showed me the ropes. There was another girl at Femme Fatale who did B&D as well, so her and me hooked up. We got the dungeon rocking, we were the top girls for quite a few years. Cops, judges, all sorts of people. Priests. One of my regular clients was a priest – he'd come every Wednesday at three o'clock to the back door and I'd grab him with his collar on his knees and drag him through. Catholics, of course – poor bastards. They got sexually screwed up – 'Don't touch it! It's not natural! You'll go to hell!' Of all my B&D clients, 70 per cent were Catholics. And 20 years ago, the old boys were still coming through that heavy-duty system of nuns and boarding schools and whips. Which is quite sad – it wrecked them psychologically. And it's a power thing – what is the Catholic church about? Dominance, power, dictatorship. Some of those men weren't allowed to talk about sexuality – they'd have an orgasm and get freaked out by it. And that's sad!

I worked in Aussie a few times – every now and then I'd fling over there for about five days. I'd stay with a friend in Melbourne and do a couple of nights at a parlour. It's a different ball game over there – they're all plastic. Well, they've got their boobs done, and their Botox, all that sort of stuff. I like it, but I'm one of those natural hookers, I don't want to go and get the boob job. When it's over, it's over, you know? Over there the clientele are more metropolitan and the girls are very professional. They do their nails and hair – they put a lot out to get a lot in, investing in themselves. High maintenance. I'm not a high-maintenance chick, I haven't got boobs done and don't get Botox, I don't even get my nails done. I'm a naturalist – I'm a bit different. Most other girls do all that. A lady I know at the moment is going to Thailand to get her boobies done. She gets Botox and that – she's beautiful, immaculate. I'm not into boobie jobs and Botox, I don't trust that. Maybe I'll wait till I'm getting up there, in the 65 department – that's when you're going to need it.

Everyone likes something different, and a lot of guys liked the natural country New Zealand chick – we're renowned for being like that. Down to earth with squidgy boobies. Asians liked me quite a lot because I'm short and blonde, blue eyes.

I worked in the industry for about eight years, then got hooked up, fell in love with a lovely man in my late twenties and left the business. I took a couple of years to break away. I was always studying stuff – I went to night school and got an accredited diploma in beautician stuff. Got into that briefly, didn't like it, so I studied a lot of spiritual stuff. I've got diplomas in aromatherapy, crystal healing, reflexology, reiki. Prostitution was still the work I seemed to like the best – it was freer, I suppose. Freedom is the thing. In the parlour days you had to be there certain shifts, but now it's a lot freer. I've done my time in factories, clocking in, clocking out. I didn't hate it, I was grateful to have a job, but it's hard work. If you can be your own boss, isn't that what life's about?

When I stopped working I studied quite hard out – I did a business course designing art, because I was always quite a good artist. That was going good, then I had an aneurysm. I was 29 – bang! The man I was with at the time did CPR, saved my life. I had a massive haemorrhage in my head and it took all my left side out. All my creativity. I couldn't read or write when I came back after the operation. I ended up in hospital for about a month – they did nine hours' surgery on my brain.

Ray looked after me. He had a good job. I had a year where I had to learn to read and write properly, walk properly, because I had a lean going on. I went and seen a woman, a spiritual healer, and my aura was all holey. She was amazing – she taught me a lot about spiritual healing. She did reiki on me and my wobble went, and I straightened up, and my speech came right. I got this little kitten, Phoenix, a little wild black cat, after I came out of hospital. That little creature was with me 24/7 every day – he just hung with me, and he was the best healer as well. We got such a bond.

After that I ended up back at Tate's. I stayed there for about nine years, a factory job again, assembling things. It was good for my brain, the coordination stuff. I did all sorts of things, got involved in things. I stayed there till about 2006, then Ray got killed in a workplace accident. Me and him were together for 15, 16 years. It was a beautiful relationship till that dreaded day. We weren't married, but we were together for so long.

So that was the end of that. I went back to Tate's after he died, but I couldn't concentrate, I couldn't function. I was making mistakes, and I was drinking, so I hit rock bottom a little bit. My job was suffering, and that wasn't fair to my boss, so I left. I was on ACC, so I was very grateful for that. I pottered round, tried to get a couple of things going on, but my heart wasn't there. I lost the plot for a while. I got back into prostitution, because financially I was struggling. I tried to go back to factory jobs, but it just wasn't working. So I thought, right, I'll get back into the bizzo. So I did.

I had always kept connected to the Prostitutes' Collective. So I went in, and hooked up with a brothel, a chick that was running a house with three or four girls. I've been there since. I try to keep a hand in my healing stuff – I do sexual healing, and then I do the other healing, reiki and massage and stuff like that. I keep it separate – I help men, I help women. I see prostitution as sexual therapy. It makes people feel good – if it makes you feel good it can't be wrong. We're not knocking on people's doors, they're coming to us. People prostitute themselves every day with what they sell. Prostitution is just the raw form – give me a bonk for some money, honey. We're all out there prostituting ourselves – 'Buy me, buy me!' in some form or another. Prostitution has been around for thousands of years, the first business thing that was needed on the planet. Food, sex, shelter.

When you're a prostitute you're so much more aware of your body and yourself and your sexuality – and male sexuality and female sexuality. I found it liberating, empowering. We're here to learn. Sex and what it's about is part of our being. We're humans, we're animals. It's a good part of your life to have – if you've got a good sexual relationship you're happy. If it's not good, if men aren't getting it, it causes issues. Same with women. And men that haven't got that – businessmen, single men, young men, men that have just split up from wives and are used to having that all the time – that's where we come in. Sex changes the chemical thing in your body – like exercise. Releases all the happy endorphins. If you've got a headache, have a wank – guaranteed to get rid of it. Have sex. People say, 'I've got a headache, I can't have sex.' I say, 'Have sex! Get rid of that headache. Have an orgasm.' People need it, it's a necessity in life.

I enjoy my job. I could do anything else if I wanted, but I'd rather be doing what I'm doing. I like men, I enjoy giving them pleasure, giving them healing. I'm here to serve, and if that's men and sexual favours, that's fine. I have a wee regular following of healing stuff as well. Guys'll get an ache or have hurt their shoulder, and I reiki it, they feel better. They'll come back if it starts to get tight again. 'Hey, that really worked, can you do that again? As well as *that*.' I'm like a physio, a spiritual healer and a sexual healer all in one. And I'm teaching them as well about spiritual stuff. So those who like that will come back, and those who aren't interested don't. I pick and choose who I'll talk to about stuff like that.

It's a wee house, just three rooms, three or four girls. It works well. People might pop in at lunchtime, late afternoon. I don't work at night. On average I do six, eight jobs a week. Some days you might do one, two, three jobs – some days I've done none. We've been caned by the computer stuff, Tinder and all that online free sex. That's knocked the industry around. There's a big price war at the moment, when things get tight girls drop their prices. It's always a wee bit quieter in winter. And we're older girls as well, we're cougars, we're not 21. A lot of boys like cougars, it's fashionable now to get hooked up with a cougar. It's a trend. So, hanging in there for as long as possible.

I make enough to make a living. Some weeks get a bit tight, but I've got to be prepared and save when I can, keep ahead of myself. I do it all alone, I have no financial support.

Men that want security and discreetness, a bed and a shower, will go to parlours and brothels. We've painted up the house. We rent it, we don't own it – the landlord knows what we do. We've done the rooms up really well, it's always clean and tidy. I've worked there for six or seven years this trip, this lag. I've been quite happy there. We all were working pretty cool, cruising along here, then the big quake struck and that rattled everyone. A lot of girls left because they were freaked out.

I was at the house. We were lucky. We had a lot of damage – wardrobes and that came down, everything fell. One of the girls was in a room putting her shoes on, waiting for a client, and the wardrobe just missed her. She was in shock on the floor. Luckily we had a client in the house – I was like, 'Quick, come in here, grab her, we've got to get her out of that room.' He put her on his back and piggybacked her, run outside – bang, another big aftershock.

All the parlours in town got munted. We were in Sydenham, which got quite caned. Things went a bit quiet for a little bit. We still had water, so that was all good. We were busy initially – a lot of hookers left town and there were no parlours. All the sex industry got wiped out, basically, in the city. A lot of girls left because of the aftershakes and that, it was a scary time. People were scared to come and have sex in case they were going to get wiped out in an earthquake.

That happened heaps of times – you'd be bonking away – 'Ooh shit, you all right? You all right babe?'

After the quakes I felt like a bit of a change, just getting onto some solid ground. So I went up to Auckland and scouted out doing some street work. I didn't want to stand around K Road because I didn't want to upset the trannies. I hired a wee room in this parlour in Cross Street, so I'd go out, hook in a client. If he wanted to go to the room I would, if he wanted to do it in the car I'd do that, depending how I felt about him. I did quite a few car jobs and little alleyway jobs as well, and that was fun. It was more of an adventure, plus to pull in some money. I'd go out, pull in a client, and if they were keen to go to the parlour we'd go up there for half an hour, whatever, they'd have a shower and take off. I'd go back out on the street, hook on another client. He might want to just go down that wee alleyway for a blowie or something, or stay in the car and do a blowie, or have a quickie in the car. I did quite a few blow jobs in cars.

I think it's more the thing of getting caught for them – it's a funny wee game, the street game. There were quite a lot of P [methamphetamine] freaks up there, I found. They were hard work to make have an orgasm if they've been on a bender for four or five days. Most of them can't come – they were just wasting their money. Some were a bit freaky, mental. You get them in the room and suddenly they start acting like a fucking monkey, or get really erratic. I had to feel my way. P makes them a bit aggressive.

That parlour I was working at, the trans were also using the rooms. I got to know them really well, quite a few of them that were up on K Road. I said where I was, and they go, 'Oh OK, that's cool.' They go, 'If you want to come up there we'll look after you, girl.' I got quite friendly with them, and they knew I wasn't a threat. I was different to them. Men want trans, that's what they're looking for, those boys. Some of them go, 'Are you a real woman?' I'm like, 'Yeah, I am.' 'Oh, OK! Choice!' They've been caught out. Some of them didn't know – 'Oh, I picked up this chick, and –' I'm like, 'That's what this area's known for, you ning-nong.'

A lot of the trans were into P as well, which was quite sad. I didn't like doing clients on that. I used to just turn the music down, not stimulate them too much. Calm, calm. I had a few incidents of ruffians and strangulations and stuff like that. Nothing I couldn't handle, though – just really rough clients, throw you round a bit. I'm pretty tough, it didn't bother me, put me off. Just, he's a bit of an idiot, and get on with it. I didn't go to the cops – it's just the drugs and the alcohol. Clients that I really didn't like the look of, I didn't do. You'd just say, 'No, sorry baby, I'm busy, ra ra ra.'

I got quite a following. I went up there for about three years, back and forth, once every two months. I'd put ads in the paper and on NZ Girls.[1] During the day I'd work off my ads, and then I didn't take bookings at night. Street work was just there, pick you up and gone, no advertising. That's how I rolled. The street work was the best – I made the most money.

I hadn't done it before, but I thought it'd be a bit of an adventure, plus some extra money. I'm a hooker – all it is is a different venue. And I'm not a sookie, I'm very assertive, so it's like 'Hi, baby.' It was a challenge and an adventure, and I made some money as well, covered my costs. Couple of times I had slower trips. I remember going up there once and there was a bloody hurricane, so that was a bad weekend. The streets were just quiet, no one was looking for nothing. Another time the cops cordoned off the street, right there, put up their cones. I was like, 'Are you staying here all night? You guys interfering with my business!'

I believe in all my protection, so I never doubted my safety. When I didn't feel safe, I moved on. A carload of guys, I'm like, 'Nah sorry mate, it's all good.' I got abused, all the normal crap and that – 'You're a slut!' 'I'm not a slut, I'm a businesswoman! Fuck off!' You get quite assertive. It's just young ones, really, young girls hanging out of cars. Nothing serious. I met quite a few people that were just walking by and they'd go, 'Hi, how are you?' A couple would stop and talk: 'What are you doing?' 'What does it look like, love?' 'Oh dear. You look quite nice.' I'm like, 'I am! What are you saying?'

I always had Christians that would be coming up to me – 'Do you know Jesus loves you?' 'Yeah, he does. Do you know that Mary Magdalene was an ex-prostitute and Jesus was fucking her?' They'd be like, 'What?!' So I ended up preaching to them.

I had a lot of fun. I hooked up with the wee street boys, young ones that live in a house, squatting. They kind of befriended me. There was one I got

---

1. The New Zealand Girls website was a common place for sex workers to advertise in the 2000s.

quite friendly with – I'd shout him a smoke, give him some food, get him some groceries. I tried to help him out and he ended up doing a course in hairdressing. They were just young, lost guys. Dad's in jail, connected to gangs, Mum's dead. They were good boys, staunch, but I always got on with them. I never gave them money, but I'd buy them food. You just naturally meet those sort of people on the street when you're hanging out – the homeless and stuff, all sorts of people.

I enjoyed my street work, I really did enjoy it. I never was scared – if you're scared you shouldn't be there. I had no fear, and the odd incident I had wasn't serious. It was just an incident, a bit of roughing up, ooh, this guy'll be gone soon, let's get this over and done with, keep it calm. That's what you've got to do. If something turns, anger or something, just keep calm and talk them down. Don't feed that anger. Also, there are times when you have to get quite staunch yourself. It depends on the mood and what's happening. A couple of times you're just really assertive – 'Hey! Enough of that!'

I got ripped off twice by clients. I should have taken the money first – you learn that very quickly. It was a young Indian boy – he just took off. Silly girl, don't do that again. Then one time a guy looked like he put the money down, but it was gone. That's OK, just silly little things you've got to watch out for.

They were easier clients to do than Christchurch clients. They don't want a hell of a lot, whereas Christchurch clients are quite demanding. They give you more money up there, and they just really want to get it on and get it off. Christchurch clients want this, want that. Good money up there, and a lot of professional men, business boys. Quite cool. On the street I was getting 170 an hour, which was pretty good. Or 80 or 100 for a quickie. Eighty was my lowest price, for about 10 minutes. Most of them gave me 100 dollars for those quick interludes. I quite like that excitement – it was fun, and you never know who's coming round that corner.

If I had a busy, busy night I'd give it up just before the day starts again, the day people come in. I'd be out there maybe half past 4, 5, then the light starts coming and people start cruising the shops, so you go and wind down and go to sleep till about 10, then get up and turn the phone on and do the day shift. Long days, long nights. My legs used to get tired from standing. I had a little Chinese man on K Road, I used to go to him for a massage. He'd go, 'You standing long time! Your legs are tired!' He didn't know what I did. 'Your calf muscles tight!' He'd sort me out – he was lovely. And I got local with all the bars and coffee bars, after a while they knew who I was and what I did. They were like 'Hi Misty!' 'Hi guys!'

When I first got up there a cop pulled me up. He knew what I was up to – I had to give him my name. He goes, 'What are you doing?' I said, 'Well, I've come up from Christchurch. I'm just here to have a bit of a change, solid ground, try and make some money, honey!' He said, 'Yep, you're good here.' He was really helpful, he told me where not to go and where to go. After that the police used to go by – they had put me through the computer and seen I had no convictions or wanted or anything.

I used to look like an American street hooker. I wore big fuck-me boots up to my thighs, black leather, and a short black dress with a little leather coat on. I looked quite hot. I had guys stop and take photos. I used to get lots of comments because I made the effort. In the winter you've got to keep warm, so I mostly didn't go up there too much in the winter.

I've been to Queenstown once – I just got a motel, put ads up, take the phone. Quite a few girls do that from Christchurch, go to Queenstown, Blenheim, Wellington, Auckland. You advertise and hopefully do quite a few clients, cover your costs and bring a little bit of money home. Sometimes you tell the motel owner, sometimes you don't. First time in Auckland, another chick and me went up and got a motel and put our ads up. Big motel so there was a lot of people coming and going – we got away with it.

I haven't been for a while, because Mum got really sick. I had to stay around and look after her, I couldn't leave her. She passed away, so that was really sad. It was awful. She died about 16 months ago, so it's still pretty raw. You've got to get on with it, and you can't stop working. We had a terrible time – but life, you've got to get on with it. I've been just plodding. I'll sort my shit out and get moving very soon.

These houses now are way better for girls like me, older girls like me. If you're in a parlour and you're waiting for clients to come in, if there's younger girls often you're left sitting there. Whereas if you put your own ad up, put yourself out there, they're interested in *you*. I prefer it way better this way. We've got more control, we're not told what to do. If I want to go and do two hours' work, or do one job, I'll do that, come home. Whereas parlours, eight-hour shifts, often nights – I don't want to do nights. I'm too old, I want my sleep at night. If you're 21 or something, all good. You're your own boss, and you get out of your business what you put into it. If you're motivated, it's like anything – if you're there to make the money it's all good. If not, that's your tough luck. Self-motivation, like any business.

I advertise on NZ Girls and in the paper. Put photos up and a wee spiel about what I do – sensual massage, stuff like that. I sound really nice and relaxing. So I go from that angle. And a wee bit of fantasy work. I don't do B&D any more, because I haven't got a dungeon. It's 170, even if you just want a straight massage, because that's my time. Same price if you just want a hand job – you're still coming.

I don't do anal sex, and I don't kiss. I don't do the Girlfriend Experience[2] – I'm old school. I'll kiss the old regular client every now and then, but nothing passionate. Mouth diseases – not into that. I don't usually let them suck my pussy cat. Not many men want that anyway – you get it on and it's all about them. I've got wee toys, wee vibrators and that that I'll pull out, throw that on their balls and they get distracted. Most of my regular clients are not kissers – they just want straight lovely sex. I find a lot of the younger ones are more into all that business – anal and stuff. It seems to be the trend at the moment. Some girls do, but I don't. I'm not comfortable with it.

I don't kiss because of bugs – flus and colds and all the bugs you can get out of a mouth. Especially if those sort of people have been going round sucking things and they want to kiss you – eeuughh. And it's very intimate. I just say, 'There's a few flus around at the moment dear, we'll give that one a miss, shall we?' Most men don't mind that. But boys that do want all that will find girls that do. There's heaps of girls that do. The Girlfriend Experience started coming in in the last five years. It means kissing and sucking pussy, and they don't want to pay any more for it.

The Porn Star Experience is probably easier than the Girlfriend Experience. Act like a porn star, that's all you've got to do. Be a wee bit naughty, rub a dub dub. More acting. I'd rather do the Porn Experience than that fucking Girlfriend Experience. I hate it. I'm not doing it. I'm not kissing, and I'm not

---

2. Sex workers in the 2000s sometimes marketed themselves as offering the Girlfriend Experience (GFE) or the Porn Star Experience (PSE).

doing that. I'm not a girlfriend. I'm a hooker. Girlfriend Experience, what are they on? I'm not your girlfriend. I don't want a man to think I'm his girlfriend. I'm a hooker. You're not going to ring me every day and say, 'Hey, babe.'

Most men know what it's about. And if they're vulnerable and they fall for a hooker – which happens, often – it's up to those two to sort that out. She has to be straight with him. He might have a mental disorder. I've had people get a wee bit infatuated, and I've had to pull the plug. I say, 'Darling, you forget I'm a prostitute.' I just pull the plug. I say I'm not available. Sorry. I've only done that once or twice. That was a simple man. I had to say, 'Baby, I'm not your girlfriend. You're paying me to have sex. This has got to stop now.' I sent him elsewhere.

There's been one person in all the years I've been working that I've had coffee with and meals with. He's a lovely regular, and I know he's OK. I know he's not going to get all dumb about it. I've been doing that for about seven years – go and have brunch and a cup of tea, then he'll follow me back to the house for a bonk. He just enjoys having a yarn and some female company. He's good, he's solid, of sound mind. But I wouldn't do that with many clients, because you're giving them the wrong idea, unless you have ideas of getting in further.

When you're a working girl you don't look at looks. I don't look at a man and go, oh, he's ugly. Old men, I think they're lovely. Lots of clients are interesting as, they're cool people. They come for company, connection, counselling, stress relief. In the earthquakes I found men were quite shooken up, out there working, doing all the hard shit. I really focused on their shoulders and their necks. A lot of men were grateful for that, because they were holding all their stress. They needed attention, they needed support, so I gave them lots of healing.

My house got caned in the quake, and it was the beginning of the end with my mother. Her house was badly damaged, so she lived with me. I had to hide, because she didn't know I worked this time round. She was too old, I didn't want to worry her and make her sicker. She thought I had a wee office job. It knocked the old around, the quakes. It knocked us all around, emotionally, mentally, physically and financially, and it still keeps coming. It was pretty tough, but we all just got on with it – we had to, really. Can't break down, got to keep going. As Churchill said, when going through hell, keep going. You can't stop, you can't go back.

Most of my friends know what I do. And a handful of family. The first time round they all found out and I got crucified. Mum found out and told everyone, as mums do. She was worried, she didn't understand. I got crucified – they treated me like shit. My uncle threatened to run me out of town because I was a hooker. Then when I hooked up with Ray, things changed. They treated me fine again and they forgave me. So I won't go back there again, I won't tell them this time round. I understood, I could see where they were coming from, and understood the stigma attached to the industry. I had a few friends turn their back as well. So I figured the ones that stayed were the ones that were good, and the ones that didn't – see you later.

My partner handled me working – but once I committed, that was a whole new relationship. I can't have a relationship while I'm working. It takes too much of your headspace, and you get involved, your heart and your emotions, and once that happens it makes the job harder. You feel guilty. It *is* wrong, to have a relationship and be a hooker, I feel personally. So I don't get involved. I might pick up the odd stray for a quick one-nighty, that's it, see you later. Not coming round, having tea. I'd rather that way – it's just easier. It never lasts long, because it's not right. I wouldn't go out with a man who was a prostitute or a stripper. I wouldn't consider it. No way. You haven't got their whole attention. Commitment is total commitment, and I can't do that when I'm working, so I don't do that. I just keep working, working, working.

I'm not going to meet someone – it's not my plan. I'm a career woman. Prostitution is my business, my life, my income. Ain't got too long left with it, I'm getting older. If I'm meant to meet a man maybe when I'm older it will happen, and if it doesn't I really don't care. I'm not needy. I can look after myself. I don't need someone to sleep with. I can live alone – I'm strong that way.

I have a plan. Prostitution is probably a bit like models – once a model starts getting wrinkly and a bit worn, you don't make as much money. I think it's got a lot better for older women in the business, because cougarism is a wee trend at the moment. With that in mind, maybe early fifties. See how I'm looking, see how it's going. But I do want to start up my own business, with candles and shit that I make. Try and retire into that business eventually and let this one go. You can't do it forever. Maybe 60! Maybe I'll get Botox at 55.

I enjoy it – I like variety. I don't think I could have a one-man relationship.

My nature's that way anyway, except when I was in love, that period of time when I was totally committed, totally loyal. And that got taken away, so I figure, I'm back to the way I was. I was always promiscuous when I was younger, always liked to have multiple partners. Always been that way except when I was committed. I like different men, different energies, different stuff. You learn more.

I was thinking about getting back to B&D again, because it's quite popular now. That could be a good retirement thing, because you could mask up, and wear a big black suit – be a mistress that no one's ever seen your face. You could work to 70 years old. That's one of my things that I have in the back of my mind – stepping back into that, and being a really mysterious mistress that no one ever sees the face. I love it. I love acting – and when you're with every man you're acting, Misty's coming out.

When I go to work I put my Misty hat on, and when I get home I put my other hat on. Misty is the sexual femme fatale. My assertive businesswoman is Misty. And my other hat is my soft, gentle, healing, cards stuff that I do, spiritual stuff. It's like white and black, black and white. It's always connected, but when I go to work I'm Misty, and when I come home I leave Misty at my work. I know how to separate. It just happens naturally. It's probably like any job – you leave your job and come home. You can't be a hooker all the time. When I go out and socialise I don't act like Misty, I just act like a normal woman.

I have a lot of men friends – I enjoy male company and conversation. I'm not really into girly stuff, Facebook and crap and nails. I'd rather talk about cars. I'm quite a tomboy really, deep down, always have been. That's probably why I'm quite strong on my own, I have got a wee bit more masculine energy.

When I'm working I'm very soft, sexy as. Hair's nice, makeup's pretty. High heels, wear naughty wee things – corsets, stockings and stuff. Lay it all on. I'm like a wee sex machine – put it all on and off we go. That makes you feel in the mood. If you're not in the mood you still do it, because it's second nature. I don't tell clients much, it's not about that. It's about them. Girls that tell them their whole life story – I'm not one to do that. People love to talk about themselves, so I always turn it around quickly. It's easy to distract people from your stuff. I've mastered that over the years. Even in normal conversation, a lot of people say, 'Oh, what do you do?' 'Oh, wee office job,' and then it's gone.

They don't want to know any more, they're too interested in talking about themselves.

I've always practised safe sex, never not used condoms, especially in the sex industry, and out there as well. I've had the odd issue with guys and condoms, and I'm very staunch – just 'See you later.' The clients, if they don't want to use one, they get a hand job. I just say, 'Nah. If you're not happy with that, you can go now, or have a hand job.' Blow job, condom, and sex, condom. They're usually pretty good – most men that come to see us know the rules. It's the boys you pick up out there that are the ones with the issues.

I'm really staunch about it, because you have to be. It's my temple. It's my body, it's my business, if it breaks down because of some fucking idiot, excuse my language – no way. And I don't trust anyone at all when they say, 'I'm clean.' They all say that. I've had lots of men offer me a grand to have sex without a condom. Nah. Nah. 'I don't want your money, honey. I don't know what you're trying to sell me, but it must be worth quite a bit.' That's always my comeback – must be a good disease, it's worth a lot. I've always been very staunch, and I've never had a sexually transmitted disease.

I've worked off and on for the Prostitutes' Collective over the years. I'm their cleaner at the moment. Around the earthquake time I was involved in the outreach project with the street girls. We'd go out and give free condoms and connect with them, make sure they're OK. Tell them about our place, all the free checkups and counsellors that we have. I've been quite involved with them over the years, and wrote to all the politicians about decriminalisation, said my bit. I was part of that movement, which was great. Bringing the laws up from the eighteenth century to the twentieth century.

Prostitutes' Collective has been really amazing for my working career and a lot of working girls. They've helped a lot of women over the years, and guided us in the right direction with the laws. Decriminalisation is great – gives us our own power to do our own stuff, to organise ourselves. Men aren't in control like they thought they used to be.

The police have got a really good relationship with the Prostitutes' Collective. Once you seen a cop coming, you'd fucking run and hide. Now it's like, 'Hi. Are you all good?' 'Yes, thanks.' 'Cheers. Have a good night.'

It will always be stigmatised. That won't change in my lifetime. People will always have moral issues, religious issues and issues with prostitutes. Religion, and the way society has trained us all to be – women hate us in case we nick their men. We're not knocking on their doors. You say you're a prostitute to a couple, and the woman stands closer to her man. Insecurities. Some things will never change. 'Oh, darling, you're going to be a prostitute when you're old enough!' 'Darling, you're going to be a nurse or a hooker!' Which would a mother prefer her daughter to be? Hmm. But it doesn't worry me, I'm not worried about that, I never have been and I never will be. I'm quite proud of what I do. I have respect for myself. I love myself and I care about my clients. I don't have any issues with self-esteem, and I feel sorry for girls that have. If it's affecting you in that way it's time to get another job. Simple. It's like any job – if it's getting you down, you're not happy, can't cope, get another job.

It's a fun job, and I'm pleased that I've been a hooker. I wouldn't do it any other way if I lived my life again – I'd probably do it again, but start younger and do it longer.

Misty was interviewed at her Christchurch home in June 2015.

POPPY

POPPY

I WAS BORN in a little nursing home in Herne Bay, Auckland, on the 5th of April 55. I was taken from there to the Sisters of Compassion, and from there I was adopted, and my name was changed. Both my adoptive parents were from Hokianga, Northland. My mother was half-caste Māori, my father was full Māori. Te Rarawa is my mother's hapū, from Mitimiti; my father is Ngāti Te Haua from Whangapē.

My parents and their sisters and brothers, coming from the country where there was no money – all the industry up there had ceased – they had to come to Auckland to work. My mother and most of her sisters started off as maids. My father was a labourer, a bushman.

My mother had previously married. She was the great beauty of the family. She was the girl – I think they call them puhi – who was expected to make the grand marriage in the family. And she did, she married a European man. But of course, my mother being the puhi in the family, and the favourite, and the beauty, she was brought up in a bit of a spoilt way. When her first husband said she would be subservient, my mother said, 'No, I will not be. I'm my own woman.' She left him and she married my father, one of the darkest, blackest Māoris of the north. He used to always laugh his head off and say, 'You had the Pākehā, but it was the black man that got you.'

My parents were very, very hard-working people – they were not the type of people that would take a day off work. Never. They'd go to work sick – my parents were workers. And on the weekend, they liked to play hard, because they worked hard. So I was left to my own devices. I'd be off to the matinees at the weekend, and roaming around town and what have you.

We were in Sandringham, and my parents owned a big Edwardian villa, very dilapidated but beautiful. Because my parents and all the men in the family worked, there was always one woman who would stay at home with us young ones. It was an extended group, mostly from my mother's side. There were kids as well.

We always had animals. My parents were from the country, so my father always had two pig dogs. I'd always have a dog, and my mother had her cats. We had Pomeranians and chihuahuas and birds. A huge chicken coop. I was brought up in the country in the city, and we ate country food. My mother knew how to cook absolutely everything. We grew everything from apricots to pears to the most ginormous plum tree you've ever seen. Walnuts, guavas, we had two types of lemon, kiwifruit, cape gooseberries, and the vege garden.

I went to Mt Albert Primary School, and I used to dream up plays in the afternoon, before we'd have our nap. The teacher would be marking things, and we were allowed to put on a little play. So I always organised it, and I was always the queen. I'd make my little crown and my little outfit.

My mother worked at Feltex, Lynn Laces, and they made laces. She used to bring home the rejects, for bring and buys, fundraising. My mother was in the Māori Women's Welfare League, and our family was fundraising to build a marae here in Auckland.[1] My friend across the road made me this Cleopatra wig out of these shoelaces. He put beads on them, and it looked so fabulous. So off I went on school gala day – they had a fancy dress thing. I was prancing round there. I wore my mother's old-fashioned black petticoat – I went as Cleopatra, with my little black wig. And I got first prize. There was some dignitary there who said, 'Oh, that little girl wins the first prize. Cleopatra.' Then he says, 'Part of your prize is, you can throw the dart for the raffles,' when they spin the thing. I threw the dart, and as I turned around I saw the principal whispering something in his ear. 'I don't think that's a little girl, it's a little boy.' And from then on that man wouldn't look at me. He just turned his back. But anyway, I got to throw the dart.

---

1   Te Ūnga Waka marae, an urban Catholic marae in Epsom, opened in 1966.

My parents were fluent in Māori – that's their first language, of course. But they didn't speak Māori to me. Any kind of teaching of Māori, or Māoritanga – none of that. You were in the city, you were going to Pākehā schools. My mother wanted me to be a priest. Your Māori side didn't count where she wanted me to go.

My mother was Catholic and my father was Church of England. My mother was the staunch, pious Catholic, but my father just let it go. The only thing he ever said to me about religion was – he put his hands over my head like this, like a steeple and a church, and he says, 'That's your church!' Meaning your body, yourself. 'That's your church. You are your own temple.' I didn't realise what he was talking about when I was younger, but now I'm older I know exactly what he was talking about. That's your temple there. He didn't believe in all that Catholic ritualistic nonsense, which I spent decades getting rid of.

I was an altar boy for many years. I served in most of the churches in Auckland. I was a believer, and I did have aspirations to become a religious. I was told that after I left school I would have two years in the world to see the world and make sure that you have a vocation before entering a Franciscan friary.

But those two years were the end of that.

Put on the wrong frock.

You knew you were different. But you didn't know, because you're a child. It's not until years later that you realise exactly what it was. You have – what do they call it – gender dysphoria. My adoptive family were really quite beautiful to me. Only one aunty called me the Q-word, and I slapped her mouth, right then and there in the passageway. I think I was about 14. I just slapped it – put a stop to that right now. But I've never had any nasty words from any of my family. When I transitioned, my uncles would hug me, kiss me and treat me like a girl. So I'm very fortunate there.

I only went to Mitimiti twice as a child. I went to a wedding up there at eight. The second time I was about 14. And by that time I was in a little miniskirt, little halter-neck top. The hair was starting to grow, the hormones were starting to work, and my cousins wanted to knock me over and part my legs to see what was in there, until I screamed my head off and my mother came running, and they all got told off.

We've been there over 700 years, our people in that spot. There's no tar-seal roads – there's tar-seal roads to Panguru, but from there it's all metal roads, potholes. No one's got any money, everyone's on benefits. Lovely little marae there – we have our own church. In the past it would have been a perfect little spot to live in. You've got an outcrop of rocks where you get all your seafood. There's all the fish there. You've got toheroa, tuatua and all that along the beach. And you have the beautiful crystal water that comes through there – Moetangi, crying waters from the mountains. Clear, crisp, freezing cold and pure. There was a creek down the side of where all the gardens used to be. It's a lovely spot – most of those places are.

When I was about 11, I used to look after a lady next door to us, Mrs Horne. She was very old, and after school I would go over and make her a slab of bread with jam and a cup of tea. I'd toilet her, help her into the bed and change her. I'd put her to bed and she'd tell me about the old days. One day she gave me three 10-shilling notes. 'Take them, take them, take them.' 'OK.' I took myself into town on the Saturday. I did two movies – the 10 o'clocks and the 2 o'clocks or whatever it was. I used one of my 10-shilling notes to take a plane ride on one of those planes that took off from the water.

Then I went to the Wimpy bar on Customs Street. I ordered my favourite, because I had all this money. There was this man there; I was eating, looking at him. I finished and I left, and I was walking up Queen Street. I glanced behind me, and that man was still there. There was a theatre, the Century, and it had two glass windows. I could see that man in the window behind me, and the shadow got bigger and bigger until I knew that he was standing right behind me. I turned around and looked at him. I was starting to get a bit scared.

He said to me, 'If you come up to Albert Park with me, I'll give you five shillings.' I went, 'Oh.' Five shillings. Not thinking of any danger or anything else – just, five shillings.

Off up there we went – I followed him up there. They used to have these huge trees, Moreton Bay figs. We went into the roots of this tree, and he molested me. I was quite put off. I didn't know anything about this, and he wanted to do oral things to me. I thought it was all highly disgusting.

I went back into the city after that. I was a bit shaken and confused and bewildered. I went to go to another movie, and he was following me. By that time I was scared. So when I got to the usherette I said, 'That man –' and I started crying. I said, 'And he gave me this!' I went to give the five shillings to her, as if you could get rid of it, the whole experience. She said, 'No, no, no.' She wouldn't take it. She said, 'You go and sit in the theatre,' so I went in. She came back five minutes later, and she said, 'It's all right, he's gone.'

I went home and thought about it all. And then your scheming little mind goes to town – *I can make money*. Even though the experience of being molested wasn't pleasant, it was in my brain that I could make money, and the person you were making money off didn't have to be a creepy old man in a trenchcoat. Because, believe it or not, he was a creepy old man and he wore a trenchcoat.

From then on, I was getting florins, half-crowns, from university students, because I was an attractive young person in those days. I'd hang around outside the toilets and be approached. I knew I could make money, and it didn't have to be with an old classic child molester. I could make money off beautiful young men who wanted me. So I took advantage of it. And I lost my virginity – anal sex. The boy who used to live across the road was with me one day. We wanted to see a movie, and I said, 'I know where to get some money.' So I took him up to Albert Park and we picked up a student. My friend and I both lost our virginity together, to the same student.

I was about 12. I was molested at 11, and 12 was when I made my move on the world. The first experience was absolutely horrific, but it gave me an insight into who I really was. It gave me an insight that I was attracted to men. It was a molestation, but it was also an eye-opener. I hadn't really thought of sex before. At 11, I didn't know much about it at all.

And I had some boyfriends. At that time – this is the 60s – I thought to myself, I'm homosexual. Must be. I'm a boy and I'm with men. So what else would you think?

I was asked to leave school at 14, because I was a bad influence on the boys at St Paul's College. By that stage I'd already made up my mind that I was going to be who I am, and the rest of the world can go jump. That was my instincts. I had to be like that.

I was kind of feminising. Pre-hormones, though. My behaviour suited me, and I wasn't going to behave how other people said I should behave. Poppy was breaking out, and Poppy was going to win that battle. And she did. And I suppose they couldn't handle it.

In my last year of school I was teasing my hair, starting to wear a couple of my mother's rings. Not necessarily outrageous, but just being a bit more open about who I am. By that stage, I was not very impressed with some of these brothers who taught us, and I had got to the point where I don't care what you think about me, I have to do what I have to do for me. If getting rid of me from your college is it, so be it. I wasn't worried about that any more. I had my own agenda. To be a girl.

I'd seen it, you see, by then. To get to school I had to catch the bus to Wellesley Street, walk the length of Queen Street, then catch the bus to Ponsonby. And in Queen Street, I used to see so many queens. There was Maiti, who used to be the warehouse worker at the Royal Albert Hotel. He used to unload all the crates of beer, and he was outrageous. From the Cook Islands. A lot of the Polynesian people, they were open with their sexuality. Then I'd go further down the road and I'd see Taina. A little Māori queen, dressed as a boy – no one was dressed as girls in those days in Auckland. He used to work for tolls. Trissing round Queen Street with his hair teased up on top and little kiss curls. Then I'd go further down the road, and there'd be all the shop queens that worked at John Court's or Milne and Choyce. I used to notice all these people. And then one day I met one of them. Phyllis. She was in drag – she was a bold person. She eventually took me under her wing.

I met some of these people, and I realised, I'm like them. They were all feminine, and most of them became sex-change women. Things changed – their environment changed and they could have these operations. Most of them lived their lives as women. Beautiful women, too. They were all shop queens, dressed as boys. But as soon as the operations became available, and the oestrogen tablets, you could be who you wanted to be, instead of being locked in your male prison. I still know some of those girls to this day. All grey-headed old things they are – but sex-change women now.

So that was our time to come out of our prisons. We had wonderful medications that could help us. The drag people before us, the transsexual and drag people, they had to live as men and they had to develop as men. They had to get the big jawlines and the muscles and all that because they didn't have the hormones. Inside they're feeling like a woman – and there you are on the outside looking like Arnold Schwarzenegger. But of course, we were the lucky generation, to get the oestrogen hormones that we could take, and feminise, and stop that development into male.

I was 14 or 15 when I started. What would we do without our hormones? Our oestrogen. I got them from Dr Jack – our wonderful Dr Jack, who had a surgery in Three Lamps in Ponsonby, and was very sympathetic to us girls and helped as best he could.

I was one of the youngest of my era to start so early. Most of the other girls around my time – 17, 16 maybe when they started, 18. But I was 14, 15. There was no communication with my parents about it. My father got a bit bewildered, because I was getting more feminine every day, and I'd started wearing little halter-neck tops, and he could see that my breasts were developing. He must have been thinking to himself, what the hell's going on here? Being from a different generation, he'd never seen any of that type of carry-on in his life.

I was still living at home. I was just me. And if anyone tried to stop me, there was trouble. My father burnt my clothes, but I told him, I can always buy more. So that stopped that pretty quickly – waste of money. My father didn't understand any of this, but I used to hear him talking – 'Oh, it's just a phase he's going through, he'll grow out of it.' I did say to him one day, 'I ain't growing out of nothing.' Because it's not a phase.

When I was about 14, I was had up for a minor theft, and I was sent to the Children's Court. I had the most beautiful blue crepe frock, a little mini with little puff sleeves and a heart-shaped neckline. I had some lovely blue open sandals. My hair was still short, because I wasn't too long out of college, so I had a little blue and white scarf, a summer scarf. I appeared in court. The judge looked at me, then looked at the policeman and says, 'What was the name?' because he'd heard my boy's name being called. The judge says, 'You've got the wrong person.' The policeman said to the judge, 'This is him.' The judge looked at me, bewildered, then got a bit angry, then confused. He was told about my charge – it was a little theft from a shop in K Road. And because I must have been one of the first to appear in the Children's Court in women's attire, I was sent to Oakley psychiatric hospital for a month's observation.

Into maximum security I went, where all the hardened criminally insane people were. There were really insane people that needed to be attended to 24/7, poor darlings. We were in there with them. My friend was in there, too, not long out of college. She was there because she was feminine and transsexual. Her mother couldn't handle it and got her committed. She was there for years. She turned out to be the most beautiful big, buxom blonde sex change. Gorgeous. Made money like nobody's business.

I was there for my month. I went back to court, then I was sent back to Oakley as a partially committed patient. I was put into Male Six – an enclosed ward. Only certain ones could leave the ward to go into the grounds, but I couldn't. I was put on a treatment called aversion treatment. It was to turn me into a heterosexual.

I would go into this room, about the size of a single bedroom. It was all painted black; there was a bar in it, with drinks, alcohol. There was a coffin by the wall. There was – you know when you look at the American movies and they show the old wooden electric chairs? There was one of those, where you get strapped in with leather straps on your ankles. And a full-length mirror, and a bag of drag – women's clothes. I was strapped into the chair. Electrodes were put on my arm. And then – if you ever see the movie *Clockwork Orange* – same thing. The electrodes were put on my arm, then he'd have his button, and he'd ask me the questions. About girls and sex and all sorts of things. And if I answered incorrectly, or what he deemed to be incorrect, zzzzzzhhhhhh [buzzing electric shock sound].

You'd get your shocks. Then you were unstrapped, and made to drink alcohol. I remember the drink I was given was bourbon. I couldn't bear the smell of the stuff for years, or a man who had drunk it. I was got drunk on bourbon, and then I was told to dress in the women's clothes in the bag, which were horrible clothes, and look in the mirror at how ridiculous I look and how ridiculous I am, and I was told that I was going to end up an old drunken homosexual in that coffin.

That was called aversion treatment, and that was given to me in Oakley Hospital, about 1970, when I was 14 or 15. That's when I ran away. It was a half-open ward, and when they'd finished that treatment with me, I was allowed to have time out in the garden. That's when I ran. Soon as that door was open, I was out of there. I ran home to my mother. I said, 'You get me out of there or else I will never forgive you.' Because part of my committal was her signature.

They came and got me, believe it or not, in a little white van, and they had their little white coats on. They took me back to Oakley, back to Male Three where I originally was, maximum security. And I received a paraldehyde injection, a very painful injection, as a punishment.

I had six or seven sessions of aversion therapy. That was in Ward M6, Oakley Hospital. I've got the files. I took up a case against the Crown. It went for about six years, but the Crown keep changing the goalposts, and I've just been informed that my case will not be eligible for any kind of compensation – the main reason being that it was normal treatment of the time. I have the documents. They were just sent to me by the lawyers about two weeks ago, when he told me that my claim would not succeed. It cost $6000 for that lawyer. It would have cost more, but he waived it.

Normal treatment of the time.

What a silly treatment that is. Fancy getting a 14, 15-year-old drunk on bourbon. You call that treatment? And electrocuting them. Crazy. Barbaric.

No compensation for me. An apology would have been nice.

Those were the times, I suppose.

History is brutal.

It was so bloody boring in Auckland. When I was 15 or so – young, pretty, miniskirt, got little boobies and that – Auckland was closed. Auckland didn't open till Thursday. You'd have all these visiting business executives, wandering round going, 'Hullo love. Where does a man find a bit of fun around the place?' And I'd say to him, 'You're looking at it.' 'Where does a man get a drink around the place?' I said, 'It's called room service.' There's no nightclubs open, no hotels, and you've got all these businessmen from all over the world.

That's how I knew about foreign dollars, was through these businessmen. There I was, 15, 16, the only prostitute in Queen Street. In *Auckland*, tell you the truth, the whole of Auckland. And there's these businessmen: 'Where does a man find a bit of fun?' No nightclubs until about Wednesday, Thursday when Embers would open. But in the meantime, here was little old Poppy making the foreign dollars. I used to take my dollars up to Thomas Cook, and they'd give me the exchange rate for my dollars. Thank you!

I learnt quickly not to dress too prostitute-looking. Dress nicely. Otherwise you'd never get into the hotels that they lived in. You couldn't just invite people up to your room. If they knew on the desk you were a prostitute, you'd never get past them. Even though you've paid for your room and you should be able to have a guest up to have a drink, 'No no no no, it's a prostitute. We know her, we know what she's up to. No, you're barred.' That happened a lot of times. But I knew how to dress – dress ladylike but attractive, so that if you were at a counter in a hotel or something like that, they wouldn't spring you for a prostitute. 'Certainly, madam, go through.' 'Thank you, dear, thank you.' It's part and parcel of chasing the dollar.

A lot of those executives, whenever they were back in the country I would meet up with them at Embers bar. As soon as I saw them come in I would go and sit by myself, and they'd come straight to my table. I had them for a long time, whenever they were back in the country for business.

It was fun. We enjoyed our life on the street, us girls. I didn't do parlours and all that business – no, if I'm going to put my ass on the line, the money's mine. Not sharing it with nobody. We had fun. We were well-known by a lot of men, us girls in my little clique of friends. We'd get home – 'How much did you make?' We'd try and outdo each other. We had our lovely little flats, and we'd go shopping during the day. Even just going shopping during the day you'd be working, getting picked up. You were cracking it all the time. It was 24/7 – whenever it was available you'd take it, unless you had enough and you didn't need it. I'd take any opportunity, day or night, any time. I'd go in cars, boats, alleys – anywhere. You know what men are like. When they need it, they'll do it anywhere. And we'd be there. Dangerous situation, you can put another 20 dollars on it. Say, 'I ain't doing it here. Another 20, please!'

I've worked in hospitals and kitchens, cafés and restaurants. I've been a wine steward, I've waitressed. I've been a landscape gardener, I've been a caretaker at a hospital. As a man, as a woman – when I worked at Cornwall Hospital, all the trans girls were working there. All pantry maids, wards maids and all that. I thought, I'm going to get myself a job there. There were no jobs as wards maid or pantry maid, but there was a job as groundsman. So I came back dressed as a boy, I got the job as the groundsman. Then when a job came up as pantry maid, I rushed home, changed, went back and got the job as pantry maid. I was interviewed by the garden people, then I was interviewed by the hospital staff. They didn't realise I was the same person. My friend Dana [see p. 171] and I both worked there – we'd poke our head down the corridor, wave out to each other. We had our own little pantries and our own wards that we looked after and cleaned.

I waitressed at the Café de Paris, one of the first, if not *the* first, open trans/gay/whatever places to open in Auckland. People flocked there because they knew all the waitresses were queens. Not only that, when they got there, gazing at us because we were all so young and pretty and outrageous, we had the best steak meals in town. Ivan, our chef Ivan, he knew how to cook a steak. Beautiful. It was good music – we had the best jukebox in town – the best meals, and all us outrageous ones, the waitresses.

For people of our inclination, it was a safe haven for them to come and congregate, have a coffee, catch up, and feel as if they can come in off the street and relax. We were all roped in under the same heading in those days – there were no such names as trans this or trans that or sexual dysphoria. We were all gay, homosexual, queer, poof, whatever you wanted to call us.

Ca d'Oro was a coffee lounge in Customs Street, which had been going since the early 60s. That area was where the girls worked. Night people went there – and queens. That's where the queens really worked from in those days. And Greys Ave, too. Carmen used to work from Greys Ave. Also I worked during the day, prostituting, in one of the early opening bars, the Schooner, on the waterfront. All sorts happened in that bar – there were drugs, stolen goods. There were people who would come and take your order, then they'd go and shoplift it for you. You had stolen clothes – there was a little room there, you could go and view the clothes. The Schooner was well known for seamen. There'd be card games going on in the corner. A lot of drugged people all over the place, and girls cracking it, queens. I'd get there about 8 in the morning. By about 10 o'clock, everyone's coming in to get their drugs and whatever. They'd pop whatever they popped, then they're there all day. It was a real fun place. People would approach me, and we'd go wherever – if they had a place. I'd have my car parked there. Men's toilet … in you'd go, into the men's toilet. Notorious little bar, the Schooner.

There were a lot of bars where girls worked from. You had the City Hotel, on Hobson Street. There was Gleesons, the Snake Pit. Gleesons was a notorious hotel frequented by the seamen, down by the waterfront. When the tide came in, the basement would flood. You'd have beer crates for chairs. You had the roughest ship molls you could ever meet sitting around that bar. A big Island queen – man queen – with eyeliner on serving behind the bar. Oh, it was outrageous. I loved it. Dana and I used to often go there – there was always something going on in Gleesons.

I first worked on a ship in the late 60s. I met some queens, and they took me back to their flat. One of the ladies that lived there was a ship moll. Later she changed and became a female-to-male transsexual. She was a big ship moll back then.

    We did all sorts of ships. Danish ships, German, Japanese, Korean, Pommie. Most of the ship men, or tima tānes as we used to call them, were gay-friendly or queen-friendly, because a lot of the staff on board were queens – the cooks, the bar staff. They were gay-guy queens – effeminate. Wear makeup and boys' clothes. You had to get along in the middle of the ocean, so most of the seamen were quite friendly to the queens.

    They had bars on the ships, lovely bars. We'd go in there and party, and then back to their rooms. If you got on well with your tima tāne, he'd be with you for the whole stay. If you got on extra well, whenever he came back to port, you were for him, you were his girl in this port. In those days we were always scouring the *Herald* – 'Oh, what boats are coming in?' It was fun.

    We'd go on board with them, or sneak on, or get passes. You'd meet them on shore, or go on with them. You'd go on, party in their bars. They had fabulous parties on the ships, and they loved us Māori girls. A lot of them stayed and are still here – married the girls, jumped ship. A lot of children I know are from seamen. One family I know, there's Japanese, Danish and German children from the seamen. You got paid – or else you went shopping, especially with the Japanese. They'd take you shopping. You'd buy perfumes, clothes, shoes, things like that.

I worked in clubs, but I wouldn't call myself a showgirl as such. In the early days you were strippers. I used to do spots at Club Exotique in Wellington, way back in 71. Emmanuel Papadopoulos had it then, and Pasi had the Purple

Onion. I used to do spots at Art-o-rama. You couldn't move if you were totally nude, because of the laws. If you were totally nude, you had to be still. You're doing tableaux, posing as this or that – Cleopatra, or Madame Pompadour, or whatever, if you were nude. But if you had a G-string on or something, you could move. That's why women had to wear the pasties, cover the nipple. As soon as you were totally nude, you had to be still.

I did spots at different places in Auckland and Wellington, but later actually worked as a showgirl at an all-male revue, it was called in those days. Today you'd say drag shows. But these weren't drag queens – these were transgender women, really. And great beauties, like Lee Mercedes, Carol de Winter, Niccole Duval. I worked at that show, at Mojo's, and it was the best all-male revue show that New Zealand has ever had.

Wages weren't all that much in in the early 70s. Outside our nightclub we used to have a little *Herald* box. And I could make more money sitting on that *Herald* box than actually working upstairs in the show. But it was wonderful to work there, because what woman wouldn't want to be covered in feathers? We had the most amazing show. There would be burlesque, of course, fire dancers. There would be hula dancers, Polynesian dancers. The girls from Tahiti used to come and work for us. We had girls come over from Australia to work – all great beauties. In those days, not many girls had had operations, but a lot of our girls had had them. Because we were billed as an all-male revue, there was always one girl in the show who was publicised as the only sex change on the stage. The rest were all trans girls. But very very trick. Quick change artists. The best New Zealand has had, in my eyes.

It wasn't that big, either, Mojo's. But we were licensed. We made all the lovely little toasted sandwiches and bits and pieces people liked to eat. Put on a good show. Of course the people came – a lot of working people who wanted to come and be amazed. And they were. As I've said, some of the girls that worked on that stage were famous New Zealand beauties of their time. A lot of them went off and worked in the shows in Hong Kong, Manila, Singapore.

When you think of Las Vegas showgirls, that's how we were. It was very glamorous. Expensive, though. We had to pay for some of our own costumes. We all lived at Maree de Maru's, where we got the boas and feathers, the beading and fabrics. Wonderful. And people went away entertained and amazed. And sometimes the husbands came back.

A lot of trans people did sex work. It was difficult to get jobs in those days when you were transitioning and everyone's anti. Plus, a lot of us girls never knew about benefits, the dole and things like that. Most of the people that I knew worked on the street. There were a lot of Island girls, too, but a lot of them had jobs. They were factory workers and seamstresses. They got their jobs through family, and most of the factories and sewing industry were Island people. So they fitted in fine with their own people, whereas we were different. People weren't as accepting towards us as the Island community were towards theirs.

I was harassed all the time. Just being called horrible names in the street – you could even get assaulted, if people sprung you for being a trans. It was quite dangerous, especially here in Auckland. We weren't out in the world like the Wellington girls. We had to look like girls, or we could be in danger. Wellington was different, because of Carmen, and because you wouldn't want to upset people like Chris Witoko. She was a big girl, so *you'd* be in trouble, not her. Chris Witoko would even take on gangs. 'Leave the girls alone.' Plus, they were outrageous, too, the Wellington girls, with their high hairdos and all the makeup. Whereas in Auckland – no. It wasn't until we got a bit more seen around the place, in the mid-70s, that things started to settle down a bit. Plus, of course, a lot of the girls up here were Māori girls. I was never a fighter, so I got hidings, but some of the girls were good fighters, and became known around town – don't mess with those queens, because you're in trouble, not them. We've all got convictions for assault.

I even have one for assault on a policeman. I was coming out of the Crypt nightclub one night, and two policemen were walking down the street. One called out the Q-word – 'You queer.' I became very annoyed, because this was coming out of the mouth of someone who's supposed to uphold our laws. I walked up to him and asked him what he said. He said it again and I slapped his mouth. Off to the central police station I went, and I got my conviction. Which isn't a good conviction to have, assault on a policeman. But a lot of our convictions were caused by the police themselves, through victimisation and harassment.

Dana and I and about 15 of us got rounded up for having our hormones prescribed under girls' names. All our houses were ransacked, tipped upside down. I was living with Dana in her mother's house after her mother passed away. They came and upset the whole house, looking for our medicine bottles. I got hauled before the courts, and it wasn't even hormones. My medication with my girl's name on it was actually antihistamines for my hayfever. There were 15 of us in court. They raided all the houses where we all lived, rounded us up. They went through all the drawers. They never had to do that – we would have given the bottles to them. But they pulled everything apart. Then the cop said to Dana, 'You people live like pigs.' Dana said, 'You're the pig.' And she was pushed into the bedroom, the door was closed and I could hear her being beaten on the other side.

We all got convicted – but what a colourful courtroom it was that day. We all went in our wigs, all our makeup, our outfits – low-cuts, everything. We dressed for the occasion.

My lawyer was David Lange in those days. Bloody good lawyer. They had me up once for prostitution. David Lange said to the judge, 'Does the court recognise the Oxford Dictionary?' They had an adjournment, talked about it, then came back and said, 'Yes, the court recognises the Oxford Dictionary.' David Lange said to the judge, 'Prostitute. A woman who sells – ' He said, 'My client is a man, but the Oxford Dictionary said that a prostitute is a woman.' I was discharged.

I fully agree with making prostitution legal. What I want to do with my body is my business. It's the same as abortion – I'm pro-choice. It's my body, it's my business. And if I want to sell it to you for such and such, who are you to poke your nose into my bedroom? What goes on behind closed doors is not your business. Same with those poor homosexuals too. Police bursting into their bedrooms to arrest them! It's all a change for the better.

My husband was my client in the beginning. He was always very good to me – he was always very nice. And we were never lost for anything to talk about. It just slowly happened, and that was that. Just one of those things – sometimes it's on top of you before you know. All of a sudden – oh, you've got feelings for this man. But he wasn't a client for long till we started a relationship. And then the lucky bugger got it for free.

The girl he was with before me, she was a working girl too. He didn't have any hang-ups about that. He got most of the money anyway. They pay our bills, honey. I'd just keep a little bit back for treats. We lived in comfort in Mt Albert for many years. He was working – I had jobs on and off. I was on a benefit also, plus I had three boarders, plus I was working the streets at night. We were living comfortably.

When I was working, I would wear my uniform. High-heeled black shoes, black stockings, they always made your legs look good. Black mini, black low-cut top. That's me. But not prostitute-looking. An ordinary woman could wear an outfit like that too, to a party or to a night out. Bit of jewellery, hair done, makeup. Show your assets. Way back, we wore wigs. We stopped wearing wigs about 74. But everyone wore wigs in those days, the 1960s and early 70s. There were wig shops everywhere.

We didn't use condoms – not many people used condoms back in those days. People were too embarrassed to go and ask for them anyway. There were no real safe-sex practices. Different for girls, I suppose, you've got to have condoms if you're a girl. Didn't want to get pregnant. Safe sex wasn't thought of back then, really.

Once we realised there was such a thing as Aids, we took the advice. I used to get condoms on script. I used condoms for oral too. We used to be offered extra money not to use them, but only the silly girls did that, and some of them paid. I had to be extra careful too because I was married. I didn't want to take nothing like that Aids home. So I was always very careful.

Most of the trans girls I knew in Auckland were on pills from about 72 onwards. So many people were on drugs – you'd see them stumbling all round the place. Myself included. One time I went into town and woke up at the bus stop, fast asleep on the pavement at a bus stop. People walking past me, no memory how I got there, how long I'd been there. It was in Victoria Street, one of the main streets off Queen Street. A lot of people were pinging up, injecting. I used to inject, but only barbiturates. I tried heroin once, but the person missed the vein and I ended up with a big bubble on my arm. I don't remember feeling any kind of stone – I thought, 'That's it, I ain't trying it again.' And thank goodness I didn't. Just that one little incident stopped me.

Girls would have a drink before they went to work – a bit of Dutch courage. Also, a lot of them were using pills. It could make them a bit messy. It was to deaden things a little bit – it dulled things. I used alcohol, just because of the situation you were in, cracking it. A lot of your clients weren't Adonises, and it just took that edge off. By that time, I'd given up pills and all that. I'd have a few drinks though before I went to work.

You had all sorts of clients. You had your old men, your young men. Sometimes you had gorgeous men, and I used to say to them, 'What on earth are you paying for it for? Can't you go to a club and get yourself a nice girlfriend? You're so nice-looking – why?' It used to bewilder me. Why are you paying for it when you could get any woman you wanted? I could never understand that one. I think it was that it was naughty. Plus a lot of the girls on the street were a bit colourful. I think they liked that. And I think a lot of men also like a bit of sleaziness. It turns them on. Plus, it's amazing how many men like queens. Married men. They go into town for their queen now and then, for their oral sex. They say, 'I've got to come in to K Road to get my blow job because the wife won't do it, and I like it.' 'Oh, OK. Keep on coming.'

The majority of your clients are your average working men, most of them married. Not with a lot of money, but he'll put his little bit aside or save up so he can go and visit a girl once a month. I had a regular client for 22 years. Dear Gerry – not his real name. He was a barman at one of the hotels I used to drink at. I used to work during the day – I used to go to the early openers, the hotels, and sit there all day. Do my work from there. I used to talk to the barman, Gerry. He became my client, fell in love with me, and we were together for 22 years. A married man.

He wanted to leave his wife for me, move into a flat together and blah blah. I said to him, 'Gerry, I'm married, and I love my husband, and I ain't leaving him. So get those thoughts out of your head and go home to your missus.' When we left Mt Albert and moved out here, I never contacted Gerry again. I presume Gerry's dead now, because he was in his seventies when I last saw him. So I'd say he's passed away now. But 22 years.

I loved Gerry, he was a darling. But he was a client. He was a darling – he'd come and tell me all his troubles. Save his pennies to come and visit me. My husband wasn't jealous. He knew that I loved him – even though I loved Gerry in my way.

Then by the early 90s I was getting tired of it, working the streets. I'd seen enough penises to last a lifetime. I was getting a bit weary of all that work. Before, it used to be fun. Going out and doing our nightly work – it was a ball sometimes, and we enjoyed ourselves. But it changed into work. And when you've got to do your hair and put all this makeup on, and go out and walk the streets, it started to get a bit too much for me. That's it – I've had enough of that. I'll settle down now.

When I stopped, I didn't miss it. The money, yes, but no. I still had two regulars until the early 2000s. I'd see Gerry about once a month, or if he'd backed the wrong horse it'd be once every two months. Silly bugger he was. He put $2000 on a horse one time and it lost by a nose. I said, 'Why didn't you go $1000 each way, Gerry?' So I didn't see Gerry for a couple of months. He had to save up again.

I've got 30-, 40-year friendships. A lot of the girls were ostracised by their families, so we became family – we are family. We're the transgender whānau. In a lot of cases, the transgender family had stronger ties and stronger love links than their own families. So we were supportive and very close.

When you see another young girl, and you see the traits in that girl, that she's a transgender girl, well, you tell them. 'These are the tablets you take, girl. Get onto these tablets as soon as you can. This is how you do your hair. This is how you do makeup.' Awhi one another, support one another. I've showed many the path.

We were stubborn Māori girls. Very stubborn Māori girls, in those days. And thank goodness for us. The majority of those who walked the streets in Auckland, dressed as women, were Māori. Who had the audacity to walk the streets as women, and when you were told to get home and change, would stand there and say, 'No.' 'No, I won't, officer.'

You should have seen us when the hot pants came out. No one had hotter pants than us. God – didn't leave much up to the imagination. To think they'd squashed a penis in there too! The police would try – 'We'll have you up for indecent exposure.' 'Go on then!' Stubborn Māori girls.

We stuck together. No one else is going to stand up for us. Nobody. You walk down Queen Street, and if they realise you're not a girl, you'll get punched in the street. And when you call a policeman, he'll abuse you too. I'm proud of it. We were tough girls. The 1960s was a tough world, you know?

Poppy was interviewed at her Auckland home in June 2011.

EPILOGUE

IT WAS MID-2009 when I began these interviews, and the book was finished in early 2018. I had interviewed people in Auckland, Wellington, Christchurch, Tauranga and Invercargill – in their homes, in my hotel room, in workplaces, and at the New Zealand Prostitutes' Collective's offices in different centres. Some of the interviews were done in one session, leaving both interviewer and interviewee exhausted and reeling slightly; others stretched out over weeks or even months, an hour or two at a time. There was often food, brought by me or made by interviewees, and, invariably, cups of tea. When I interviewed people at their homes (and even in one NZPC office), pets were often present – Stevie's grey-and-white cat Taxi, Dana's poodle Tinkerbell-Noir and her black cat Rap, Jeanie's dog Roscoe (whose ear-splitting bark interrupts the recording a few times).

And if this talk of food and tea and pets makes the whole process sound very cosy and domestic, that is my abiding sense of it. I had begun with some nervousness about these interviews, but eight years on, the Māori word 'awhi' – to embrace or cherish, often with the connotation of support or encouragement – was what came to me if I tried to sum up the interactions. I felt I had been awhi'd (if I can be excused for mixing a Māori word with an English construction). I had been welcomed into homes, over and over; the Wellington office of NZPC also felt like a kind of home (although I was still terrified of its small, shaky lift). The collective operates in a remarkable way, with an open door and a relaxed, perpetually welcoming attitude; at any given time the office might be the venue for meetings with government officials or overseas researchers, or for counselling sessions and a medical clinic, with sex workers popping in and out informally to chat or catch up, or pick up condoms and lube. Here too, cups of tea are always on offer, and staff can be doing things as varied as supporting a sex worker in negotiations with a brothel owner, preparing a paper for an international conference, talking to a journalist or helping a sex worker move house. There was, I found, a real community of sex workers and sex-worker activists and allies; I felt I had made new friends, as well as reconnecting with some old friends and acquaintances.

As the project drew to a close, the book almost finished, I contacted the interviewees to see what they were up to now. Jeanie wrote back that she was working as 'a city ambassador, walking the streets on the lookout for anyone who needs help, from tourists to our vulnerable street people. After many years of working in costume and fashion, it is refreshing to not have to sell anything to anyone … Add to that keeping fit from walking up to 20 kilometres a night, and being paid for it, and I think I have the perfect job.' Allan remained 'happily partnered' in his 18½-year relationship and was now a grandfather of two (as well as a father of four). He continued doing sex work in Auckland as both a male and a cross-dresser, as well as providing clinical therapeutic massage and mirimiri (Māori massage), and was a board member and volunteer for NZPC.

Shareda continued to work as NZPC's community liaison with transgender sex workers, a position she'd held for 15 years. She was studying Wing Chun martial arts and the Mandarin language; she also taught poi to, and performed with, Tīwhanawhana, a takatāpui kapa haka group in Wellington. Stevie was involved with community organising and was one of the founding members of the transgender group Gender Minorities Aotearoa; they continued to do sex work and lived in Wellington with their fiancée, son and cat.

Mistress Margaret, now in her early seventies, had retired from her dominatrix business three years previously. She emailed from England, where she was visiting family and helping her sister redecorate her house, and was 'looking forward to a few days in London going to galleries and museums'. Anna Reed, also in her seventies, had retired in 2016 after almost 30 years as Canterbury regional coordinator of NZPC, to quite a lot of media fanfare. She had taken a six-week holiday in Cuba and Mexico straight after, and had come back to receive three awards – the Public Health Association's public health champion award, shared with Catherine Healy; a life membership award from the AIDS Foundation; and the New Zealand Police district commander's commendation for her 'invaluable' work with the police since the mid-1980s. In 2017 she was tending to sick friends and had a daughter and young grandson living with her. 'I just wanted a quiet and peaceful retirement!' she complained cheerfully. Her interview had, of course, taken place before the Christchurch earthquakes, at the NZPC office in a now-demolished building on Lichfield Street. Misty, too, was in Christchurch; she texted me, saying that she was still doing sex work and volunteering for NZPC.

Poppy rang for a chat and told me she was 'happy, living a quiet life in the suburbs', though thinking of downsizing to a smaller, easy-care house; she was 'playing Florence Nightingale' to her husband, who was on the mend after breaking his shoulder in a golfing accident. She had been to Dana de Milo's lavish 70th birthday party in Wellington the previous year, and to the Hui Takatāpui in Auckland. 'Life is good.' Kelly had changed jobs and was working for a district health board. Catherine Healy, now in her early sixties, continued as NZPC's national coordinator, and the organisation celebrated its 30th anniversary in late 2017. In June 2018 she was made a dame in the Queen's Birthday honours.

Dana continued to live in the Wellington hills with her beloved animals; asked what she was up to, she messaged back via Facebook, 'Same same – work etc, but very happy'. Sadly, she was diagnosed with liver cancer not long after and died in Wellington in early 2018, surrounded by her many friends, some of whom had come from as far away as Vietnam and Australia to be with their much-loved 'sister'.

In the 15 years since sex work was decriminalised, the dire predictions of those who so strenuously opposed the law change have in no way come to pass. Instead, the industry continues to operate quietly for the most part, and the lives of sex workers are easier, particularly as (like other New Zealanders) they are able to rely on the protection of employment law and the police. While there are occasional outbursts from a small handful of abolitionists who (giving little credence to the views of actual sex workers) insist all sex work is slavery and should be eliminated, and local authorities have sometimes attempted to limit sex work, there is generally little appetite among politicians from any part of the political spectrum – or indeed the wider public – to recriminalise sex work overall.[1] The decriminalised status of sex work is as much an accepted part of the political landscape as the decriminalisation of sex between men or the more recent introduction of same-sex marriage – both issues that were also initially contentious but have come to be accepted by most New Zealanders and generally recognised as important victories for human rights.

CAREN WILTON
June 2018

---

1. See Gillian Abel, 'In search of a fair and free society: Sex work in New Zealand', in Eilís Ward and Gillian Wylie, eds, *Feminism, Prostitution and the State: The politics of neo-abolitionism.* Abingdon, Oxon; New York: Routledge, 2017, p. 149.

GLOSSARY

awhi – help, aid, embrace
back slang – a spoken code used by ship girls and transgender workers, mostly to talk to one another covertly in front of clients or others; sometimes called 'gibberish'
beat – area, usually in a street, park or public toilet, where transgender or gay male workers meet clients or sexual partners
bog – public toilet, particularly one in which males meet for sex
cisgender, cis – having a gender identity that matches the gender a person was assigned at birth; not transgender
cracking it – doing sex work
K Road – Karangahape Road in Auckland, long a home to many sex-industry businesses
kanikani – dance
men's kākahu – men's clothes
mimi – urinate
moana – sea
moonlighting – stealing clothing from a washing line
non-binary – identifying as neither exclusively male nor exclusively female
plucked – to be picked up by police in an undercover operation
queen – a mid- to later-twentieth-century term for a transgender woman (also sometimes then known as a drag queen) or effeminate gay man (sometimes called a butch queen or boy queen)
ringbolting – stowing away on a ship to travel to other ports
roll – steal from
ship moll – a woman who forms temporary relationships with visiting seamen, sometimes involving the direct exchange of sex for money
snowdropping – see 'moonlighting'
sprung – revealed as transgender (or sometimes as a sex worker)
straight – referring to a client's engaging a sex worker without the intention of paying for sexual services – usually in a massage parlour, where the

client would pay a door fee for the massage but negotiate sexual services directly with the worker

takatāpui – Māori term traditionally meaning 'intimate friend of the same gender', now used to refer to lesbian/gay/bisexual/transgender (etc) people, particularly those who are Māori

tima moll – see 'ship moll', above; 'tima' is a Māori transliteration of the English word 'steamer'

tima tāne – male seaman, from the Māori words 'tima' (steamer) and 'tāne' (man)

taping – concealing male genitalia by taping it between the legs

trick sex – sex in which a male partner is led to believe they're having vaginal intercourse when they're actually not

tucking – hiding male genitalia by pulling it back between the legs

unspring – term referring to a transgender person who does not appear to be transgender

ure – penis

wairua – spirit, soul

whakamā – shame, embarrassment

whāngai – customary Māori practice of fostering or adoption

working – doing sex work

THE PHOTOGRAPHS

WHILE SOME of the interviewees provided me with photos (or were photographed by me), and would have been happy to have these published, others were strongly committed to remaining anonymous, and did not want their faces to appear in the book. It felt like a conundrum; if we included photos of some but not all interviewees, then it would seem as if those with photographs were being given more prominence, were more vivid and visible and fully represented than those without.

In the end we chose to move away entirely from literal representations of the narrators, and instead to work with a photographer, Madeleine Slavick, whose luminous, reflective and multi-layered photos of Hong Kong, shown at Aratoi museum in Masterton, had impressed me. I felt that Madeleine's style would offer a fitting take on the sex industry, with its layered, complex and sometimes veiled and secretive nature. Our budget didn't allow her to travel far afield, so she focused on the Wellington region, photographing sites that are, or historically have been, associated with the sex industry or with sex-worker activism. She also selected four photographs previously taken in Brazil, Hong Kong and the US that aligned with the theme and imagery.

Her photos are a wonderful addition to the book.

CAREN WILTON

PHOTOGRAPHER'S NOTE

What is photography but seeing – more than once.

I seek complexity in images, with layers, movement, spatial relationships, multiple perspectives, a quantity of quiet and subtlety, the unknown, and sometimes, humour.

The images in this book are primarily daytime photographs, to mirror the openness of the workers with their life-affirming stories, and to align with the fact that many of them prefer the day shift, when their children are in school.

While working on this assignment, I meet a woman who runs a wheelchair-accessible sex establishment with glorious bedrooms, massage rooms and a dungeon. Another has been renovating her gentlemen's club, which used to be a squash centre. The day I meet the founder of the national prostitutes' collective, I also meet a beautiful sex worker, activist and parent who enjoys working doubles whenever possible; and I am reminded of my prose poem written after a four-hand massage:

I Pay Them to Touch Me
They pray before they touch me, before they speak. There is oil, lemongrass, towels, paper panties, a melody I am not supposed to remember. The room is warm, or I am, as four hands swim down my arms, waist, thighs, legs, and I become a place with no memory. Do I sleep?

I leave alone, seep into evening, a city, raining. Their four hands keep remembering, and I feel no edges.

MADELEINE SLAVICK

Madeleine Slavick has exhibited her photography internationally and has authored several books of photography, poetry and non-fiction. *Round: Poems and photographs of Asia* won the Bumbershoot Book Award; *delicate access* includes a Chinese translation by Luo Hui; *My Favourite Thing* achieved bestseller status in Beijing; and *Fifty Stories Fifty Images* accompanied her exhibition Hong Kong Song. Madeleine has lived in North America and Hong Kong, and now lives in Aotearoa New Zealand.

PHOTOGRAPH LOCATIONS

All photographs by Madeleine Slavick

Cover: Funhouse, Wellington.

p. 2 New Zealand Prostitutes' Collective office, Wellington. NZPC produced the 'We are professional' poster in 1989.

p. 7 Mannequin in window, San Francisco.

p. 19 Columbia Private Hotel, Wellington, previously Lloyds, where during World War II proprietor Clara 'Ma' Hallam rented rooms by the hour to US servicemen and sex workers.

p. 37 Interior, Paris, Lower Hutt.

p. 61 Sex worker mural, painted by Michael Ting and Michael Bensemann in 1990, Bicycle Junction, Marion Street, Wellington.

p. 85 Dungeon, MM Club, Wellington.

p. 107 Exterior, Il Bordello, Wellington.

p. 127 Stairwell and sculpture, Henry Pollen's restaurant (previously the House of Ladies and Number 12 massage parlours), Wellington.

p. 151 Dildos, MM Club, Wellington.

p. 169 Carmen Rupe cross-light, Cuba Street, Wellington. Pedestrian traffic lights featuring Carmen were installed at a number of Cuba Street intersections in 2016.

p. 197 Car and home, New Mexico.

p. 215 Exterior, Paris, Lower Hutt. The building was previously a squash club and sauna.

p. 235 Ceiling light, Paris, Lower Hutt.

p. 253 Woman in a lift lobby, Hong Kong.

p. 273 Woman, Tijuca National Park, Rio de Janeiro.

FURTHER READING

Abel, Gillian, Lisa Fitzgerald and Cheryl Brunton. *The Impact of the Prostitution Reform Act on the Health and Safety Practices of Sex Workers: Report to the Prostitution Law Review Committee*. Christchurch: Department of Public Health and General Practice, University of Otago, 2007.

Abel, Gillian, Lisa Fitzgerald and Catherine Healy with Aline Taylor, eds. *Taking the Crime out of Sex Work: New Zealand sex workers' fight for decriminalisation*. Bristol, UK: Policy Press, 2010.

Agustín, Laura María. *Sex at the Margins: Migration, labour markets and the rescue industry*. London; New York: Zed Books, 2007.

Armstrong, Lynzi. 'Decriminalisation and the rights of migrant sex workers in Aotearoa/New Zealand: Making a case for change', *Women's Studies Journal*, vol. 31, no. 2, December 2017, pp. 69–76.

Armstrong, Lynzi. 'Managing risks of violence in decriminalised street-based sex work: A feminist (sex worker rights) perspective.' PhD thesis, Victoria University of Wellington, 2011.

Belgrave, Kate. 'My average life as an average whore', blog post, 7 October 2010: www.katebelgrave.com/2010/10/my-average-life-as-an-average-whore/

Bellamy, Paul. 'Prostitution law reform in New Zealand.' New Zealand Parliament, 2012: www.parliament.nz/en/pb/research-papers/document/00PLSocRP12051/prostitution-law-reform-in-new-zealand

Brennan, Mary and Eleanor Black. *Some Kind of Fantasy: The amazing life story of New Zealand's top dominatrix*. Auckland: David Bateman, 2015.

Casey, Cathy. *Change for the Better: The story of Georgina Beyer*. Auckland: Random House, 1999.

Charlton, Thomas L., Lois E. Myers and Rebecca Sharpless, eds. *Handbook of Oral History*. Lanham, MD: AltaMira Press, 2006.

Delacoste, Frédérique and Priscilla Alexander, eds. *Sex Work: Writings by women in the sex industry*. London: Virago, 1988.

Ditmore, Melissa Hope, Antonia Levy and Alys Willman, eds. *Sex Work Matters: Exploring money, power, and intimacy in the sex industry*. London; New York: Zed Books, 2010.

Eldred-Grigg, Stevan. *Diggers, Hatters & Whores: The story of the New Zealand gold rushes*. Auckland: Random House, 2008.

Eldred-Grigg, Stevan. *Pleasures of the Flesh: Sex & drugs in colonial New Zealand, 1840–1915*. Wellington: Reed, 1984.

Farvid, Panteá. 'The politics of sex work in Aotearoa/New Zealand and the Pacific: Tensions, debates and future directions', *Women's Studies Journal*, vol. 31, no. 2, December 2017, pp. 27–34.

Gira Grant, Melissa. *Playing the Whore: The work of sex work*. London; New York: Verso, 2014.

Global Network of Sex Work Projects. 'History of the NSWP and the sex worker rights movement': www.nswp.org/timeline

Gluck, Sherna Berger and Daphne Patai, eds. *Women's Words: The feminist practice of oral history*. New York; London: Routledge, 1991.

Green, Anna and Megan Hutching, eds. *Remembering: Writing oral history*. Auckland: Auckland University Press, 2004.

Hanson, Jody. *The Business of Sex*. Sydney: Lulu, 2007.

Hazenberg, Evan and Miriam Meyerhoff, eds. *Representing Trans: Linguistic, legal and everyday perspectives*. Wellington: Victoria University Press, 2017.

Healy, Catherine, Ahi Wi-Hongi and Chanel Hati. 'It's work, it's working: The integration of sex workers and sex work in Aotearoa/New Zealand', *Women's Studies Journal*, vol. 31, no. 2, December 2017, pp. 50–60.

Hill, Julie. 'When the vice squad came calling.' *The Spinoff*, 24 February 2017: https://thespinoff.co.nz/society/24-02-2017/when-the-vice-squad-came-calling

Human Rights Commission. *To Be Who I Am: Report of the inquiry into discrimination experienced by transgender people*, 2008: www.hrc.co.nz/files/5714/2378/7661/15-Jan-2008_14-56-48_HRC_Transgender_FINAL.pdf

Ings, Welby. 'From the beat to the SOOB: The language of the male sex worker in New Zealand.' *NZWords*, no. 12 (May 2008), pp. 2–5.

Jordan, Jan. 'MacKenzie, Flora', first published in the Dictionary of New Zealand Biography, vol. 5, 2000. Te Ara – the Encyclopedia of New Zealand: www.TeAra.govt.nz/en/biographies/5m19/mackenzie-flora

Jordan, Jan. *The Sex Industry in New Zealand: A literature review*. Wellington: Ministry of Justice, 2005.

Jordan, Jan. 'Sex work.' Te Ara – the Encyclopedia of New Zealand, 2011: www.TeAra.govt.nz/en/sex-work

Jordan, Jan. 'User pays: Why men buy sex.' *Australian and New Zealand Journal of Criminology*, vol. 30, no. 1 (March 1997), pp. 55–71.

Jordan, Jan. *Working Girls: Women in the New Zealand sex industry talk to Jan Jordan*. Auckland: Penguin Books, 1991.

Lévesque, Andrée. 'Prescribers and rebels: Attitudes to European women's sexuality in New Zealand, 1860–1916.' In Barbara Brookes, Charlotte Macdonald and Margaret Tennant, eds, *Women in History: Essays on European women in New Zealand*. Wellington: Allen & Unwin in association with Port Nicholson Press, 1986, pp. 1–12.

Macdonald, Charlotte. 'The "social evil": Prostitution and the passing of the Contagious Diseases Act (1869).' In Barbara Brookes, Charlotte Macdonald and Margaret

Tennant, eds, *Women in History: Essays on European women in New Zealand*. Wellington: Allen & Unwin in association with Port Nicholson Press, 1986, pp. 13–33.

Macdonald, Charlotte. *A Woman of Good Character*. Wellington: Allen & Unwin; Historical Branch, Department of Internal Affairs, 1990.

Martin, Paul. *Carmen: My life*. Auckland: Benton Ross, 1988.

Mayhew, Pat and Elaine Mossman. *Exiting Prostitution: Models of best practice*. Wellington: Ministry of Justice, 2007.

Mossman, Elaine. *International Approaches to Decriminalising or Legalising Prostitution*. Wellington: Ministry of Justice, 2007.

Mossman, Elaine and Pat Mayhew. *Key Informant Interviews: Review of the Prostitution Reform Act 2003*. Wellington: Ministry of Justice, 2007.

Museum of New Zealand Te Papa Tongarewa. 'Queen of the Evergreen': collections. tepapa.govt.nz/topic/3751

Museum of New Zealand Te Papa Tongarewa. 'Wellington nightlife 1960–2000': collections.tepapa.govt.nz/Topic/10131

Nagle, Jill, ed. *Whores and Other Feminists*. New York: Routledge, 1997.

New Zealand Prostitutes' Collective. 'Decriminalisation of Sex Work in New Zealand: Impact on Māori', 2013: www.sexworklaw.co.nz/pdfs/Decriminalisation_of_Sex_Work_in_New_Zealand_-_Impact_on_Maori.pdf

Newbold, Greg. *Crime, Law, and Justice in New Zealand*. New York: Routledge, 2016.

Perks, Robert and Alistair Thomson, eds. *The Oral History Reader*. 3rd edn. Oxon: Routledge, 2016.

Petro, Melissa, ed. *Pros(e): A collection of writings by individuals with experiences in the sex trades*. New York: Red Umbrella Project, 2012.

Prostitution Law Review Committee. *The Nature and Extent of the sex industry in New Zealand: An estimation*. Wellington: Ministry of Justice, 2005.

Prostitution Law Review Committee. *Report of the Prostitution Law Review Committee on the Operation of the Prostitution Reform Act 2003*. Wellington: Ministry of Justice, 2008.

Radačić, Ivana. 'New Zealand Prostitutes' Collective: An example of a successful policy actor', *Social Sciences*, vol. 6, no. 2 (2017): www.mdpi.com/2076-0760/6/2/46/htm

Rickard, Wendy. 'Collaborating with sex workers in oral history', *Oral History Review*, vol. 30, no. 1, pp. 47–59.

Ritchie, Donald A., ed. *The Oxford Handbook of Oral History*. New York: Oxford University Press, 2011.

Roche, Lauren. *Bent not Broken*. Wellington: Steele Roberts, 1999.

Roguski, Michael. *Occupational Health and Safety of Migrant Sex Workers in New Zealand*. Wellington: New Zealand Prostitutes' Collective, 2013.

Schmidt, Johanna. 'The regulation of sex work in Aotearoa/New Zealand: An overview', *Women's Studies Journal*, vol. 31, no. 2, December 2017, pp. 35–49.

Schrader, Ben. *The Big Smoke: New Zealand cities 1840–1920*. Wellington: Bridget Williams Books, 2016.

Siren. New Zealand Prostitutes' Collective, 1988–.

Sterry, David Henry and R.J. Martin Jr., eds. *Hos, Hookers, Call Girls and Rent Boys: Professionals writing on life, love, money, and sex*. Berkeley, CA: Soft Skull Press, 2009.

Sweetman, Bridie. 'The judicial system and sex work in New Zealand', *Women's Studies Journal*, vol. 31, no. 2, December 2017, pp. 61–68.

Tolerton, Jane. *Ettie Rout: New Zealand's safer sex pioneer*. Rev. ed. Auckland: Penguin, 2015.

Wagenaar, Hendrik, Sietske Altink and Helga Amesberger. *Designing Prostitution Policy: Intention and reality in regulating the sex trade*. Bristol: Policy Press, 2017.

Waitai, Rana. 'Modes of a dress: Drag queens in Wellington.' In Michael Hill, Sharon Mast, Richard Bowman and Charlotte Carr-Gregg, eds, *Shades of Deviance: A New Zealand collection*. Palmerston North: Dunmore Press, 1983, pp. 126–39.

Ward, Eilís and Gillian Wylie, eds. *Feminism, Prostitution and the State: The politics of neo-abolitionism*. Abingdon, Oxon; New York: Routledge, 2017.

ACKNOWLEDGEMENTS

IT'S PROBABLY a cliché to say that it takes a village to write a book, but in this case it is true. I am very grateful to many people for their input, kindness, support and guidance, usually far beyond the call of duty.

First and foremost, the interviewees, who were so generous with their time and their stories. Those whose narratives are included in this book put in even more time going over their chapters and discussing changes with me. My greatest respect to you all; I am deeply grateful and hope that this book does you justice.

A big mihi to the people of the New Zealand Prostitutes' Collective – particularly Catherine Healy, Annah Pickering, Anna Reed, Chanel Hati, Ahi Wi-Hongi and Calum Bennachie – for all their help and encouragement, for putting me in touch with potential interviewees, lending me books, letting me use their offices for interviews, making me cups of tea, and sometimes trying to keep me in line, with varying results!

Alison Parr, formerly senior oral historian at the Ministry for Culture and Heritage, has supported this project in a number of ways from its rather inchoate beginnings almost nine years ago. I have been very grateful for her kindness, guidance and advice along the way. Thanks also to Megan Hutching, Linda Evans, Lynette Shum and Sue Berman of the oral-history community. This project received three New Zealand Oral History Awards over its duration, which were hugely helpful in allowing me to travel to other cities for interviews, and take time off work.

Alison Parr, Basil Keane, Calum Bennachie, Chanel Hati, Claire Baylis, Hinemoana Baker, Jared Gulian, Jan Farr, Jan Jordan, Johanna Knox, Madeleine Slavick and Megan Hutching read and commented on different sections of the manuscript, providing me with invaluable feedback. Jane Cherry transcribed a number of the interviews; Nancy Swarbrick and Kerryn Pollock gave me some helpful input when I needed it. Rachel Scott at Otago University Press has been a thoughtful, perceptive and supportive publisher;

Madeleine Slavick's beautiful and sensitive photographs are a marvellous addition to the book. My thanks also to Erika Bűky for her very sharp-eyed copy editing, Fiona Moffat for her great design, Imogen Coxhead for her careful proofreading, and the two anonymous readers who made some very helpful points.

My earliest thoughts about the possibility of an oral-history project looking at the sex industry were stimulated and encouraged by Ben Schrader, Jock Phillips and Malcolm McKinnon (my then colleagues at Te Ara – the Encyclopedia of New Zealand), and by Jan Jordan.

My husband, Colin Dowd, has been unstintingly patient, kind, supportive and funny, and gives great advice; thanks too to my friends for being smart, thoughtful, hilarious and good listeners.

I met Dana de Milo when I interviewed her for this project; she became a friend. She passed away in February 2018, as I was completing the final draft of the manuscript. This book would be much poorer without the inclusion of her remarkable story. Moe mai ra e te kahurangi, moe mai ra; you are much missed, and will always be remembered.

CAREN WILTON

I thank all the people along the way: Denise Batchelor, Bicycle Junction, Chan Wai-fong, Julie Clifton, Common Ledger, Rosalind Derby, Catherine Healy, Kakapo Ink Tattoo Studio, Mary Brennan of Funhouse and MM Club, Heather Main, Danny McGrath of Henry Pollen's, Bev of Paris, Kedron Parker, Ian Saville, Rachel Scott, Ahi Wi-Hongi and, most of all, Caren Wilton.

MADELEINE SLAVICK